THEY CALLED ME CHOCOLATE ROCKET

CALLED ME

THEY CHOCOLATE CALLED ME ROCKET

John Paris, Jr.
with Robert Ashe

Formac Publishing Company Limited
Halifax

Formac Publishing Company Limited recognizes the support of the Province
of Nova Scotia through the Film and Creative Industries Nova Scotia. We are
pleased to work in partnership with the agency to develop and promote our
creative industries for the benefit of all Nova Scotians. We acknowledge the
financial support of the Government of Canada through the Canada Book Fund
for our publishing activities. We acknowledge the support of the Canada Council
for the Arts for our publishing program.

Library and Archives Canada Cataloguing in Publication
Paris, John, Jr, author
      They called me Chocolate Rocket : the life and times of John Paris, Jr.,
hockey's first black professional coach / John Paris, Jr. with Robert Ashe.

Includes bibliographical references and index.
ISBN 978-1-4595-0331-1 (pbk.).-- ISBN 978-1-4595-0332-8 (epub)

      1. Paris, John, Jr. 2. Black Canadian hockey players--Biography.
3. Hockey players--Canada--Biography. 4. Hockey coaches--Canada--
Biography. 5. Hockey coaches--United States--Biography. I. Ashe,
Robert, author II. Title.

GV848.5.P368A3 2014   796.962092   C2014-903338-9

Formac Publishing Company Limited
5502 Atlantic Street
Halifax, Nova Scotia, Canada
B3H 1G4
www.formac.ca

Printed and bound in Canada.

TABLE OF CONTENTS

INTRODUCTION 7

1 Curry's Corner 11

2 Scotty 28

3 Chocolate Rocket 40

4 The Way It Is 56

5 Last Chance 69

6 Sixty-seven Pounds 85

7 Strike 108

8 The Blues 128

9 Turner Cup 144

10 Crossroads 166

11 Macon Whoopee 184

12 One Night in Huntsville 199

13 Marc-André 216

14 Rocky Mountain 232

15 Reflections 246

APPENDIX 1 First-, Second- and Third-Rounders 262

APPENDIX 2 Ten Commandments for Coaching Success 264

ACKNOWLEDGEMENTS 267

INDEX 272

INTRODUCTION

I was at a coaches' seminar in Toronto in the late 1980s, after-hours in a lounge area, where a small group had engulfed Jean Perron to listen to one of his spontaneous lectures. Perron had recently coached the Montreal Canadiens to a Stanley Cup, so in the hockey world his words were gold, although, with his unusual cadence, sometimes a little hard to understand.

As Jean yakked away, some men at another table across the room began mumbling insults and mocking his fumbled English. Jean couldn't hear their foolishness, but from my table across the room I could hear it all. One fat-faced guy in particular was making certain that someone noticed him. "Fuckin' frogs can't even talk!" A few of his companions snickered. "Chickenshit frogs. They'll take *anything* in Quebec. They all slept with squaws anyway."

That was it for me. I pushed back my chair and charged across to his table. When I got there I stood over him. "If you've something to say to him, why don't you go up and do it? Otherwise, cool it!"

His table went quiet. The guy twisted in his chair and stood up. Not especially tall, he was still a half-foot above me. We stood, glaring, inches from one another. I could smell the booze on his breath. I told him that he should keep his views private and show some respect.

"You speak French, don't you," he said. "You coach with *them*."

I told him I coached in the Quebec Major Junior Hockey League and was proud of it. "So what's your point?"

He smirked and looked back at his table. "Not only do we have to put up with the fuckin' frogs, but with *him*, too. I can't get a sniff and *he's* coaching."

Wrong answer, *mon ami*.

I drove my face up into his, then in one motion placed my left hand on his shoulder and my right hand down against his jewels, prepared to yank those babies until he squealed like a pig. I looked him in the eye and spoke calmly. "If you say another word, if you *move*, I'm gonna hurt you. I've had it with you. You ready to put your life on the line? Don't move, man, because if you do you'll have to kill me to stop me."

Silence. His eyes widened. I think he stopped breathing. A few seconds passed. Finally someone said, "It's okay, it's okay." Our eyes were still locked as I backed away and returned to my table. I didn't hear his voice again that night.

Through all this, Perron kept talking. He didn't hear or see a damn thing. When I talked to Jean years later he never even mentioned the incident. I thought: *I could have had my butt kicked and no one would have noticed!*

So would I have done it all over again?

Absolutely.

* * *

To understand my life, and me, there are some things you should know.

First, I am an idealist. There's not much grey in my world. I feel strongly that things should be a certain way, and that wrong is never right. Period. All my life I have tried to live by basic principles of integrity instilled in me by my parents, including the golden rule of doing unto others. When I see or hear something bad, I move quickly to address it. It's my reflex. Others may turn away, but I step forward. Sometimes at a considerable risk.

Second, I am a proud black man. But this does not mean I am obsessed with race — although twenty-five years ago a man who would go on to become an assistant coach of the Montreal Canadiens accused me of being exactly that. I live in the real world where there is no denying my race has played a significant role in my life. So far I've been a Negro, coloured, black, African-Canadian, brown, a minority and bi-racial, not to mention a tidal wave of racial slurs and insulting descriptions. That said, I believe the colour of one's skin is no excuse not to strive to be the best in one's field and to live and behave with honour.

Third, I consider myself religious. Too many strange things have happened in my life to allow me to deny the existence of a supreme being or to disrespect formal religion. I was raised a Baptist and perhaps this fuels my idealism. In any case, I don't want to knock on the door of the Lord one day and say, "I'm sorry, but I believe in you now." I just don't want to take that chance.

Fourth, I adore women and admire the intuitive, balanced way they see the world. Perhaps this appreciation comes from studying the dignified way my mother went about things. Whatever its roots, I have enjoyed the romance. In the company of women I have learned many things about life and about myself. Women — including the incredible young woman to whom I am now married — have played a major role in shaping the person I am today.

Fifth, sports fascinate me. Especially hockey. I love its fabric, its textures and its sensual qualities. I love the times when I stand in the middle of it all, the chess master. Hockey has introduced me to the famous and the great and afforded me a ticket to see much of the world. In fact, when I was very ill hockey may have saved my life, offering me the promise of something special if I could just hang on. On the other hand, hockey has been a harsh mistress, unapologetically costing me at least one marriage and several relationships, as well as introducing me to dark sides of many people.

The final thing — and maybe the most important thing — you should know about me is that there ain't no quit in this dog. None. I believe that perseverance is the central theme of my life story, permeating moments big and small, evident when I was very young and continuing to this very day.

So this is my story. Triumphs and tragedy, warts and all. Enjoy.

— John Paris, Jr., September 2014

CHAPTER 1
Curry's Corner

The brilliant Georgia sun followed our convertible like a spot-light, bathing our victory procession as it slowly left the Omni Coliseum and headed for Atlanta City Hall. The city was paying tribute following our championship of the International Hockey League and on this perfect Friday in May 1994, however briefly, the Atlanta Knights owned the place. My heart was pounding.

The whole thing had a carnival feel: a high school band, a fire engine, police vehicles, our Zamboni and a giant float carrying our mascots, Sir Slap Shot and Claude the Happy Trumpeter. Most of our players rode in open convertibles. A couple drove new Harley-Davidson motorcycles and one even brought his own car. Hard-core fans and curious lunchtime onlookers lined the route, waving and shouting congratulations as we headed up Martin Luther King Boulevard. "Coach! Coach! Right on, coach! You the man!" I reached out and grasped the hands of people who ran up to our car.

At City Hall hundreds of fans in Knights jerseys and cham-pionship T-shirts cheered, rang cowbells and tossed confetti as

*Atlanta Knights Day, May 1994. I'm with players and their families on the
steps of City Hall.*

one of our players carried the Turner Cup up the front steps
and placed the glistening trophy on a table. An official from the
mayor's office took the microphone and proclaimed "Atlanta
Knights Day" and our general manager Richard Adler boasted
to the crowd that the team now ranked with the other sports

franchises in the city. Several players thanked the fans. When it was my turn, I said that the Knights, with all their cultural and language differences, worked together and won. Atlanta can do the same, I said. "All you have to do is to remember the Knights!"

Almost all of our players were under contract with the Tampa Bay Lightning and many of them still aspired to catch on with the parent club or another NHL team. A few would fulfill that goal, but most would continue in the minor pro leagues for a few years then settle for more conventional jobs. And the dream would end.

For me, the first black man ever to coach a professional hockey team, on this day in the Southern sun, all this seemed plenty. I couldn't stop smiling. For while the parade from the Omni to City Hall covered only a few blocks, the journey had taken me most of my life.

* * *

That life began on August 1, 1946, in Windsor, Nova Scotia, Canada, the birthplace of hockey and the self-proclaimed Pumpkin Capital of the World. I was the third of five children of John Paris, a local post-office worker and modest entrepreneur, and his wife, Annie Paris. We were the town's only "coloured" family.

Windsor is a resilient, middle-class community about sixty kilometres northwest of Halifax, on the eastern cusp of an agricultural belt called the Annapolis Valley. Farming, textiles and gypsum mining at various times have been staples of the town's economy. A British stronghold in the 1700s, after the American Revolution the area became home to a large wave of United Empire Loyalists, including newly freed slaves, my ancestors among them. In the late nineteenth century it was a major port for shipping and travel. When the age of sail disappeared, the town persevered and adapted. When fire gutted the town —

in 1897 and again in 1924 — Windsor bounced back. Since the early 1900s its population has hovered around 3,500.

Pumpkins aside, Windsor's current glory is linked to a popular belief — at least, it's popular among us Windsorites — that the town is where the sport of ice hockey was born. The town's claim is supported by Windsor native Thomas Chandler Haliburton, Canada's first internationally acclaimed writer. In his book *The Attaché*, published in 1844, Haliburton reported seeing King's College boys playing "hurley on the ice" when he was a student at the school, around 1800. Apparently it's the earliest reference in English literature to a stick-ball game being played on ice in Canada. So far this has trumped any evidence presented by other Canadian communities seeking the distinction as hockey's birthplace.

The Windsor I knew as a youth had no McDonald's or Burger Kings, no taverns or night clubs. Restaurants were few. Downtown was dominated by small shops and the usual civic structures such a fire station, a post office and banks. We had two prestigious private schools: King's College for boys and Edgehill School for girls. For a small community there were ample recreation facilities, including the main hockey rink, the Hants Exhibition Arena. Security at the dances at the town community centre was just one local fellow, Norman Skelhorn, who collected the entry fee. When I was very young I was in charge of giving out pop and potato chips. When a fight broke out, usually over a girl, it was taken to the field across the street. Never on the community grounds.

At our town movie theatre, Kirk Frederick was the supervisor and a lady with a beautiful smile took the tickets at the window. Entrance to the theatre was ten or fifteen cents, but the lady would usually let me and my friends in for free. It was a ritual for Kirk to come by and look aghast at the handful of us and joke, "Aw, you got in again!" Small things. Sweet memories.

Windsor had a community solidarity. So when outsiders

rolled in to town to cause trouble, young men from across Windsor would band together and take care of business. However, inside the town it was a different matter. Around Windsor your area of town was fundamental to your identity. I lived in a section called Curry's Corner — a kilometre from downtown — so I ran proud with the boys from Curry's Corner. If you were a Curry's Corner Boy, you'd *die* a Curry's Corner Boy. There'd be seven or eight of us, aged about ten to thirteen. Hardly a gang by today's standards, but we *did* have a youthful swagger and didn't hide when trouble presented itself, especially in the form of our main rivals, the O'Brien Street Boys, named after one of the town's main drags.

Our tiffs with the O'Brien Street Boys ended up with roughly equal numbers. A few O'Brien boys had the mentality of being tough. But *believing* and *being* are two different things. Often they were just bullies. Typically, a bully is a bully because he's *allowed* to be a bully. If a brother or friend wanted to avoid a bully, I would not let them. I insisted they confront him — with me at their side. And I was prepared to battle.

I had my approach down pat. First, I'd look the bully in the eye. *"We don't have to do this."* If he didn't back off, I escalated things. *"You're not going to win. Even if you beat me physically, you can't beat me mentally."* I'd pause and give him a mean little smile. *"But you're not going to beat me physically, either."* And then I'd shock him. *"Are you ready to die?"* He'd look stunned by this, but I meant it. I *would* die. No one was taking my dignity! I'd die for that — even today. While he thought things over I'd add, *"This is going to be the worst war you've ever been in. Because I'm not going to stop. If you knock me down, I'm going to get back up. And I'm going to come back at you. And if you beat me tonight, I'm going to fight you tomorrow. Until I beat* you. *What's it gonna be?"*

Usually the bully backed away. If he didn't, I could hold my own — and then some. My little secret was that this older guy named Ralph Geezer was teaching me some self-defence and karate. I wasn't working towards a belt or anything, but I learned a few useful moves and it helped my confidence in a fight.

At Curry's Corner, neighbours were more like extended family. People fed you, wiped your nose and even scolded you when you deserved it. I spent many days at the home of the Reddens or the Paynes or the Kendalls or the Taylors. I slept in the same bed with my friends and ate at the same table. There may have been race wars in the United States, but in Windsor, Nova Scotia, in the late 1950s, they seemed remote.

Then one day, for me, reality hit.

I was sitting on my living room floor one afternoon, laughing with a friend, when the news came on the television. We went quiet as we watched cops hose water on black people and growling dogs chase and bite women and children who screamed and ran. I stared at the screen, straining to process it all. I will always remember how I hurt when I heard it was just "negroes" under attack. No one else. I had nightmares for years, so searing were those black-and-white images, so commanding was that moment. Powerful people attacking helpless people. Name-calling and violence. My friend had tears in his eyes. We slowly got up and went outside on the lawn where we stood, two adolescents — one black, one white — neither of us knowing exactly what to do or to say, but both realizing this day and this event had meaning. He kept saying he was sorry and then began to throw things. I finally stopped him. "You didn't do anything to be sorry for. We're friends."

In the coming days I began to recall comments by older people, about me not letting my guard down, about being beaten or killed just for being coloured. Watching those horrid TV images I began to understand. I swore then that I'd never accept such treatment. Not from cops, not from anyone. Was I really a marked person? Over time, as I moved through my adolescent and teen years, things happened to make me wonder.

. . . Like the adult sister of one of my baseball teammates one afternoon running from her house and screaming at me to go back to Africa, that niggers have no place in Canada. I looked at her and stopped. At first I was embarrassed. One of my friends yelled at her, "Shut up! You're crazy!" We walked away. But from that day on I made it a point to pass by that house, finding an excuse to stop by tying my shoes or dropping a ball, just to show that I could not be intimidated. I would never say a word to her, just look at her defiantly when she came to the window or came out on her front porch.

. . . Like the cluster of older boys from outside town who yelled at me when I was walking to the movie threatre. "Hey, Buckwheat! Hey, monkey!" I walked up to the biggest one, a Caucasian with a darker skin tone, and told him that someone in his family likes black, that he may even be related to me, that he should go home and ask around. He didn't appreciate my advice. When he menacingly stepped towards me, I kicked him in the testicles. Bang! I then quickly turned to one of the others and punched him in the face. Smack! Just then Norman Skelhorn, the security man from the community dances, came by and told the boys to scram. They did, swollen testicles and all.

. . . Like the time in Truro, seventy-five kilometres from Windsor, when I was in a car with three or four of my friends and an RCMP officer stopped us. He walked over to our car and pointed at a chocolate bar wrapper on the ground a few feet away. He then looked inside the car, saw me and ordered me to pick it up. I protested, but he told me to shut up and get out and pick it up. Now, I had nothing to do with that damn wrapper. I was sitting on the opposite side of the car from where it was lying. Plus, it was an Oh Henry! wrapper, and I never ate bars with nuts. (I was a Hershey's man.) Eventually I got out, picked up the wrapper and then contemptuously thanked the cop for proving that a uniform alone does not make a man a good person.

. . . Like one summer when I was socializing with friends in downtown Halifax and was refused entry into a club on Spring Garden Road. A woman at the door bluntly told me, "No niggers allowed." First she said *Negros*, and then on the second mention it was *niggers*. I braced myself and complained she couldn't do this because it was against the law. Hearing my protests, a heavy-set guy with a cigarette hanging from the side of his mouth came over and glared at me. I thought about calling the police, but, remembering my experience in Truro, I concluded it was likely futile.

* * *

I attended Curry's Corner School, just across from my house. School bored me and my grades were often poor. I had problems concentrating and was usually daydreaming. However, when I found something interesting I had no difficulty and could speed-read material with high comprehension (today I can read five or six times faster than the average adult). But mainly I would go into a shell, stubbornly refusing to volunteer an answer even when I knew it.

School went from frustration to dread when they rolled out material such as *The Story of Little Black Sambo,* the illustrated children's story that portrayed black people as gluttons and contained illustrations showing blacks wearing bizarre clothing and having grossly exaggerated facial features. The book came under attack in the 1960s and has since almost disappeared. But at Curry's Corner School, *circa* 1958, it was part of the curriculum and tolerated through ignorance. Some of the kids found the book funny, but they didn't mean any harm. Finally, one day I told the teacher that it was not believable, and that I should not have to listen to it. Teachers would say I was being too sensitive, although, softly, one teacher, Mrs. Brighton, told me that I was right. My parents complained to the school. Eventually, along with others, they were able to have the book removed.

The family Paris, 1952, left to right: father Buster, me, Mike, Cecil, mother Annie May, Percy, Faye.

Teachers often perplexed me. One teacher, herself with brown skin, once accused me of talking in class even though I was not saying a word. (For the record, it was a kid named Doug Taylor who was talking and carrying on — and she knew it.) I lost all respect for her. Whatever pressures she had, she was still wrong and I didn't let it slide. I still can't, all these years later. I'm not going to let anybody off the hook. If you are wrong, you are wrong. Colour is not going to buy you any grace with me.

Although it didn't help me in grade school, as a youngster I began displaying the faculty of precognition. In other words, being able to see into the future. My premonitions occurred in my dreams and would scare the sweet bejesus out of my Aunt Viola. One evening I awoke and began to tell my mother, in front of Aunt Vi, what I had just dreamt. I pointed to my lower stomach and spoke of being sick and having a bag on me (my ileostomy) . . . I said I would move away and speak other languages (I've lived in several places and learned to speak French, Italian, Mandarin and Spanish) . . . I described that my wife will have long hair and speak other languages (my first wife was French-Canadian) . . . I would have four children and lose one (this proved exact) . . . I said that I was going to carry a large trophy (the Turner Cup is huge) . . . I would "make history" (the first black professional hockey coach).

My mother and aunt were both quiet as I went through this list. Finally, Mom said, "What else, John?"

Aunt Vi couldn't handle any more. "That's enough! The boy is crazy!"

Many years later my mother, who lived to witness several of these events, asked me if I remembered talking to her and Aunt Vi that night.

"Yes, every word," I said. Mom gave me a knowing smile.

* * *

The greatest influence on me was my family: a strong, supportive brood led by two parents who opened their arms to extended family and friends. We weren't the richest, but we lacked for nothing. We had clothes. We had food. We were happy.

The Paris children were (in order of birth) Cecil, Faye, me, Percy and Mike. Cecil was a free spirit whose work life included running a dry-cleaning business and importing. He also modelled male clothing for a time. He died in 2008 of a heart condition. Faye worked for a bank in Montreal and then for the Nova Scotia government in family and children services. In many ways she became the spiritual centre of our family after the passing of our parents, who she cared for in their latter years. Percy played hockey for St. Mary's University where — joined by Bob Dawson and Darrell Maxwell — he was part of the first all-black line in university hockey. After university, he scouted in junior and pro hockey, taught at Dalhousie University in Halifax, and then went into provincial politics where he held three port-folios: Minister of Economic and Rural Development; Minister of Tourism, Culture and Heritage; and Minister of African Nova Scotian Affairs. Mike became a very skilled draftsman and artist-architect. He had incredible hand-eye coordination as an athlete, but was always more artistically inclined.

In addition, three cousins became part of our family and were considered our siblings: Lorne, Carol Ann and Marvin (who went by "Pop"). Two more cousins, Andre and Tammy, lived with us for a considerable time when their house was being rebuilt after a fire.

Also, there were "uncles," who were not even uncles at all, but just people who came to be part of the family one way or another. Freeman, for example. I called him Uncle Freemo. He had been with the family before I was born, an old man whose exact age no one knew, but we think he was over a hundred when he passed on. We all loved him dearly. I was told that he joined the family when my grandfather found him sleeping in a barn where he worked and took him in. Uncle Freemo would spoil us kids every Friday evening by bringing us comic books and candy, and by giving us money for the movies. He adored my parents and made certain that he spoiled them, too. "This is the only family that I have," I once heard him say. "They treat me as a man, and that's worth more than anything in this world."

We would have uncles and aunts around all the time. Some aunts were so familiar to our white friends that they often started calling them "Aunt."

Our home was a stopping point for many in the local black community when they were coming in to Windsor, and again before they left town. From our two-storey house at 125 Cottage Street, high on a hill, we had one of the better views in Windsor. We could see all the dyke land, the old high school and the police station. The house was purchased in 1854 by my great-great-grandfather Issac Paris. My dad inherited it. It was old-style, on a nice piece of land. When I was about nine or ten, Dad tore it down and built the new family house on the same piece of land.

The new house was okay, but that old house was special. Today

The Paris family home on Cottage Street in Windsor, Nova Scotia.

archaeologists and historians would not have allowed it to be demolished. Over the years we found artifacts — coins and arrowheads and the like. It had a fireplace in almost every room, a large veranda in the back and a porch on the front. The basement had thick walls of cement and stone. A small passageway led to the basement, and smaller passages connected several rooms. All my aunts on my mom's side were afraid to go to the basement because it was rumoured that an old sea captain had killed his wife down there. True or not, kids from all over the neighbourhood played there a lot and never once saw any ghosts or sea captains . . . or aunts.

The living room became part of our family folklore because that's where, while playing cowboys and Indians, I tried to make smoke signals by building a fire right there on the rug! A good whuppin' from Mom followed. To go from upstairs to downstairs we slid on a rail — a feat my younger brother Percy could never master. Unlike everybody else, who just coasted off, Percy would slip and fall on his head. *Always* his head. Whether this was early training for his future political career, I can't really say.

We had most of the appliances of the day, including two freezers and a washing machine where one of my aunts got her braids caught in the wringer. In the mid-1950s we bought a television set — one of the first families in Windsor to get one — where I sat for hours mesmerized by the "Indian chief" test pattern. I used to love cowboy shows, like *Roy Rogers* and *Hopalong Cassidy*, and movies where the hero rode with his posse into the sunset.

To keep warm in the old house we had three or four kids in a bed. Sometimes there would be twenty around the table for meals. I don't know how my mother did it, but nobody left our house hungry. And everyone was well-behaved. If they did something wrong at our house, they got spanked. Not violently, just a slap on the bum. The same held for us when we went to friends' homes. Their parents would spank us, too. (Today, no reasonable adults would *think* about spanking a child not their own.) Incredibly, even with all this traffic in our house, we had just *one* bathroom. First come, first served.

* * *

Mom came from nearby Three Mile Plains, one of the larger black communities in the area and the home of my cousin, boxer Clyde Gray, who in the 1970s fought twice for the world welterweight title. The Plains was poor, but interesting. Bootlegging was big by both blacks and whites, and, frankly, back then the Plains didn't always have the strongest family structure. We weren't always sure who was related to whom. Secrets were well-kept. Interracial dating was generally frowned upon, but clandestine black-white "encounters" happened frequently. Mom used to say when the lights go out colour disappears. (One day on the television news she and I noted a very influential, wealthy, white Maritimer. Without hesitation or emotion she said, "John, that's your cousin, but no one will ever admit it." That was the end of the conversation. Neither of us ever broached the topic again.)

My mother's actual name was Annie May, but everyone just called her Annie. She was one of six States sisters, all strong-willed and protective of one another. Several were servants to business people in Windsor. Her parents died when she was relatively young and Mom, on her mother's request, tended to the needs of many of our aunts and uncles into their declining years.

Mom was sensitive, proud, thoughtful, smart. A slight woman who in later years had a bit of a posterior, in her youth she was truly beautiful. She never worked outside the home, but was active in the community in the ladies' auxiliary of the Royal Canadian Legion and the Windsor United Baptist Church. Mom was also a neighbourhood resource. When other women needed something or other, they'd always check to see if Annie had it. Often she did. She and my sister Faye once started a little business in front of our house, selling vegetables from our garden. It didn't go well. Seems my father had given *carte blanche* to our neighbours to come into our garden and help themselves. Mom protested. Dad just shrugged.

In some ways, Mom was a contradiction. On the outside, she was soft-spoken and reserved, a great listener sought out by neighbourhood kids who would come and talk to her about their troubles. On the inside, however, she was tough and resolute.

Once Mom and Aunt Viola were downtown getting groceries when they encountered a local character known as Judge Baxter, who drove a horse and buggy. He lived with his long-haired sister, who played the piano late at night in front of the living-room window with the blinds open. (This spooked all the Curry's Corner Boys, who were a little timid about passing that house after dusk.) Well, this day in the store Judge Baxter barged in front of Aunt Vi and my mother without excusing himself. Even worse, he then bent over and farted. When George straightened up and didn't apologize, my mother knocked him back into the aisle. The judge got the message.

In another store, when I was seven or eight, I was with Mom in a checkout line cradling a couple of big boxes. The clerk blankly looked up at her and asked, "Is this all?" Mom said, "Yes, thank you." The clerk took her money and flipped the change on the counter. She then quickly gave a very warm greeting to the next person in line. Mom started to pick up the money . . . then stopped. I saw *that* look on her face. She said to the clerk, "Pick that money up and place it either in my hand or lay it down respectfully." I jumped to do this but she put her hand out and said, "Not you, John. I'm speaking to this lady who threw it down." I was shocked. But I knew Mom was upset and would not back down. "I am not leaving until you do it," she told the woman. The clerk turned red, then slowly picked up the money and handed it to my mother. I felt proud, without fully understanding why.

* * *

My father's name was John, but everyone knew him as Buster. He grew up in the 1920s and 1930s, the only black student in his elementary school. Little Buster Paris was a charmer. He overcame racism by using basic smarts and a strong, winning personality that in his youth made him the perfect choice for mascot of local senior hockey teams.

Dad could be boisterous, but at the same time humble. He could spin a yarn with the best of them, often adding details that became more and more absurd until people caught on that he was just joking. He never lacked for pleasant conversation with anyone, and every woman who entered his post office, where he worked for more than twenty-five years, received a polite compliment. Dad also owned what we think was the first steam-operated laundry in Eastern Canada. The business was started by his great grandfather and at one time did all the laundry for Windsor's King's College. It lasted a few years then folded.

While he stood only about five-foot-five, he was wiry, agile and muscular, with strong hands and great balance. Excellent at hockey, he was even better at baseball. He played several positions for the local senior team in the 1930s. His ability was confirmed when the New York Giants, the storied National League team, wrote to invite him to a tryout camp. Probably someone had told a "bird dog" scout about him, who in turn informed people in New York. However, along the way someone forgot to mention that this prospect named Buster Paris was a Negro! Back then blacks were banned from playing in the major leagues, so it was a significant oversight. In any case, his mother feared for his safety so Dad didn't go to the camp. But it would have been interesting.

My father was a decorated World War II veteran, fighting in Italy and France, returning with an injured shoulder. One of his friends, a local Esso station owner named Sonny Brown, himself a veteran, told me that during a surprise confrontation overseas, Dad stayed behind and fought to allow others to safely escape. Each Remembrance Day we'd watch him quietly leave the house, loaded down with medals. He rarely discussed his war experiences, a peculiarity shared with many veterans. When Dad died in 2007, at age eighty-seven, I was struck by how many grown men — black and white — were moved to tears. That says plenty.

For many years my father was one of the best known men in Windsor, rarely seen without his trademark pipe. He was extremely active in the community: the Air Cadets, the Royal Canadian Legion, the Lions Club, several town committees and the church choir. I believe one year he was named the Nova Scotia Volunteer of the Year and recognized by the Canadian government. But he's most remembered for minor sports. Over the years dad coached and mentored hundreds of kids, one of many people in Windsor who gave of themselves in this way, often behind the scenes. He taught me baseball fundamentals and how to appreciate the game. Often he and I would be out in the summer sun, Dad hitting balls to me on a pothole-filled school yard to hone my reflexes on ground balls.

As much as I relished those baseball sessions with my father, the true cement of our relationship was our shared passion for another sport — hockey.

CHAPTER 2
Scotty

As kids we dove into sports. All sports, all the time. Serious stuff. On rinks and on ponds and on the street, even pick-up hockey games had gravity. For our "Spring World Series" it was as if Hammerin' Hank and The Mick walked among us.

Where sports were concerned I was a quick learner. Unlike grade school with its numbing structure, at the rink and on the baseball diamond I was a sponge. Details intrigued me and strategies fascinated me. I could easily recite histories of all NHL teams. I learned to watch and interpret and absorb *everything*.

We learned from many sources. Television helped, but back then sports coverage was minimal and not the quality we enjoy today. We studied our local senior baseball and hockey teams, the latter featuring future pros Simon Nolet, Serge Aubry, Jacques Allard and others. Mostly, we'd watch the older kids. My pal Brian Redden and I would scrutinize how they played and then go off and emulate them. Sometimes, on the pond, when the stars aligned and they needed a body or two, the older kids let us join in. But usually we stood in the plowed edges of the rink . . . and

At hockey school in Kentville, NS, 1957.

waited. We weren't allowed to barge in. The pecking order was fixed and, at that point, our place was the bottom. So we'd clear a little section and play our own mini-game until, on that magical day, *our* names were called.

We played hockey everywhere we could, including church leagues and Boy Scout teams. We even helped out at the arena to get free time on the artificial ice. I spent many winter nights on an outdoor rink — with lights — in the backyard of a local butcher named Bud York. Dad knew I was sneaking out, but since he knew exactly where I was headed, there was not a problem. Bud would turn on the lights even if just one of us showed up and sometimes his wife would make us hot chocolate. Brian and I learned to play with our heads up by having the lights turned off.

Summer hockey schools were few in the 1950s. At one school, about forty kilometres from Windsor, in the town of Kentville, I won the "best player" and "meanest player" awards, for which the prize was a small medical kit. They even gave me a nickname, Sputnik, after the Soviet satellite. Often these hockey schools would entice NHL players. But it was chiefly to lend their names to the advertising because usually the stars did very little teaching. In Kentville, for example, there was a young Eddie Shack, then a New York Ranger, along with Montreal Canadiens' stand-out goalie Bill Duran. I doubt either broke a sweat with us.

* * *

Windsor's minor hockey teams in the 1950s and 1960s were remarkably business-like. If we talked at all in our dressing rooms it was in hushed, short sentences that focused on the game. This was *hockey*, this was *important*. Local minor hockey was run by an athletic club, which received some funding from the town. There was no registration fee so all boys — there were no girls in the system at that time — played for free. I played with some fine players. Joey Robertson was our goalie, although he later changed to forward and signed with the Boston Bruins organization. Brian Redden also signed with the Bruins. Others included Doug Miller, Delphis Caldwell, Howie Fish, Billy Boyd, David Boyd, Jake Miller, Richard Redden, Billy Foley, Chook Smith and Claire "The Snake" Weir. All my brothers were good players as well.

Boys from peewee to juvenile were organized into teams and then leagues, with "rep" teams selected according to ability and — please note — character. A youngster's attitude mattered. Chippy kids were not tolerated for long. Nor was gauche celebration after a goal, chest-pounding or trash-talking. We showed respect for opponents and celebrated only *after* the game. Show respect, get respect. True then, true now.

The epicentre of minor sports in Windsor was Murray "Moe" Smith. For baseball as well as hockey, Moe was the man. "Coaching minor hockey is certainly a privilege and a joy," he once declared in the local weekly newspaper.

Moe was not long-winded. In fact, he was kind of a loner. But he understood sports and he understood us. He'd skate us hard during practices and teach positional play, basic skills and responsibilities away from the puck. Otherwise, Moe just let us play. He rarely scolded or screamed at a player and we worked our butts off for him. During games he'd keep his instructions simple: "turn it up," or "let's go, boys," or "pick it up now," or "stay out of the box." Stuff like that.

Moe let me hang around his family's sporting goods store downtown where he often gave me any stick I wanted. Other than an occasional errand, I don't remember doing much to earn those sticks. If I was there and he was eating, then I was eating, too. I wasn't the only kid he treated this way. On his teams the skates were always sharp and the sweaters always clean and mended. Never a charge.

* * *

My first racist experience in sports happened when I was still playing minor hockey in Windsor. It took place in Greenwood, Nova Scotia, a site of a military base. I was eight or nine years old and like our other players I was thrilled to play in a different arena and in another town. The thrill ended, however, as soon as we stepped on the ice and local men began screaming at me, calling me "Buckwheat," "monkey" and "nigger." A player on the other team actually cried because of all the hostility. I persevered that day, putting my head down and trying to ignore it. But I still feel pain in the pit of my stomach when I think of that episode — the first of many. Fortunately, my father was not there. If he was, something very bad would have happened.

In 1963 we beat North Sydney to win the provincial midget championship. They had a big star named Miles MacDonald, who we had heard a lot about. I took it upon myself to outperform him, to make him chase *me* and not the other way around. We won, 7–4, in a packed Windsor arena. I scored three goals and had two assists. The championship was Windsor's biggest provincial win in two decades. That night there was a big dance at the Memorial

Center. No alcohol, but plenty of 7 Up and Pepsi, all the Scotties potato chips we could eat, and — let's get real here — lots of girls. Years later, in the 1990s, at a function at the Windsor Lions Club, a middle-aged woman told me she had an additional reason to celebrate that victory. Seems she used to lay bets on games when I was playing. "I made *a lot* of money on you," she grinned.

A lasting treasure for me from that time came from Moe Smith, who wrote in the local newspaper, "[One player who oozed a winning attitude] was John Paris who comes from a family whose motto seems to be, 'Never Quit.' With his speed, expanding skill and determination, John soon became a leader in his team and was often called up to play with the older division teams. Being a very positive person, John's remarks in the dressing room or on the bench were heeded by all. He inspired his teammates to greater things . . . John Paris may not be the biggest guy on the block, but pound-for-pound you won't find a finer warrior. [I]t's heart that makes a winner and I know John is well equipped in that department. You will not find a more loyal person than John Paris."

* * *

It was an afternoon in May 1963 and my friends and I were in the middle of our Spring World Series when my little brother Percy puffed up to the field on his bike. "John, you gotta come home. Right now!"

I tried to ignore him. "Not *now*. We're playin' . . ."

Percy's annoying little-brother voice strained to take on some authority. "Right now! Mom and Dad are there with Mr. Bowman, from the Montreal Canadiens. They're waitin' for *you* in the house. Now!"

With Percy in the lead we all sprinted towards my house. A little out of breath, I burst through our front door and walked into the living room where my parents were chatting with a trim, dark-haired fellow in a nice sports jacket with no tie. When he saw me he stood up and extended his hand and smiled.

"I'm Scott Bowman with the Canadiens, John . . ."

I reached out and shook his hand. He then sat back down on the sofa next to my father. My mind was exploding. I am thinking *this is unbelievable!* I was aware of some interest in me because I'd received letters from other organizations: Detroit Red Wings, Toronto Maple Leafs and Boston Bruins. While they were great for my ego, I also knew that many kids across the country got such letters. It was a way that teams made their interest known and official. But certainly no one had bothered to come see me . . . until now. And the fact that he represented the Montreal Canadiens — my team, our family's team — made this momentous.

Bowman looked over at me. "You're quite a hockey player, John. What do you think of the Montreal Canadiens?"

I replied that I liked them a lot. Bowman smiled. Dad smiled. I smiled.

At that time Bowman was the Canadiens chief scout and just twenty-nine years old. Of course I didn't know I was looking at the man who one day would be widely recognized as the greatest coach in hockey history, winning nine Stanley Cups, holding countless NHL coaching records and acquiring the nickname "Rain Man" for his memory of statistics and general hockey knowledge.

Bowman probed a little deeper. "So, John . . ."

I felt my whole body tighten. A little voice inside was reminding me to keep my answers short and be polite. I was really just trying not to jump out of my skin.

". . . what are your interests? What do you like to do?"

I replied that my main interests were sports, primarily baseball and hockey.

Bowman nodded. "What are your plans?"

Plans? I forget what I answered, exactly. I think part of it mentioned sports.

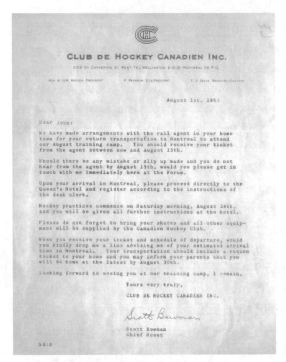

My official invitation to tryout camp of Montreal Jr. Canadiens, 1963. Signed by Scotty Bowman, who scouted me.

"I know you have talent, John, and we're interested in you — seriously. Or else I wouldn't be here."

"Yes, sir," I said, with a little nervous grin.

The conversation continued for a while, with Bowman and my father doing most of the talking. I could tell that Dad, a good judge of character, was impressed. They seemed to be bonding. (About forty-five years later I was in Florida and ran into Bowman at a conference. The first thing he asked about was my father. He remembered after all those years, demonstrating not just his own astonishing memory, but my father's ingratiating personality. "You didn't say too much that day," Scotty Bowman laughed. "No, sir," I replied.)

After Bowman left that day, I could see that Dad was excited. "When someone like this takes the time to come here — *to our house* — then this is important," he told me.

A week or so later I was again at the ball park when Moe Smith came up and handed me an envelope that showed the Canadiens' letterhead. Inside was an invitation, signed by Bowman, dated August 1, 1963 — my seventeenth birthday — to attend the training camp of the Montreal Junior Canadiens, the NHL team's junior A affiliate and the most prestigious junior team in the country at that time.

* * *

I'll never forget the train ride to Montreal. I was too excited to sleep the night before. At the station in downtown Windsor that Thursday morning were my parents, coaches, friends, relatives, teammates and others all wishing me luck. I vividly recall how they were beaming, proud of my success. I felt such love that day. I think I hugged everyone.

I was the first player on the train, but as it looped down to Halifax I was joined by other Nova Scotian prospects invited to the camp:

Norm Ferguson, of Sydney, would make the Junior Canadiens the following season, and also play there in 1965–66. In 1968–69 he was the runner-up for NHL rookie of the year, setting the rookie scoring record.

Darrell Maxwell, of Truro, another black kid, would play junior in Quebec for a few seasons and then join the St. Mary's University Huskies.

Brian O'Byrne, of Amherst, ended up playing that year for the Peterborough Petes, in the Ontario Hockey League. The following season he had a stint with the Montreal Juniors. He ended his junior days starring with the Halifax Junior Canadiens. He also played for St. Mary's.

Miles McDonald, from Cape Breton, who I faced in the Nova Scotia midget championship the year before, and **Gerard Pellerine**, from New Glasgow, were also part of our group. There may have been one or two other players on the train, but no more than that. Our chaperone was a Canadiens scout from Prince Edward Island.

We all shared a nervous energy that helped us connect right away. Normie Ferguson, who I think was a year older than the rest of us, was the calmest of our group. It was an overnight trip so I had a berth, but I had trouble sleeping because of the noise of the tracks and — never having been so far from home alone — I missed my parents, especially my mother.

We pulled in to (coincidentally) Windsor Station in Montreal the next morning and exited the train. The people! All shapes and sizes and colours, scurrying madly in tight spaces. I looked at Normie and Darrell. We were mesmerized. Country bumpkins just standing there, eyes wide, mouths open. It was scary. I thought: *What am I into here?*

* * *

We were met at the train station by two young Canadiens scouts, Cliff Fletcher and Ron Caron, both future top-notch NHL general managers. Fletcher would oversee the Calgary Flames in 1989 to their only Stanley Cup, and the colourful Caron in St. Louis would become the stuff of hockey lore. (Caron would one day hire *me* as a scout.)

Cliff escorted us the short distance from train station to the Queen Elizabeth Hotel, then just five years old and one of the grandest in the country. (Notable guests: Queen Elizabeth, Charles de Gaulle, and John and Yoko.) We checked in, went to eat, and walked to the Montreal Forum. Although I was very young I understood what a privilege all this was. The Canadiens were a dynasty and just to be noticed by that organization was an honour. If you were not selected for the big team, then other junior teams at a lower level, on hand to assess the talent, could make you an offer. If you didn't draw an offer, you simply returned home and continued to play, humbled, realizing every region, city and town had good players. There was no such thing as an "open camp" or "pay-to-come," as you see today, especially in the States. My parents didn't send me to multiple tryout camps or compose gushing letters to influential people or move me from place to place just so I could be seen. Nor did the parents of the other prospects who travelled with me to Montreal that fall. We all *earned* that train ride on our own.

* * *

At the Forum we were assigned our dressing room and each given equipment for the duration of our stay at the camp. I weighed only about 135 pounds and the pants they had for me were far too big. An assistant had to rush out and find a smaller pair, in Canadiens blue. The other stuff fit well enough.

In the dressing room before that first session my heart thumped so loudly that I wondered if anyone else could hear it. Everything had a dream-like quality. Several of the players, mainly from Quebec, huddled and laughed as friends do, all in French. Those of us new and unknown strained to take in the whole scene. No one more so than me.

Stepping onto the ice surface of the Montreal Forum took my breath away. The Forum benches! The Forum walls! The lingering bouquet of greasy food, cigarette smoke and perfume fused in to the corridors and the wooden seats. The ice glistened, but it was softer than I had expected. Our blades cut the surface, making a deep, rich sound. I was hyper-conscious of every stride.

Yves Nadon, a former American Hockey League goalie, was the Junior Canadiens' coach that year. It would be his only one. From the outset, I realized that making the team was a long shot for me. Many players were assured spots, deservedly so. That first day I would share the ice with Jude Drouin, Carol Vadnais,

Jacques Lemaire, Serge Savard, André Lacroix, André Boudrias, Christian Bordeleau, René Drolet and Bob Charlebois, among many others. Yvan Cournoyer was not there the first day, but he showed up the second day, dressed only in a warm-up suit. Man, that guy was fast! Looking back, I appreciate that all these players were teenagers with insecurities like me — although most of them hid any self-doubt rather well.

As I circled the Forum ice my inner voice was working overtime. *"Time to show up, John . . . Time to apply yourself . . . You can play with these guys, John . . . Play with abandon . . ."* After a few laps I felt more relaxed. I was able to look around at the other players and my breathing returned to normal.

At this camp there were no protracted skating drills with stop watches or agility exercises with ropes and pylons. Rather, the prospects were divided into teams and evaluated by their performance during formal scrimmages with a referee and two linesmen. We were not there to get in shape; we were there to show what we could do. Each day we had a session in the morning and another in the afternoon.

Cliff Fletcher seemed to be one of the people in charge of the camp. I occasionally looked up in the stands and would see him sitting with Ken Reardon, Canadiens vice-president, and Sam Pollock, soon to become the general manager. To be frank, I dominated the first two or three days of that camp. I had jump. It was easy for me. I felt strong and I was healthy. It was my ice! Oddly, it some ways, it's easier to play with elite players. I didn't have to be the one directing traffic. Feedback on me was positive; the vibe from the coaches was good. After the second day the scout from Prince Edward Island, who escorted us on the train, told me, "You're not goin' anywhere. You're staying here."

It was interesting to watch players' performances rise and fall. Adrenalin can carry a player for a while. But when the adrenalin reduces, one has to know how to continue. A lot of players come to tryouts and shine early on. Then you see character come out. If he doesn't know how to maintain, he slips back. In those days you got tested. You were hooked and held with impunity. I went to the hard areas and I got hit a lot.

Darrell Maxwell was released fairly early. The day he was sent home he told me that he thought I was going to make it. I was sad to see Darrell go, but consoled myself in that I now had a room to myself.

I was there for one full week. By then the camp was down to essentially one team, and Yvan Cournoyer was in full equipment. While my performance was good, they felt that as a kid barely seventeen years old I was not ready physically or emotionally to make such a significant jump. They had a point, but I was still disappointed by the decision. My last day there they told me I was going to be assigned to the Rosemount Bombers of the Metropolitan Montreal Junior Hockey League. They said to go back home and wait for their call.

Returning on the train to Windsor, I became ill. Itching, feverish. When I got home I broke out in a rash all over my hands and half my body. I was treated by our family doctor, who previously tended to stomach problems I had. I am certain he did his best. This was, however, the early stages of a major health crisis that the medical community, without the benefit of today's knowledge of intestinal and bowel problems, would misdiagnose for several years.

I waited for two weeks — no phone call came from Montreal. My family was becoming concerned as arrangements had to be made for school. Finally, the Canadiens suggested that I stay home, play hard and return next year.

It couldn't come soon enough.

CHAPTER 3
Chocolate Rocket

Back in Windsor I settled in to my usual life while restlessly marking the months until I could return to Montreal. During this time I occasionally felt a little drained, and once or twice my arms were inexplicably weak, but I thought little of it and didn't bother to mention it to my parents or anyone else.

Finally, in mid-September 1964, an invitation arrived from the Maisonneuve Braves of the Metropolitan Montreal Junior League, a feeder league for Ontario Hockey Association junior teams, especially the Montreal Junior Canadiens. Maisonneuve was a working-class neighbourhood in the east end of the city, landmarks being the 5,000-seat Maurice Richard Arena, where the Braves played their home games, and, as of the 1970s, Olympic Stadium. They were coached by Herve Lalonde, a veteran of the Eastern Hockey League.

A short, thickly constructed man just thirty-one years old, Herve rarely gave accolades and didn't have strong interpersonal skills. Otherwise he was a good coach. He taught hockey basics well and was ahead of his time in his belief in preseason training.

I left home in June and stayed with my uncle Junior in Montreal just to take part in the program Herve devised. We trained that summer at Centre Père Marquette, off Rue Pie IX. While not as sophisticated as today's regimes — we didn't have high-tech machines and blood testing — it was hardly prehistoric foolishness. Calisthenics, weights, stretching, sprints, distant-running, balance, agility. We even watched training films, albeit on 16 mm reels. There was no loafing. I and about eight others were there for a purpose.

The Braves' lineup that season was an eclectic blend of attitudes and backgrounds that included future Montreal Canadiens all-star defenceman Guy Lapointe. Guy was an easy-going lad with a big, open smile. He didn't speak much English, and my French was still weak, so our communication was minimal, but I still liked him. We had one tall fellow from Saint-Hyacinthe, Denis Duchesne, who was a die-hard separatist. He wouldn't stand up for the Canadian national anthem, but no one — even us English players — seemed to care. Denis and I would talk and laugh about all sorts of stuff. Hockey is hockey, even in the middle of the Quiet Revolution. Other teammates included Ted Ouimet, Peter White, Rocky Farr, Guy Barrette, Tommie Angle, Michel Jacques and Cape Breton's Phil Obendorf.

I got off to a terrific start with the Braves. By December the media was declaring me the league's best rookie. In time I even picked up a nickname: "The Chocolate Rocket." I think it originated in the Halifax media, but the Quebec press seized on it.

The Chocolate Rocket.

I doubt it was intended as an insult. Frankly, I took it as a compliment. Anything "rocket" was positive, evoking Maurice "The Rocket" Richard, the greatest hockey player of his era. It was also an apt description of my prime asset: my speed. It certainly confirmed that I was standing out from the crowd. Chocolate Rocket or Blue Rocket or Pink Rocket. For me, conditioned by the social filters of the 1960s, it was the "rocket" part that mattered. As for the "chocolate" . . .

There were not the same sensibilities back then. What today would be an objectionable inference to race or ethnicity or gender or appearance, in the 1960s was simply accepted or considered clever and cute. I reasoned: what athletes get nicknames? The answer: good ones. Nicknames usually paid tribute to athletic prowess. For example, basketball had "Chocolate Thunder," a tag given forward Darryl Dawkins by soul singer Stevie Wonder. Boxer Joe Louis was "The Brown Bomber." Baseball had "The Flying Dutchman" (Honus Wagner). Hockey had "The Chief" (George Armstrong) and "The Flying Frenchmen" (the Montreal Canadiens).

While I was, at worst, ambivalent about the name, my father was not pleased. He thought it might be a slur, regardless of the intent. Dad was well aware of the social currents of the day and the race issues boiling in the United States. Nova Scotia, thanks to its large black population — at least for Canada — was sensitized to this social change. I think he complained to some hockey officials as well as to the rather creative Halifax newspaper reporter who he thought came up with the name, but I wasn't directly involved. In any case, the name stuck. In the end, no harm, no foul.

* * *

As Braves players we got special passes to NHL games and were allowed in the Forum during Canadiens' practices. Sometimes I'd slowly walk by the Canadiens' dressing room before their practice and discreetly peer in and see many of the players I had idolized just months before back home in Windsor. In the early weeks there'd be the occasional gestures hello and maybe a few quick pleasantries with them, during which I always made it a point to call everyone "sir," including the Canadiens' support staff. One afternoon their assistant trainer, Larry Albut, came out and said, *"Hey toi, Paris, pour toi. Ne dites rein."* ("Hey Paris, something for you. Keep it to yourself where you got them.") He handed me three sticks. One of them — since bequeathed to my grandson — belonged to Jean Beliveau.

During our training camp that year several Canadiens veterans joined us to get the kinks out before their camp opened. Unlike today, when professional and junior players train all summer, many of these men had not been on skates or near a gym in four months. Several had other jobs to supplement their annual hockey salary, which in some cases was barely more than that of an experienced tradesman.

For one Braves scrimmage I was on a line with Henri "The Pocket Rocket" Richard. Just a couple of years before, playing on Long Pond in Windsor, this was a fantasy. I think I grinned the entire session. But Henri was serious that day — as usual. I always wanted to ask him certain questions, but I never did. Like other Braves players I was intimidated by Henri. He would dress quickly and quietly and we didn't have the nerve to go into that space. He'd nod and maybe give you a little smile. But that was it. If any Canadiens player wanted to talk with you, they would talk with you. Their choice. There was a pecking order in hockey. You just didn't walk up and say, "Hey, what are you doin' here . . . ?" It was about respect.

At that same scrimmage was hard-scrabbled, square-jawed winger Claude Provost, the sturdy "shadow" of superstar Bobby Hull. Provost, who skated with a pronounced bow-legged stride, advised me about looking before I went into corners and how to tuck in my elbow on an opponent. He also showed me how an extra step would take away an opponent's lane. (I tried this move in a game that season against Michel Bergeron, the future fiery NHL coach known as *Le Petit Tigre*. Bergeron was not pleased with me.) Defenceman J.C. Tremblay, a puck magician, was one of the more generous with practical tips during these sessions. He demonstrated how to pretend to lose the puck then adroitly pick it up with a skate. Tremblay always had his head up, explaining "you have to see first what the others cannot see."

At these workouts when a Canadiens player shouted for you to dig deeper and skate harder, you dug deeper and skated harder. A nod from the Pocket Rocket after you made a good play was worth a million bucks. I was actually as fast as some of these pros, but they could execute so well, with remarkable situational awareness. We strained to keep up with them for that reason. Some Canadiens would come to our practices during the season to rehab after an injury. And they would take part in a *full* practice, doing all the drills and exercises, not merely go through the motions. It always amazed me how hard they would work and how business-like they were. Yet, they were truly enjoying themselves.

I recall a few other Canadiens fondly. John Ferguson, himself a rookie, often took the time to ask me how things were going. Despite his well-deserved reputation as a tough guy on the ice, he was one of the more genteel Canadiens away from the rink. Jean Beliveau was very kind and always greeted me warmly. Many years hence Beliveau and I became a little closer when we spoke at conferences together. I was also there when he received his honourary doctorate from St. Mary's University in Halifax. A true gentleman, he remains the perfect corporate image of the Montreal Canadiens. Goaltender Jacques Plante, while not technically a Hab at the time, much to my surprise greeted me by my first name one day at Place Versailles, a downtown shopping complex. The friends I was with were impressed, needless to say.

One time I encountered Canadiens coach Toe Blake in the Forum when I was there seeing physiotherapist Bill Head for a groin injury. (Head had placed a tube on my upper thigh, which was then the standard treatment for a groin pull if you wanted to try and play that evening.) I was slowly preparing to leave the tiny examination room when Mr. Blake walked in, looked at me and paused. Fedora, suit and tie, intense eyes, the full deal. He asked how I was doing.

"Fine, Mr. Blake, thank you." *Mr. Blake.* It would have been unthinkable that a young person call him "Toe" or his actual first name, Hector. Mr. Blake placed his hand on my shoulder.

"I've watched you. Don't let anybody tell you can't do anything."

I nodded.

"Have you ever thought about coaching?"

I was flattered. Probably someone had told him that I was rather assertive and liked giving directions to teammates.

"You know the game. That's good. When you were yelling at that winger to get there and you pointed, we saw the puck go right on his stick. That's good. Where'd you get this?"

"My father," I said.

With Mr. Blake, it was never a long narrative. Just right to the point. Sometimes with a cuss word for affect. ("Shut the fuck up, now.") Some saw Toe Blake as a bear in a fedora, which he wore constantly. I found him considerate. In the several conversations I had with him he never chastised me in any way. Rather Mr. Blake would just pat me on the back and tell me to keep on going. This small gesture meant a lot. He'd hand me a few dollars on occasion and always make it a point to ask if anyone was bothering me. I'd tell him they weren't.

"Well you let me know if they do," he'd say. I know he meant it.

* * *

Maurice Richard may have been the most astounding hockey player ever. For an entire population he was certainly the most *important* hockey player of his time. As author Roch Carrier wrote in *Our Life with the Rocket: The Maurice Richard Story*, "Around the ice in the Forum, the crowd has found a world in which they are not powerless. Their province is being torn apart by the debate over conscription, divided by language, culture, economic disparities. Workers and bosses, English and French, Jews and Gentiles: with one voice, the population of Quebec cheers the French Canadian. And through this ritual, French Canadians feel a little less defeated, a little less humiliated, a little stronger."

For more than a decade the Rocket carried the torch. Guided by his famous glare the Canadiens won and won and won. But while the fire still burned, by the late 1950s the skills had dimmed, requiring others such as Jean Beliveau, Boom-Boom Geoffrion and his own little brother, Henri, lead the charge.

By the time I met Maurice Richard he was in the middle of a transitional period in his life. He had retired, reluctantly, four years before and had been give a $20,000 annual salary to be what the Canadiens were calling a vice-president. He had an office and other trappings, but his duties were unclear and the Rocket was struggling to find a sense of purpose. Two years later he would resign in frustration and for many years there was an uncomfortable, strained relationship between the hockey club and its most celebrated player. For me, as an eighteen-year-old gazing upon this hockey icon, all this was either unknown or unimportant. I was too busy being star-struck.

The first time I saw him he was entering the Montreal Forum, dressed in casual street clothes. It was September. I knew that some people thought he was gruff, and a person just didn't run up to someone like the Rocket. So that day when I saw him coming I held my distance. As he moved alongside me, without breaking stride, he nodded — to me! I had to pinch myself. I doubt whether I have ever had a bigger smile. Long afterward I boasted that the mighty Rocket had *talked* to me that day. Okay, I exaggerated.

Eventually, however, we did speak. I would see him at the Forum or — appropriately — at the Maurice Richard Arena. Each time our conversations were a little longer. Almost from the start he took an interest in my personal welfare. One of the first such talks happened near the Forum early that first season. It began when he briskly walked up to me.

"Are you OK?" he asked.

"Yes, sir. I'm fine." By this time I was having serious health issues with cramps and fatigue, so the answer was untrue. However, the last thing a person in my position needed was a reputation as a complainer. Unless a limb was about to fall off, there was *not* a problem. But I could tell the Rocket didn't believe my answer. He looked at me with those famous dark eyes.

"Do you like it here?"

"Yes, I do. It's different from Nova Scotia, but I like it a lot." (That answer *was* true.)

"Do you speak French?"

"Pretty good," I answered — in English. "I'm just starting. I can understand more than I can talk."

This drew a knowing smile from him. Richard was sensitive about learning the other language, having laboured for years to learn English, often being mocked by opposition players when the words did not come out perfectly.

"I expect you to be one of their leaders," the Rocket said, referring to the Braves.

I was thrilled. Then, hinting that he did not trust what I told him about my health, he repeated: "Feel good . . . ?"

"Yes, sir. But sometimes I get a little tired."

He looked at me, reached into his pocket and gave me a couple of dollars. Then he tapped me on the shoulder. "You'll be OK."

As we parted he said something in French that meant I shouldn't tell anyone that he had given me money. I didn't. This went on every time he'd see me. He'd ask how I felt, followed by words of encouragement, then reach in his pocket, take a two-dollar bill from his wallet and stuff the money in my shirt, usually with a couple little pats on my pocket. I always said, "Merci." Nothing more.

* * *

It was during the second half of that season that I started to feel extremely ill. The fleeting fatigue and weakness that I fought off the previous summer back in Windsor were now more frequent. As a result my play became unpredictable. Some games I would dominate and draw comparisons to the Pocket Rocket. Other games I was ineffective, practically invisible. I knew deep down that something was wrong. I was eighteen years old and fit and strong . . . and tired. Often *very* tired. I had no idea why. Many days even just touching my abdomen or lower area caused me sharp pain. I can remember going to a bathroom and crying while trying to eliminate. Often there was blood in my stools. Concentration became difficult. Every time I received or gave a body check, it was like death.

One time, before a game in Montreal North, I felt especially weak and nauseated. Blood was coming out of both ends and I was swollen around my neck and my arms. During the game I had sharp pains and trouble catching my breath. I was sweating even more than usual. One instant I was very hot, the next I was cold and shivering. Yet, I scored twice that evening and managed to finish the game, even as the cramps grew stronger. Team staff took me to the hospital immediately after the game, but I was sent home with assurance that I was OK. They said it was just the flu. As they would do many times in future, doctors that night gave me a bottle of stomach medicine and told me to take it easy for a day or two.

Over subsequent weeks I tried hiding my discomfort by adjusting how I played. It didn't work well. I ended up looking like I was lazy or scared, and especially timid about going into the corners. My inconsistent performance was not lost on the Braves management. Our assistant coach, Gene Cloutier, always seemed to read when there was something wrong with me. He'd say, "This is not normal. Are you certain that you are feeling okay, John? Are you telling me *everything*?" I was, sort of. I would parrot the doctors and reassure him that I was fine, that it was the flu. However, the fatigue, diarrhea and occasional dizzy spells continued.

Gene Cloutier was a terrific guy. If I needed something he was always there. He had a couple of memorable arguments with Herve Lalonde concerning me. One evening after a game I overheard him saying loudly, "I told you John was in the bathroom with diarrhea and he has a fever. But he still got dressed, played his game and never said a word about it. You yelled at him for not winning a corner battle against *two guys*. He didn't say a word to you, did he?"

Lalonde said no.

"Well, what does that tell you? He is complaining only about ice time, but you never took the time to tell anyone about what he's going through."

After that, things changed a bit.

One morning at the rink, Lalonde saw me and immediately told me I didn't look well. "Have you eaten?"

I said I hadn't. In fact, I had not eaten for a couple of days. I was hungry — sort of a sick-hungry. So he took me to a nearby restaurant and bought me eggs, bacon and toast. Herve could show a tough side, but he was also compassionate and was now more sensitive to my situation thanks to Gene. I ate all the breakfast — Herve stayed there until I did — but soon after I had severe diarrhea. My weight had dipped to about 125 pounds, ten or fifteen pounds under where it should have been. But I had natural muscle, so I was still strong. In any case, I was hoping all this internal upset would just go away . . . in time.

My play continued to decline. Some shifts I had jump; other times I was so fatigued I could barely move. It would come and go. Consequently word circulated that I did not give my all every time. In such a competitive atmosphere no one could afford such whispers. Herve sent me to the hospital a couple of times. I'm certain he didn't know the extent of my illness. How could he? I didn't know myself.

But I still had fight. One night against the Lachine Maroons I bodychecked their big defenceman so hard that I knocked him out cold. So the next game in Lachine they were waiting for me. The Maroons ran at me all night, but I held up, performed and fought back. A day or so later, near the Forum, I bumped into the Rocket and he beckoned to me.

"Good game," he said.

"Merci."

He then paused, squeezed my shoulder and said, "I know."

I was not exactly sure what he meant. *I know.* He had done this same thing a few other times. Hand-on-shoulder, then "I know."

I'll never know for sure what "I know" meant. But I treasured every encounter with the Rocket. We seemed to have a special bond. That I know.

* * *

While hockey was my focus, overall life in Montreal, so different from Curry's Corner, challenged me in other ways. There were significant adjustments to be made. Three in particular.

The first concerned the French environment. For the first year or so most people accommodated me and switched to English. Fortunately I can learn languages easily and picked up French rather quickly. By my second year it was much less an issue with me. Interestingly, most Quebec hockey dressing rooms and chatter during games featured a flowing combination of both languages. (One time after I assisted on a goal, Serge Savard, who was on the other team, skated by and patted me on back, "Way to go, *mon p'ti*.")

Whether playing or coaching, I never had anybody tell me not to speak English in the dressing room. However, I did hear Anglophones tell Francophones not to speak French. This bothered me. (As a coach, I always told my players that if you are so insecure that you try to dictate to another person what language they should speak, then *you* have a problem. On my teams, if it was French, speak it! If it was English, speak it! If it was Russian, speak it! There are bigger things in life to worry about.)

The second adjustment I had to make in Montreal related to the attention I was receiving just by being part of the Canadiens family. Frequently there'd be people hanging around asking me for autographs outside the Montreal Forum or the Richard Arena or elsewhere. At the hotel or on the street, people would say hello or bonjour and then pass me a piece of paper to sign. I did a few media interviews as well. This was flattering at first, as it would be for any eighteen-year-old. But I have a "loner" side to my personality so I rapidly stopped enjoying the recognition. In Windsor, I always had space. Not so in Montreal. I was unsure how to handle it all. But I learned.

The final adjustment was school. In the fall of 1964 I enrolled at Dunton High School in the east end of the city. Not a bad experience, but during my time there I faced a few issues because of my race. For example, in geography class the topic of climate and native people came up. When the teacher asked why tribes changed locations so frequently, one student stood up and said, "Well, the niggers want to eat." I looked around to see if the teacher — or anyone — was going to say something. No one did. I lost it. I jumped up and ran across two aisles and put my face an inch from the kid who spoke. "If you ever say something like that again when I am in the room, we'll make it your birthday . . . and I will be the only one with a gift for you."

The teacher tossed me out of the classroom. Later, in the school director's office, with the teacher there, I was told that I could not create such havoc or threaten anyone. I pointed out that I hadn't actually hit him, but I couldn't let something like that go unchallenged. I looked directly at the teacher. "*You* didn't say anything to him, no response at all." In the end, there was nothing said by the school director, either.

I concluded that there were two playing fields: one for *them* and another for *us*. When I asked a couple of the other black students in the class why they remained silent, their answer was, "Well, you saw what it got you. They don't care about us." I was amazed and frustrated that they had given up hope of receiving respect. Thankfully, not everyone felt that way. Others agreed with me: if you are black and you accept it, then that makes you wrong and no better than them.

The nasty incident may have been worth it. I soon heard about more kids saying: uh-uh, no more of this. A white student, John Purcell, unexpectedly came to see me one afternoon. John played for Verdun in the Metropolitan league. "I heard what happened in your class," he said. "I just want you to know that if I was there, I'd have punched him out." Knowing how he played hockey against me, I believe he would have. I have never forgotten his support.

* * *

Not all the adjustments to big city Montreal were so taxing. The vast cultural possibilities of Montreal were thrilling. One example was the vibrant nightlife. As a young person I couldn't avail myself of the full palette, but I still had many growth experiences.

Cabaret clubs were a big part of the Montreal nightlife in the

1950s and 1960s. Lucky for me, the Braves' assistant coach Gene
Cloutier worked as a doorman at the Casa Loma, one of the top
establishments. The Casa Loma was located on St. Catherine
Street, near St. Laurent Boulevard in the iconic section known
as The Main, and hosted some incredible jazz with the likes of
Miles Davis, Duke Ellington and John Coltrane. I didn't go to the
Casa Loma a lot as Gene was not comfortable with me in the club
environment. Still, teenage curiosity ablaze, I did go a few times,
hoping among other things to get a peek at a stripper like Lili St.
Cyr, who one time I *did* see . . . from far back, unfortunately.

In addition to the great music, the club was a favourite hang-
out for Montreal's underworld. This included members of the
Cotroni family. Linked with the powerful New York mob, the
Cotronis controlled Montreal's drug trade as well as other dark
activities in Quebec and Ontario. I met a few family members
who were high on the corporate ladder, including Joe di Maulo,
a major ally of the Cotronis, and Frank Cotroni, son of the family
boss. These guys were the real deal.

Di Maulo was well-dressed and looked me directly in the eye
when he spoke. A little disconcerting, but that's the way he was.
(Di Maulo was executed mob-style outside his Montreal home in
2012.) Frank Cotroni was even more of a straight-talk guy. He'd
curse or intimidate and he had an edge. You just knew Frank was
hard-nosed and not to be messed with. He was given the red car-
pet treatment all the time at the club. Once I met his brother Vic,
also a family boss. Vic seemed a little different than the others.
He was a top-notch dresser, very articulate and much softer in
his mannerisms. I was actually surprised to learn that Frank and
Vic were brothers.

It was obvious to everyone at the club who was street-wise
— and this was *most* of the people at the club — that I was not
street-wise. Frankly, I didn't care. I was really there just for the
music, always off to the side, always quiet. Gene had explained

to the mob guys who I was, so they didn't have an issue with me. And if those guys did not have an issue, then *no one* had an issue. They were always pretty polite to me as I sat there passively sipping on my 7 Up. If someone approached me, one of the "wise guys" would wave them away. One evening in there when a man called me "snowball," a couple of the Cotroni associates quickly came over and made him tell me that he was sorry. Then they told him to get the fuck out and not to come back. He left quietly.

During those years I saw a grand menu of legendary jazz, R&B and blues performers: Joe Tex, Wilson Picket, Aretha Franklin, The Paris Sisters and Fats Domino. Then I'd switch to French clubs where I enjoyed Little Caesar and the Romans, Ginette Reno, Les Baronets, Jenny Rock, Bruce Huard and Nanette Workman among others. I would listen and study how they were playing. Some of the biggest thrills happened by chance when a performer would go to another club and jam into the wee hours. I took in Eddie Floyd and saw the great blues organist Jimmy Smith this way. Amazing.

One well-known club, Le Mocambo, on Notre Dame East, provided me with maybe the richest experience of all. One night I was in the big room upstairs, at my table with my usual glass of 7 Up — for which I would give the waitress $15 and a big smile — waiting for the attraction to come on stage. Eventually one of the band members came out and asked if anyone in the audience could play a keyboard. Seems the regular guy was delayed for some unannounced reason. My hand shot up.

I can play keyboard, piano and organ and can read music, having been tutored back in Windsor by a former nun named Yolande Poirier. (Friends say I also have a darn good singing voice.) The keyboard they had on stage was a Yamaha. It was set too high for me, but I didn't bother to make them adjust it. I just asked them to write down the chords for me, which they did very quickly. They played a 2-6-5-4-1.

Finally, the star came out on stage.

Ray Charles.

Ray turned his head in my general direction as he settled in and said to make sure I hit the right chord. I did, luckily. I soon learned that he was not the easiest guy in the world to accompany because he would modify everything according to how he was feeling. His riffs, everything. So understandably this was a challenge for me. In addition, I wasn't experienced standing up to play and couldn't reach the top of the keyboard because of my height. So that night I worked only on the bottom keys.

I played one set. *Let's Go Get Stoned. Georgia. Hit the Road Jack*. I did about six songs in all before the regular guy came back, looking ill but well enough to take over. No problem. I had my moment with The Genius.

* * *

I continued to struggle all that season. It didn't help when late in the year the Braves traded my on-ice bodyguard, a huge black player named Gerry Rodriguez (son of Hollywood actor Percy Rodriguez). Without Gerry riding shotgun for me, opponents took liberties and bumped me around pretty good. Even so, if I had been healthy and able to freewheel, perhaps the Braves would not have been eliminated in the league semi-final. But after Christmas, as my illness advanced, there was little I could do about it. I was just too sick, too often. I scored seventeen goals in the first half of the year but only a few after that. Talk of my winning the top rookie award stopped. My future in hockey was suddenly murky.

CHAPTER 4
The Way It Is

In the summer of 1965, Butch Marchand, a scout with the Montreal Canadiens, gave me a choice: I could stay in the Metropolitan league and throughout the season play a few games with the Montreal Junior Canadiens, or I could transfer to the Sorel Black Hawks, of Quebec Junior A Hockey League. Butch favoured Sorel. I liked Butch. I selected Sorel.

The decision set the course for the rest of my life.

Located east of Montreal, at the convergence of the Richelieu and the St. Lawrence rivers, Sorel was a working-class city of forty thousand, known for heavy industry and the Hell's Angels, the world's most notorious biker gang, which would soon make Sorel its Canadian headquarters and more or less take over the place. The city operated almost entirely in French, as did the Black Hawks — a point Butch Marchand failed to mention to me. The team was a junior affiliate of the NHL's Chicago Blackhawks (although Montreal retained my rights) and owned by a couple of businessmen and a lawyer, all from the area. Marchand was also the Sorel coach, but was soon replaced that

Leading the charge for the Sorel Black Hawks in Halifax against the Junior Canadiens in 1966. Halifax captain Brian O'Byrne is in pursuit.

season by John Choyce, a former scout with a crusty demeanor and little patience.

Unfortunately, from the time I arrived there, my health issue — again cramps and again fatigue — made my play uneven. Even getting dressed for games became an ordeal. Yet Choyce was not sympathetic and attributed my dips in performance mainly to simple laziness. When I told him that I had no energy he responded by telling me to take better care of myself and to get to bed earlier. Once when I tried to elaborate, Choyce pushed me aside and said, "I didn't ask you for a song and dance." That ended the discussion.

By late December I had just four goals and seven assists, far below what I and others had expected. We were scheduled to play a couple of exhibition games with the Halifax Junior Canadiens just before Christmas, and I was hoping to get a boost from the trip home. I thought maybe playing in front of friends and family would recharge my batteries, although my parents seemed apprehensive about my playing in Halifax. Mom rarely attended games so this was a big deal to them. I was determined to make everyone proud.

* * *

The Halifax Junior Canadiens are a storied Maritime sports team, despite lasting just three years — 1965–66 to 1967–68 — and never coming close to winning the national junior hockey championship. This failure deeply disappointed Halifax businessman Fred MacGillivray, who had formed the team with that singular goal in mind. Roughly affiliated with the Montreal Canadiens, it was largely an all-star team drawn mostly from talent across the Maritimes. They played only exhibition contests, mainly on weekends, against local senior and university teams, plus games against junior teams from Ontario and Quebec. Crowds in the creaking, venerated Halifax Forum were large and enthusiastic, and Halifax players, despite being in their teens, were minor celebrities around town, accorded "adult" perks such as booze and gambling money.

My homecoming did not go unnoticed. I rated a mention or two in the local daily newspaper and on a couple of the Halifax AM radio stations. In addition, the Halifax Forum's in-house publication, *Sports Weekly*, featured "The Chocolate Rocket" in one of those classic, full-body, deer-in-the-headlights posed photos. The attention was nice. But things soon took a nasty turn.

It started during the warm-up for the first game. Standing behind our net I could hear the taunts coming from more than one place in the arena.

"Nigger! Hey, boy! Here nigger-nigger-nigger . . ."

My first thought was, "*Oh-no, not tonight. Mom's here.*"

This garbage escalated after I scored the first goal of the game, halfway into the second period, when I took a pass at the Halifax blue line and went in and deked their goalie, Gary Withers. Through the wire mesh screen that rimmed the rink I saw the ugly, distorted faces of people acting like complete idiots as they made monkey sounds and gestures. "Your mother's a gorilla, boy."

Seeing it all . . . and hearing every word . . . were Buster and Annie Paris.

"Scum! Nigger!" People were almost frothing. I was spat on more than once and coins were tossed at me through the screen when I went near the boards. I also got it from in back of our bench. My teammates didn't know how to react or what to say. Defenceman Max Goudreau tried. "Don't pay any attention to them," he said in French, and gave me a supportive squeeze on the shoulder. I took a deep breath. The idea of giving in to these bastards never crossed my mind. No surrender. Ever.

To make matters worse, it looked like I was hot-dogging as I leapt in the air to get around Halifax players. To some, it came across as cowardly. What the spectators didn't know — and not even my own team realized — is that it hurt even to lightly touch my body. So I desperately tried to protect my abdomen, and jumping usually diminished the impact. The flimsy padding of the day absorbed very little of the jolt, so when I got nailed into the boards or knocked to the ice the pain was excruciating. I found ways to survive. I avoided certain areas of the ice, such as the corners, or I crunched down and let myself go by relaxing my entire body. But when contact was inevitable I'd try to shield my right side by making a quick spin or pivot. The taunts and obscenities increased when the Halifax crowd saw me maneuvering like this.

"Nigger! Hit the nigger! Chickenshit!"

The police on hand certainly heard it. As did the Forum security guards. None of them reacted. How much vulgarity and racial slurring would it have taken for them to show the slightest concern? I wanted to fight someone. I wanted to explode. It was horrible. Somehow I managed to get through the game, which we won 2–1. Nothing about any of the taunting or racial slurs appeared in the Halifax press.

I was left utterly depleted. I was ashamed for teammates, several of whom saw how upset I was. Richard Charron, our captain and my linemate, came to me and said only, "*Ils sont malades.*" (They are sick.)

But I was especially embarrassed for my parents. During the game my mother, a stoic woman, stood silent, slowly shaking her head. She always refused to speak about the incident, but I know it left an emotional scar. Mom never again entered the Halifax Forum. On the other hand, my father was visibly angry. To his credit he was able to put things in some perspective — even to find a small silver lining. We talked immediately after I left the dressing room. "Son," he said, "it goes with the territory. As long as they're hollering at you, they know you are there. You're *doing* something."

Dad was right, but the incident at the Halifax Forum shook me for a long time afterwards. I was hurt and confused. Something like this I couldn't just push aside and I remember that evening finding a quiet place by myself to think through what had just happened. Although I was not being hosed or attacked by vicious dogs, I reflected on those TV images from Alabama and Mississippi and I wondered about Nova Scotia and how I could trust people again.

Sometime later John Choyce told me he had heard the taunts and chose not to do anything. "You have to get used to it," he said, offering a familiar mantra. "This is the way it is." A couple of teammates told me that, too. I was expected to swallow it all.

I was relieved that during subsequent trips to Halifax there was nothing as blatant, although I heard a few insults each time.

Mind you, on those other visits I didn't exactly slip under the radar. *Sports Weekly* ran my photo with the headline *Go John Go!* It wrote: "Young John Paris, who first showed in Halifax as a member of Sorel Black Hawks, appeared again Sunday and Monday . . . There's one thing that can be said about "The Chocolate Rocket," he knows how to put the puck in the net and he knows how to set up plays . . . In Sunday's game, the Windsor, NS, native picked up two assists. He came back on Monday to score two lovely goals. When he gets the disc anywhere close to the scoring position he's a sharpie. There's a couple of things we notice about the lad. One is that he loafs a bit and another is that he isn't too solid on his skates and is off his pins quite often. However he may get over these two faults with more coaching."

Oh well.

* * *

Shortly after the Halifax incident I ran head-on into another episode that further underscored the racial temper of the era. It happened in Thetford Mines, Quebec, against the Junior Aces. A bench-clearing brawl had broken out and I was involved in one of the many fights. My particular battle was a long one. True to my roots as a Curry's Corner Boy, once engaged I refused to stop. Nor would my equally stubborn adversary — their goaltender, Michel Dumas. (Dumas would briefly back up Tony Esposito with the Chicago Blackhawks in the 1970s, and is now the team's chief amateur scout.)

Finally, exasperated at our marathon scrap, the referee yelled at me: "Stop nigger! You hear me? Stop right now, nigger!"

A linesman heard him, as did several other players. He looked around and realized he had just stunned everyone. Seeing this reaction he quickly said to no one in particular, "I'm sorry. I shouldn't have said that."

Too late, ref. At least for me.

But what could I do? I was going to drop the ref right then and there, but teammate Max Goudreau grabbed my arm. "He's not worth it, John." Then Max proceeded to call him every name in the book. The ref just took it from him. After the game the ref came up to me and said he was sorry. In fact, whenever he saw me afterwards he would apologize. I know his name, of course, as do others. But his apology seemed sincere, so I'll not name him here. Did he receive any sanctions? No. But neither did I for the fight or Max for his over-the-top ranting at the ref that night.

The whole thing just seemed to disappear — until now.

* * *

It was during the pregame warm-up for an exhibition game in the Colisée Cardin in Sorel when I glanced into the stands, as young athletes do, and noticed a teenage girl with long hair and green eyes, wearing a blue hat with a white pom-pom on top. I looked at her for a second or two and smiled in that innocent, flirty way, then went back to the warm-up.

In that fleeting moment my life had changed.

At the time I was still living with Rodrigue Lemoyne, one of the Black Hawks' owners and also the local crown prosecutor. Our team bus driver was a young man named Georges Desmarais and one day he suggested I should come live with his parents. He explained that a few junior players had stayed there and they had plenty of room. I gratefully accepted. When I arrived at the Desmarais house I was struck by how warm and friendly everyone seemed. Then I looked up and saw their daughter. It was the girl with the hat from the arena! We introduced ourselves. Her name was Louise. For some time Louise and I kept our distance. She was a very hard worker and never stopped between school, babysitting and other chores. And I had school and hockey.

Our courtship was gradual, heating up for a while and then cooling. We were cautious. She spoke almost no English and would guide me in French and we'd have playful conversations and giggle a lot. Eventually we fell in love. I gained an entire second family: Solange and Alfred (who I called Ma and Pa) and their seven children: Georges, Jacques, Alain, Jean-Marc, Aline, Lucette and . . . Louise. I felt as loved by the Desmarais as I did by my actual family — a very high standard.

* * *

Partway through the 1965–66 season I was traded from Sorel to the Thetford Mines Aces for a high-scoring forward named Jacques Lepage. Thetford Mines lost in the league final series that year, with my patchy play being one reason. An even bigger reason was that late in the season the Montreal Canadiens, with a raft of injuries within their system, decided to turn our star goalie professional and assign him to the Quebec Aces of the American Hockey League. Our goalie was Rogie Vachon.

For Thetford Mines he had won twenty-five of his thirty-nine appearances that season and was spectacular in most of them. As one of the top junior goalies in the country, he could carry a team on his shoulders. Naturally he was a first-team all-star.

Rogie was a good friend to me. He and I hit it off instantly. In fact, we were roommates, billeted with the Perron family in Thetford Mines, along with Michel Ringuette, a forward from Baie-Comeau, Quebec. Rogie and I talked about personal things, stuff you tell only someone you trust. We made all kinds of plans and promises like young men do. He would say that when he gets married I have to be at his wedding. Stuff like that.

Rogie was a year older than I was and kind of took care of me. As a roommate he saw my health problems, but certainly didn't know all the details. Still, he could see my discomfort and noted all the time I would spend in the washroom. Rogie would always ask if I was okay. More than once he went to team management and told them I needed medical attention and that I was too sick to play. As the star of the team Rogie commanded a good deal of respect, but even his words fell on deaf ears. When I'd pass out in the dressing room — and this happened two or three times in Thetford Mines alone — he was one of the first people to come to my aid. He'd scream at the coaches: "I *told* you he was sick!"

The next year Rogie would play for the Houston Apollos of the Central Professional Hockey League. With a few weeks left in the season he was called up to the Montreal Canadiens and led them to the 1967 Stanley Cup finals, which they eventually lost to the Toronto Maple Leafs. The series prompted Toronto coach Punch Imlach to snort that there was no way Montreal could beat his club using "a junior B goalie" like Vachon. The outburst has become part of Maple Leaf lore and, thanks to Rogie's strong play, Imlach almost had to eat those words. It was the beginning of a Hall-of-Fame career for my friend, who was one of the nicest gentlemen I've ever met.

* * *

When the Thetford Mines Junior Aces moved to Quebec City to become the Quebec Junior Aces for the 1966–67 season, I moved with them. I wasn't pleased about it, but that was life in major junior hockey in the 1960s. Len Corriveau, a former referee, was selected as coach.

Corriveau's lineup was not strong, but did feature future Boston Bruin goalie Gilles Gilbert and, briefly, a fourteen-year-old from Thurso, Quebec, named Guy Lafleur. (Interestingly, Gilbert and Lafleur would be key participants in the infamous Don Cherry "too many men" goal during the 1979 Stanley Cup playoffs.)

I didn't get to know Lafleur well. He would play only nine games or so with the Junior Aces that season, spending most of his time in junior B. So he and I mostly missed each other. However, even in his short stint with the team in 1966–67, it was clear to everyone — including me — that this kid, who in training camp weighed just 135 pounds, was special. You could just tell. It was the way he looked when he grabbed the puck. He just *launched*. Lafleur had the hands and he could skate. There was no way that he was going to be anything but a star. Like many of the true greats there was something special about the way he carried himself on the ice. You see it. The way a Mercedes floats on the highway, the way it takes the curves. Like that. It's also the hips and the thighs. How he put the butt to the glove and the shoulder to the chest, stick down. It's that simple. Guy Lafleur made it simple . . . and poetic.

On the other hand, Len Corriveau did *not* make things quite so beautiful. Perhaps it was fortunate that he was not there when Lafleur returned the next year. Corriveau was old school. Very direct. He meant well, and I am certain he wanted to help us out. Away from the rink he was not a bad a guy. But as a coach his message was not getting through. Not even close. There was absolutely no life in that dressing room. I could feel the frustration welling. Sooner or later he was going to detonate because he was not getting the response he wanted from this group of young men.

With me, it was an old story. I was ill, but I kept it to myself. I certainly was not going to tell Len Corriveau. The pain and the cramping were almost unbearable, but I stuck it out even though I had trouble moving my feet — let alone my whole body — on the ice.

We got off to a poor start and we all recognized the team was struggling in many important areas. However, it was out of the question that we would go *en masse* to discuss our feelings with our general manager Paul Dumont. Such insurgence, even if justified, was not acceptable in those days. Dumont, a meticulous civil servant who we all liked, was also the director of the annual Quebec peewee hockey tournament and one of the province's most influential hockey people. Indeed, he was becoming known as the "godfather" of Quebec hockey. It would be Dumont who a few years later would lead a merger of existing junior A leagues in the province to form the twelve-team Quebec Major Junior A Hockey League. He would also be an important factor in Lafleur's early years.

In retrospect, if we had gone to Dumont it is quite possible he would have taken action regarding Corriveau. Instead, we hesitated . . . and waited for the inevitable explosion. It happened in our dressing room between periods of an early season game we were losing. One of my teammates, defenceman René Lavigueur, was sitting quietly as Corriveau was trying to make some point when all of a sudden Corriveau walked over and slapped René in the face. Bang!

René was stunned. We all sat there trying to process what we just saw. No one made a sound. Finally, I said — it seems it was always *me* in such circumstances — "Hey, that's wrong!"

Corriveau twisted around and glowered at me. "Mind your own fuckin' business, Paris!"

That voice inside me started. *"Stand up to him now! This is your teammate he just hit!"*

I stood and stared defiantly at Corriveau while most of my teammates just looked at the floor. Their body language told me that I was going to be alone in this battle, just as I was in that classroom at Dunton High School. So firing back right then would have accomplished very little, except maybe a suspension for me. Truth is, I was not on firm ground. I knew that my play was not where it should be, and to stand up to a coach in a full dressing room would be a kiss of death — especially for an underachieving *joueur de couleur* in the mid-1960s. I slowly sat back down but continued to glare at Corriveau, who turned away and continued his rant.

Nothing was said about the slapping incident. I don't know how René remained calm. Maybe it was fear. Whatever the reason, I respect him for handling it. If this happened today there would be an uproar and the coach would be charged with assault. In any case, I was determined to be proactive. I called Sorel Black Hawks owner Rodrigue Lemoyne and pleaded, "Rodrigue, get me out of here. Our coach just slapped a guy!" He promised to see what he could do. Soon after, Paul Dumont called me in his office. It appeared he wanted to be reaffirming and told me that I was one of the players he wanted to rebuild the team around.

"That's fine," I said, "but I don't feel well enough. I'm not comfortable, and I don't think that would work for either of us." We parted that day without a resolution. I suited up with the Quebec Junior Aces for a few more games. When Mr. Dumont called me in again, a week or so later, the mood was different. His tone was not that of a man willing to negotiate. The godfather of Quebec hockey was about to make me an offer I couldn't refuse. "We've got two choices here," he said. "We can send you to Sorel or to Montreal — and we are *not* sending you to Montreal. You're not happy here, so I'm sending you to back to Sorel."

I tried not to smile.

"I don't understand it," he said as I was leaving. "There's just something I'm missing on you. Some days you go out there and you can do what you want."

"I don't really understand, either," I said. "I just get so tired. I get diarrhea . . ."

So, in late October 1966, I was sold to the Sorel Black Hawks for an undisclosed amount of cash, leaving the Quebec Junior Aces with my thanks — and the godfather of Quebec hockey with visions of my diarrhea.

Sorel Black Hawks, Quebec junior A, circa 1966. I am on the far right.

* * *

Back in Sorel the cramps at times were so intense that I would fall on my knees and squirm. My whole body was weak. The rest of that season I would have prolonged bouts of shivering. I was always cold. The pain would be so great that I'd lie in a ball and put some object in my mouth to keep from screaming. I went through so much clothing it was incredible. I practically lived on the toilet, praying it would all just please go away.

Rodrigue Lemoyne would again send me to the hospital where the doctors repeated that my problem was viral, that it would pass. More medication. I continued to play — or tried to. That no one took the time to investigate the fall-off in my abilities now seems very strange to me. How could an athlete be so good one game and completely ineffective the next? There just *had* to be more to it. Maybe team officials rationalized that it was my lack of size or a lack of courage. I never knew.

CHAPTER 5
Last Chance

I spent the summer of 1967 trying to reconcile my hockey future with a debilitating, mysterious illness that was beginning to take over my life. I still believed in my ability, but my career options were dwindling. So I was encouraged when a letter arrived from Frank Carlin, general manager of the Quebec Aces of the American Hockey League, inviting me to the joint training camp in September with their NHL parent club, the Philadelphia Flyers. The Flyers, one of six new expansion teams, had purchased the Aces and its affiliated Quebec Junior Aces.

This would be my second pro camp. The previous year, 1966, the Junior Aces had acquired my rights so as a twenty-year-old junior I had attended the AHL Aces training camp. I remember getting on a bus in Berthierville, Quebec, attempting to deal with abdominal pain during the ninety-minute trip to Quebec City. When I got there I headed directly to the bathroom and vomited. The pain was severe, but I never missed an on-ice session. Still, I was relieved when they sent me back to junior.

The Flyers-Aces camp in 1967 was held in Quebec City and it was huge. A total of eighty-three players (nine goalies, twenty-six defencemen, forty-eight forwards) were looking for a job with either of the teams. While younger players like me were tagged to try for a spot on the Aces, there were lots of border-line players hoping to crack the Flyers lineup. Many of these were "unprotected" players plucked from the existing six NHL teams, mostly veterans in mid- or late-career. Among them: Gary Dornhoefer, Ed Van Impe, Leon Rochefort, Joe Watson and Lou Angotti. The Flyers got lucky in goal when they landed a couple of twenty-two-year-old gems, Bernie Parent and Doug Favell.

The camp also had lots of long-time minor-leaguers, salt-of-the-earth types who saw this as their one — and maybe last — big chance.

One such player was burly thirty-two-year-old defenceman, John "Junior" Hanna, from Sydney, Nova Scotia, who had played the last several seasons with the Aces. John wasn't fast — he didn't learn to skate until he was thirteen — but he could fight and play smart in his own end. In many ways, an early Flyer prototype. That September, Hanna and I became chums off the ice. Although I was not a drinker, I would accompany him and a few others after practice when they would "go for a couple of pops." Just thinking of John makes me chuckle. He could spin a good yarn, but was a straight-shooter and highly regarded.

Cut from the same cloth as Hanna was thirty-three-year-old Cleland "KeKe" Mortson, an Aces veteran and a 100 per cent bona fide character. KeKe was simply one of the most fun-loving people I have ever known. He even looked the part. He owned a wardrobe that someone once wrote made him look as if he dressed in the dark, and he had a walk that resembled a duck. He also had an endless supply of huge, cheap cigars that unmistakably announced his presence. There is no shortage of KeKe stories. One year, when he concluded that he hadn't received enough ice time, he sawed off the end of the team bench, explaining that it was his personal souvenir of the season. Booed by fans in a visiting rink, he fed them peanuts after the game through the wire mesh. When accused in Houston of flipping a puck in practice and deliberately hitting the big, expensive clock, KeKe rationalized to management that he was just "trying to kill time."

Nevertheless, KeKe Mortson was a great friend to people. He seemed to have an immediate fondness for me and I certainly enjoyed being around him. Just about everything with KeKe was spontaneous. One day he suddenly decided to take me out to eat. He flipped me his car keys. "Rookie! You drive!" He had this old car — I was never sure if it was actually *his* car — and I'm driving. The fact that I didn't have a driver's license didn't trouble KeKe in the least. With him barking directions and me squeezing the wheel, we somehow arrived at the restaurant in one piece. Once there, KeKe paid for everything. As usual.

Mortson was taller than me, but actually wasn't all that big. He was sort of sinewy, country-boy slim, but really strong. He'd always put me in a headlock and squeeze. Often there were stars when he finally released me. That was his way. KcKc would always be joking. And he would take care of you. He'd look at me — worrisomely thin and drained — and say, "Rookie, you need to have a good steak! That'll fix you up." So he'd buy me a steak. No questions asked.

Sometimes on the ice he'd have a little fun at my expense. Nothing malicious, but stuff that a rookie could expect back then. Once at an intrasquad game KeKe cruised over to me and whispered, "I'm going to throw the puck in and want *you* to go in and get it."

This maneuver would have placed me in the territory of one big, nasty veteran named Ralph McSween. My head jerked around and I glared at KeKe, my eyes three times their usual size. "Me? KeKe, he's huge!"

KeKe gave me this little smile.

"KeKe, why me?"

"Because if you go in and you hit him, then I'll get the puck."

I quickly offered up an alternative plan. "KeKe, why don't *I* throw the puck in and *you* get hit and *I* get the puck?"

"You think I'm crazy, kid?" He laughed and skated down the ice.

He did have a serious side, however. One day we were in a motel lobby and this young guy whom we didn't know said something about me — I never heard exactly what. But KeKe heard. He went over and pressed his hand into the guy's chest. "Don't ever say anything like that to him. Don't even *think* it." The guy melted away, mumbling to himself.

* * *

While hardly a boot camp, the Flyers-Aces training camp was well-organized and tightly run. We were all housed in the Orleans Motel, in nearby Giffard, and had to keep our rooms neat. Players were frequently reminded that discipline was expected and we were to behave like "professionals" around the rink and in Quebec City. We were also told to co-operate with the media and dress present-ably. Proper attire for meals meant shoes, socks, dress shirts (never T-shirts). On the road it was a shirt and tie and a sports coat.

Rules and regulations were listed in the camp manual, and spoke to the apposite comportment of the era. There were nine-teen rules in all. Here are some of them:

- You are responsible for placing your own wakeup calls. [There] will be no excuses for tardiness.
- Curfew will be 11:00 p.m. This means being in your own room. There will be a fine of $100 for violation of this rule.
- Drinking of intoxicants is forbidden. Players are not to enter taverns or other drinking places. There

will be a minimum fine of $100.

- [Help] out your trainers by hanging up your equipment. It only takes a minute.
- Smoking is not permitted in the dressing rooms and no cigars are permitted on the bus.
- Sticks must not be given away, taken from the dressing rooms after practices or broken in fits of temper.
- Many youngsters as well as adults attend practices, games, etc. Let us curb bad language.
- No gambling.

* * *

Flyers general manager Bud Poile and coach Keith Allen were the principal architects of the new team. Another key man at camp was the Aces' new coach Vic Stasiuk. Countless others were there to assist and advise. One was Phil Watson, who that season Stasiuk had replaced behind the bench in Quebec. Watson seemed to be keeping a close eye on me. He was an interesting man. *Sports Illustrated* had once described him as voluble, choleric, fire-breathing, temperamental and tactless. It's fair to say that by 1967 men with Phil Watson's hard-ass approach were less suited to a game that was evolving and a league where players were seizing more power. Case in point: defencemen Ed Van Impe and Joe Watson (no relation to Phil), two players that Philadelphia was hoping to build around but who in the early days of the camp went on strike for richer contracts.

Each day Van Impe and Watson would come to the rink, sit high in the stands, and watch the workouts. I don't know if I did myself any favours by going up and talking with both of them. But they were always receptive to my company and seemed to appreciate my gesture. They were great guys — in Boston, Watson had been Bobby Orr's roommate — and they were gutsy for standing up for what they thought was right. During one chat Van Impe told me, "If we are on the ice and anybody bothers you, I'll handle it." Nice to know, although I never got a chance to cash that cheque.

It was a thrill to skate with such talent at that camp and to score a few goals during the scrimmages. I was struck by how pleasant the players were to me — one of the lower guys on the totem pole. Lacroix, Dornhoffer, Angotti and winger Pat Hannigan would all talk with me at the Coliseum between the twice-a-day ice sessions and make me feel accepted.

Two guys I particularly enjoyed were Bernie Parent and Doug Favell. They went out of their way to include me in some of their outings and were cool to be around. We'd travel around in Bernie's little red sports car. They didn't have to take me with them, but that was the type of guys they were. Over the years I read that Doug was a heavy drinker. For the record, while I'm not saying he never had a beer or two in those days, when I was with them Doug consumed only soft drinks. Bernie was also fun-loving. Ultimately they would both go on to have long NHL careers. Parent is in the Hockey Hall of Fame and considered one of the greatest goaltenders ever.

One task I got roped into a few times was to drive players who had just been released to the airport. This was the "human" side of these camps that the public never saw. It was seldom pleasant. I saw grown men cry and fret about their future and their families. I didn't know what to tell them. One player said, "How am I going to tell my wife and the kids that I don't have a job anymore?" I offered him a hundred dollars from my pocket. He smiled and said, "No John, but thanks. No one has ever done that before." (I later remembered that was my last hundred dollars, given to me by Marcel Pelletier, the Flyers' director of player development. Without it, I would have been in bad shape. But I would've given him the money anyway.)

As far as my health was concerned, the good-day, bad-day pattern continued. I survived. That was all. Flyers physician, Dr. Stanley Spoon, eventually noticed my depleted condition and stopped me from going on the ice until I went to the hospital for tests. I thought to myself, *"This is it. I'm fried. It's over for me."* But the doctors at the hospital took blood, x-rayed my top half, and seemed to focus on my lungs. Safe again! But Dr. Spoon was not satisfied and I never got back on the ice. The Flyers were not sure what to do with me.

Phil Watson took me aside and said he thought I had a strong camp. He explained that the Aces could possibly carry me for the season, but my development was best served elsewhere. Marcel Pelletier took a different tack. I already knew that the NHL was out of my reach, so when Pelletier offered me a scouting position with the Flyers, I thought about accepting. However, I declined. As puzzling as it now seems, I still held out hope. I was not willing to give up, not yet. *"If I can just get some strength back, if I can just persevere, everything will be fine."*

I told them I'd like to play on, figuring that even though my health was not good, I may as well give it one more look-see.

"Okay, John," Pelletier said. "We'd like to send you to Knoxville."

This stopped me cold. "You mean Knoxville . . . *Tennessee*?"

Now this was 1967. The year of the movie *In the Heat of the Night*, the year of race riots in Newark, Detroit, Milwaukee and Minneapolis. There were surely better places for a twenty-one-year-old black kid to hang his hat than Knoxville, Tennessee.

"How do you feel, John?" Bud Poile asked me. "Can you do it?"

I collected myself and nodded. "I don't know how long I'll stay, but I'll give it a try."

So, with a trio of other players from the camp, in early October I was sent to the Knoxville Knights of the Eastern Hockey League

Promising Rookie

Knights ~~Get~~ Negro Center From Flyers

Knoxville's Knights will have the first Negro to play with a Southern team in the Eastern Hockey League.

Coach Pat Egan today said one of the rookies turned over to him by the Philadelphia Flyers is John Parish, a 21-year-old Negro center from Windsor, Nova Scotia.

"He's a good position player with good agility and plenty of confidence in his ability," Egan said of Parish. He will report with other Knight candidates here Oct. 8 when the training season will open.

NASHVILLE has lost veteran goalie Marv Edwards and winger George Standing because of the expansion in the National Hockey League. Edwards will be with the Pittsburgh Hornets and Standing with the Memphis Stars.

Clipping from The News-Sentinel in Knoxville, Tennessee announcing my arrival with the Knights, 1967. Note the references to race and that my name is spelled "Parish".

for what the team termed "seasoning." Because of red tape, I had to try three times before I got through customs. American officials didn't exactly buy the story of a black hockey player in Tennessee. It took a few well-placed phones calls by Ma Desmarais, of all people, to resolve the matter. I hoped it was worth the effort.

* * *

The Eastern Hockey League was the backdrop for the classic movie *Slap Shot*. That should tell you plenty. *Slap Shot* was actually based on one of the league's more successful franchises, the Johnstown Jets. And if the EHL had a poster boy, it would have been a leather-faced Halifax-native named John Brophy — thought to be the inspiration for one of the lead characters in the movie.

Brophy, who would retire as the all-time league leader in penalty minutes, was a defenceman for the Long Island Ducks. I actually respect John. I saw him play an exhibition game during my time in Knoxville and, frankly, he was a pretty good player. But as I watched the game it was clear that others on the ice were well aware of his wild reputation. In fact he was already something of a league legend. One of many Brophy tales has him being spat on by a fan in an opposing rink, then later butt-ending the fan in the mouth through the wire mesh, knocking out the guy's teeth. Brophy smirked at him triumphantly. "Now spit, motherfucker!"

Brophy also had a lengthy professional coaching career, highlighted by eleven straight seasons guiding the Hampton Roads Admirals in the East Coast Hockey League and three truculent seasons as head coach of the Toronto Maple Leafs. (In Hampton, Brophy and his assistant coach Al MacIsaac — yet another Nova Scotian — would send me French-speaking players during my years with the Macon Whoopee.)

Brophy was equally formidable as a coach. Once when a rookie on one of his teams came to him for advice on stick-fighting — a skill that Brophy had mastered — he faced the youngster and told him to drop his stick. When he did, Brophy raised his own stick and cracked the kid on the head. The rookie dropped to his knees, blood spilling on the ice. "That's lesson number one," Brophy said. "Don't ever drop your stick first."

There were twelve teams in the Eastern Hockey League in 1967–68. All were based in the United States and split evenly into north and south divisions. The Knoxville Knights played in the south. EHL rosters included young men, just a year or two out of junior hockey, playing alongside pugnacious long-time pros with little hope of ever cracking an NHL lineup. Few EHL players made more than $4,000 a year, so nearly all of them had other jobs in the off-season. Knoxville Knights' defenceman Harley Hodgson, for example, sold insurance. Forwards Ken Schutz and George Anderson worked in a fruit-packing plant and in the stock yards, respectively.

Knoxville was the third-largest city in Tennessee and a busy manufacturing centre. It supported the Knights rather well, with crowds of 3,000 or so in the 7,000-seat Civic Coliseum located downtown. Game attendance was the main source of revenue for most teams, and a good ticket cost $2.50.

The Knights were coached by Pat "Boxcar" Egan. As coaches go, they didn't come much tougher. This is not surprising because Egan was mentored by the legendary Eddie Shore, likely the meanest, most unorthodox S.O.B. in hockey history. Egan was forty-nine years old when he assumed the reigns of the Knights. A veteran of World War II, he had an outstanding NHL career in the 1930s and 1940s as a "hardrock," rambunctious defenceman, mainly for the Boston Bruins. In the early 1960s he coached the Springfield Indians of the AHL to three straight Calder Cup championships — the only time that has ever been done. Knoxville would be his final coaching job.

Egan reigned supreme. "Breaking rules is something I will not tolerate," he told the *Knoxville News-Sentinel*. As if to prove his point, that same day at training camp he cut a winger from Ontario for "breaking training rules and reporting late to practice." It didn't take much with Pat. When he had a contentious issue with a player, Egan was known to call that player in to a room, clench his fists and ask, "How are we gonna do this?" He was playing with minds. Would he have actually fought? I doubt it. Pat was gruff, but not nuts. It was his way of getting the message across, particularly if he was challenged. Pure old school. I warned Egan that if he tried such a stunt with me, we *would* fight. I was forthright: you can't intimidate me. I think he respected that.

When I arrived in Knoxville in early October, I was accorded more attention than the average new player because I was reputed to be the first "Negro" to play on an EHL team based in the South. The *News-Sentinel* ran my picture with a short feature that bore little similarity to the actual interview I did with the reporter. For example, the story stressed how much I liked to shoot pool. I actually said that I prefer to play chess. The story also noted that I was a fan of James Brown, who was performing in Knoxville around that time. "Jazz and rhythm-and-blues are my kinds of music, and Brown is my favourite." Well, I actually said I like all kinds of music, including R&B. I guess pool and James Brown fit the stereotype better. In another story, I was called "a promising rookie," although my name became John

Parish, "a 21-year-old Negro center." They quoted Egan: "He's a good position player with good agility and plenty of confidence in his ability." I think it was Pat's way of calling me cocky.

Most of the Knights were straight-up guys. Our best overall player was Bob Stoyko, a twenty-eight-year-old centre from Winnipeg, Manitoba, who had skills better suited to the higher-level American Hockey League. Stoyko was a gentleman, too.

Nevertheless there was a distinct wild-man undercurrent that pervaded the club. A few players were just idiots. Perhaps the biggest jerk was a forward from Minnedosa, Manitoba, named Dave Lee. He thought himself a star. Ever the smart ass, Lee would always offer up some stupid prejudice remark or other inane comment. "I know a black boy who's going home!" he once shouted in the dressing room, in my direction. A few players snickered. I remember telling one of my friends on the team, Claude Rondeau, that I was going to plug Lee to stop him from spewing this crap about me. Claude told me not to fight him, but one day after practice, in the dressing room, Claude himself, normally quiet and polite, wanted a piece of him. This time *I* intervened and I warned Lee that the joke was over, that if he said another word all hell was going to break loose in the room. Things quieted down and Lee more or less shut up for a while.

Lee also loved to ridicule our French players. "Frog" this, "frog" that. In the dressing room I would speak French with Rondeau and goaltender Ronald Gilbert, both from Quebec. This bugged a few people. But we didn't care. Claude, Ronald and I developed a strong bond. In a city that was still racially segregated, we lived in the "coloured" area of town. I stayed there because I had to; Claude and Ronald stayed there because they were good friends and came with me out of solidarity, enduring "nigger lover" invectives. It took us a while to find a room, but a guy at the rink gave us a lead and drove us to a place with a very nice exterior in the black section, on McCullough

Street, where the black ball players on the local minor-league team stayed.

The landlady explained the rules and said that it would be $7 a week. We looked at each other and smiled. Deal! (This was a time when a hamburger was 11 cents and a good breakfast was 45 cents.) They were fine people. Her husband had just one leg and was in a wheel chair. The landlady would often give us extra bits of food and kept the place very clean. We would take a bus or taxi to the arena, or sometimes just walk, depending on how strong I felt that day.

When we went to the movies I would warn Claude and Ronald not to make any loud comments if there was an offensive part of the story. But they did anyway, reacting to racism more blatant than anything they had witnessed back in Quebec. We were young and we were brash and — I now realize — we were lucky. Lucky, because our comments never fell on the wrong ears. Otherwise we could have found ourselves bound and gagged in the back of a pickup truck headed for a big tree in a nearby field.

One time we were told to leave a Knoxville restaurant and we refused. Then one of the white patrons whispered to me that we had better leave because if the police showed up we were going to have to fight our way out. "They'll beat you bad," he muttered, convincingly. There was no flight in us, but we were not foolish enough to test the situation. We left quietly. At another restaurant we were eating breakfast when a white woman approached me and said, "You're a lucky young man to have two friends stick by you like that." She handed me five dollars and told me to pay for the breakfast. She then smiled and left.

"You know that lady?" Claude asked me.

"No, but I guess she likes how we're sticking together."

Ronald laughed. "We have no choice. No one wants you, and no one wants us."

He had that right.

Knoxville in those days was filled with interesting people, not necessarily malicious, but individuals with a narrow view of the world. One such fellow was a barber I met one day when I entered his shop for a trim.

"Where ya'll from?" he asked as I settled in to his chair.

"Canada."

"Ohhhh, I know 'bout Canada. Yes sah, I know 'bout the Eskimos who live in Ottawa, yes sah, living in those snow houses . . ."

"You mean *igloos*?" I asked.

He ignored my question and announced that he knew that *I* was an Eskimo.

"No sir," I said, "I'm not an Eskimo."

"Don't try to fool me, now. I know you're an Eskimo 'cause I know an Eskimo when I see one. Y'all think I can't see straight?"

I smiled. "I've never been called an Eskimo before by anyone."

"That's 'cause they don't know people like I do, y'all understand. I *know* you're an Eskimo, 'cause ya'll got that hair and I look at your face and you're short. Yeah, you got that Eskimo look. Can't fool me . . ."

I explained that I was actually black, and that we come in many packages.

He suddenly had a very serious expression on his face. "I *know* you're an Eskimo. And I know that Eskimos don't trust blacks 'cause blacks pretend all kinds of things. Some of 'em are smart, educated. Can't fool me, though. I know all about 'em. Don't like 'em. Never have and never will."

Finally, when he finished cutting my hair, I got up from the chair and passed him a paper bill. I waited for change.

"Ya'll want it *all* back?" he asked.

I nodded. "Sir, I thank you for the trim, but us Eskimos, a few of us can be cheap. And you just learned a valuable lesson today."

I shoved the change in my pocket and walked out.

* * *

One morning Pat Egan called me to his office and asked me about Ronald Gilbert. He said he was going to let Ronald go. "He's a drinker, isn't he," Egan said, presenting me with a falsehood that would give him justification to get rid of Ronald.

I replied, "No sir, he's not an abusive drinker. In fact, I've never seen him drunk. He hasn't even had a beer that I've seen . . . I think he's better than your other goalies here. Where'd you ever get an idea like that?"

"Well, I heard it."

"Well, where'd you hear it? Who'd you hear it from?"

Suddenly Pat Egan, who summoned me looking for an excuse, was not enjoying this conversation.

"From the guys he lives with."

"That's a lie!" I blurted out. "That's a lie because he lives with me and Claude Rondeau, and we're always together."

End of the conversation.

He cut Ronald anyway.

* * *

In Knoxville, the locals told me where *not* to go. Somehow they thought I would listen. I was warned not to venture down to Northern Florida, for example, but I was too naive to heed this tip. I didn't believe it could be that bad. I soon found out to the contrary.

One evening on a sidewalk in Jacksonville, a policeman put a gun against my head and told me, "Get out of town, and don't come back. If you don't, nigger, I'm going to kill you. Understand, you little black bastard?"

All in front of other cops and other people, some of whom were egging on the guy. "You tell the nigger!" someone yelled. "Just shoot the coon!" another said.

I looked at this big white man in uniform and something in me snapped. I yelled, "Shoot me, you son of a bitch, because I am not moving. Shoot me! Pull the trigger, you sick son of a bitch!"

This surprised him, to say the least. And my voice quickly drew a crowd, including some black faces. The cop surveyed the situation and backed away, but not before warning me, "I'll get you, nigger." And I knew he would have. I'd embarrassed him and called him out — a big no-no in the South. (I didn't return to Jacksonville until the mid-1990s. At that time I had a gun, legally registered.)

Not surprisingly, girls were part of my Southern experience. I would walk into restaurants with my pals and flirt innocently with the young ladies — black *and* white. They flirted back. In Knoxville I even briefly dated a pretty, elegant white girl from the so-called upper crust of society. As you may surmise, this created a bit of a problem. Her dad was an affluent WASP and *very* unhappy about this situation.

This girl was soft-spoken and feminine. But she stuck by me and fought for me, one time literally, with her hands and feet, jumping in to assist me when we encountered an unpleasant situation concerning my race. We drove around in a Corvette as if we didn't give a damn who saw us. (We *did* care who saw us, of course. And we were well aware of the statement we were making.) Her parents finally sent her off to Europe, I think mainly to get her away from me and break us up. But we still stayed in touch.

My time in Knoxville was brief. I played just nine games for

A practice session with the Knoxville Knights, 1967. I am in the back row, third from left.

the Knights before deciding that it was not something I could sustain, given my health issues. I was still weak and frequently tired, and food didn't always stay down even when I was hungry. I returned to Quebec, adrift and ill.

CHAPTER 6
Sixty-seven Pounds

I've always been around rinks and arenas, so when my junior days ended it was hard to let go. I think that's why I went to play senior hockey, in Amqui, a small town at the base of the Gaspé Peninsula. I didn't tell the team about my health issues, but it didn't take long for everyone there to see I was sick. I was having trouble sleeping and holding down food, and I felt sluggish most of the time. The team owner offered to have me help coach, but I realized it was time for me to explore other avenues. I believe the non-hockey world calls it "getting a job."

To work in the Sorel area I first had to improve my French. I began carrying a French dictionary and reading only French newspapers, while Louise, my girlfriend at the time, worked patiently with me. I enrolled in French classes at the local college, where I studied accounting and psychology as well.

My job hunt was aided by a few connections. A friend of Louise's family, Joseph Tellier, the superintendent of Saint-Joseph-de-Sorel, one day asked me if I needed a job. The next morning he personally drove took me to the field plant section of the large mining company, Quebec Iron & Titanium Corporation. "You need an office guy, don't you?" he asked the manager with Hoey Limited, a subcontractor with the mining company.

Essentially, I was the office manager for Hoey. I worked with payroll, purchase orders, contracts, reports and the like. It was a fine situation overall. My pay was good for the late 1960s — I easily cleared $100 each week — and I had a great boss, Lucien Labine, who set a pleasant work atmosphere and treated his employees as people first. He also allowed me to take my college courses. My co-workers were super, too. I was soon hired on by Quebec Iron & Titanium as a construction clerk and then promoted to cost analyst. My main sidekick was André Provencher, a contracts administrator and hockey enthusiast who covered for me when I was too ill to function well. Another good fellow was Alfie, our janitor. Alfie had only one lung and was a very nervous person. A couple of foremen sometimes made a loud noise just to see his reaction. Big joke. To his credit Alfie played along. I never got involved as I was uncomfortable with pranks. I still am.

Female employees occasionally had to cope with sexist jokes and harassment — at least, that's how we label it today. Although I was younger than just about everybody there, I spoke up a couple of times when construction workers and other male staff crossed the line. This didn't make me popular, but right is right.

Gradually over the months my mind drifted more and more to hockey. I knew it was only a matter of time before I re-entered my natural habitat. I already had taken the first step and was coaching *five* teams for the Saint-Joseph-de-Sorel hockey association. Plus, I was assisting the local junior B team (coached by my former junior A teammate Max Goudreau), as well as helping out with the Sorel Black Hawks.

* * *

My office at Quebec Iron & Titanium. The eyes are closed, but I was not asleep —
trust me.

There were other huge changes in my life around that time, too.

On November 23, 1968, in the parish of Saint-Joseph-de-Sorel, Louise and I were married. I was twenty-two, she was nineteen. We were very much in love. Although not a huge wedding, it was nice, with a reception that featured fine roast beef, considerable wine and live music.

A little more than a year later, on December 11, 1970, our first child was born. Marie-Chantal was a true beauty: bright, alert, healthy. As the weeks passed she would peek at me and smile and I would melt. Sometimes she'd turn her head to find me, then hold out her little hands to me. The doctors assured us that she was advanced for her age.

When she was eight weeks old we took her to the hospital in Sorel for a routine check-up. Staff decided to keep her there for further examination. She seemed to be experiencing a bit of colic, but this didn't worry us much because otherwise she was so healthy. The test results were fine, so we were told to pick her up Monday morning and bring her home. But at 5 a.m. that Monday our telephone rang. I sprang up in bed. "She's dead," I said. Louise rushed to answer the phone. She came back and blurted out that we had to get to the hospital right away. All the way there I hung my head and didn't speak. We dashed into the hospital and saw the doctor with his head in his hands. He said he couldn't understand what happened. She'd been fine at 2 a.m. when the nurses last looked in on her. The next time they checked, Marie-Chantal lay lifeless in the crib. They couldn't revive her.

I stood there in her hospital room and just gazed at my little angel who seemed to be sleeping, with a speck of blood on the side of her mouth. I touched her cheek and told her I loved her. I felt numb all over.

The official cause of death was listed as sudden infant death syndrome (SIDS). In the many years since this tragic event, I've never stopped wondering if there was something more to the story. Louise asked a few questions at the time, but the answers she received were vague. In our grief we elected not to press the matter. In those days in Canada you did not routinely sue, although no one advised us of our options. Today, I am confident there would have been a painstaking investigation and, at the very least, a more thorough explanation provided to us.

For a long time afterwards people would call Louise to ask how Marie-Chantal died, or want to know if it was true I found her dead at home in her crib. This was an extremely delicate matter for us and I made it clear that I didn't appreciate the intrusion. Others, however, offered comfort and sympathy.

It's true that one never completely gets over the loss of a child. Louise and I struggled to work through this period in our lives and for many years after we were still unable to really talk about our loss. Even now there's a sting when I think of her death.

But we managed to move on. For me, that meant dealing with considerable resentment for which I used music as therapy and hockey as a diversion.

Of course, I will always have the question: why?

* * *

One Thursday evening when I was practicing with a local senior hockey team at the Colisée Cardin in Sorel, I was inexplicably doing things I had not been able to do on the ice in years. I felt strong. I mean, *really* strong. After the practice when my teammates offered me a drive home, I declined and walked. As I went along I began mentally celebrating. *I am cured! Freed from my living hell* . . .

By the time I reached my apartment door, I felt cold. I went right to bed. Around 1 a.m. I woke up sweating with a fever of 103 F. I was rushed to the Sorel hospital where I stayed for two or three weeks until I was transferred to the cancer ward in the Hôtel-Dieu de Montréal. There, a biopsy and blood tests showed I had Hodgkin's lymphoma.

Hodgkin's lymphoma is a relatively rare cancer in which a type of white blood cell infiltrates and affects the lymph nodes. Since lymph tissues are connected throughout the body, the disease can spread outside the lymphatic system. Symptoms include recurrent fevers, night sweats, weight loss, persistent fatigue and a lack of energy. Of the two main types of the disease, I had classical Hodgkin's lymphoma, which strikes about 70 per cent of patients, often young adults.

So began the first of two titanic battles for my health . . . and for my life. My recollection of this whole period is foggy. Mostly, I remember disconnected images and fragments of conversations. However, I recall in the cancer ward that the young man in the next room recognized me as a junior hockey player and remembered one game he saw when I was crushed by a big defenceman. He asked for my autograph and I happily obliged. He seemed like a teeny-bopper to me, although at age twenty-four I wasn't much older.

In those days you'd get your radiation treatments and then, like clockwork, you'd get sick. My skin would peel. It was agony. I kept pillows between my knees to prevent my legs from touching.

One time after we had finished our treatments for the day, the young man and I were chatting in his room when he asked me if I had a lot of pain and if I was tired all the time. I replied yes. "Sometimes I'm so hot that I want to jump out that window." He laughed. "Me, too, John." As I began to wheel back to my room he passed me his headphones. "You're not going to sleep anyway, so take them and give them back to me in the morning." I thanked him.

"Will you spend some time with me tomorrow?" he asked, as I rolled out.

"Of course," I said. "Hey, we're not going anywhere other than to have our tests and our serum changed."

He smiled at me. "Everything is going to be fine, John. You'll be okay. Trust me."

The next morning I awoke as if someone had touched me or called my name. Through my haze I noticed movement in the next room. I strained to see, but a nurse told me to wait and quickly shut my door. But it was too late. I saw his bed being wheeled away. He was covered by a white sheet. My friend had passed. I still had his headphones.

I cried that day. And it has bothered me all my life that I never even knew his full name.

* * *

My path back was rough and slow. Although I responded reasonably well to treatment, for the next two years I was in and out of hospital. During one of those prolonged stays, another health issue was diagnosed. Doctors told me I had a bowel problem: technically, ulcerative colitis (UC), an inflammatory bowel disease. A main symptom of UC is constant diarrhea, mixed with blood. Very painful. Recalling my childhood cramps and diarrhea, I now realize that I had this condition from a very young age. Other symptoms are a lack of strength and a diminished appetite, both which I had endured throughout my years of junior hockey. Doctors were astounded that, with this condition, I had been able to skate, let alone play competitive hockey.

This bowel issue made it difficult for me to ward off common viruses, transmitted through coughs or casual contact. The fact that I was allergic to many medications compounded my predicament. With such a weak defence system, plus the cancer treatment's toll on my kidneys and other areas, I had to take precautions. (This included not shaking hands, something that many people in the hockey world would misunderstand as me being discourteous.)

During one stay in hospital, in December 1972, our daughter Chantal was born just one floor above me. In one of my lucid moments staff put me on a stretcher and rolled me up to see her. I looked at this innocent face, there in a sea of other newborns. I was intrigued because she didn't resemble either Louise or me. My sister-in-law Lucette volunteered that she even looked a little . . . odd. Then Louise arrived.

"What are you two doing?"

"Looking at our daughter," I beamed.

Louise laughed. "Actually, you're not. You're looking at the wrong one. Look over there."

There, a few feet away . . . tiny perfection, with familiar facial traits.

Deathly ill, being comforted by my angel Gilberte "Titou" Robert, the Desmarais family housekeeper.

* * *

My strength gradually returned and, with it, something close to a normal life. While going back to work full-time was not possible, there was still hockey. After I coached the Sorel midgets to victory in an international tournament, Rodrigue Lemoyne started to give me local scouting assignments. "I'll never hire you as a coach," he avowed to me one day, "because I'd never want to have to fire you."

That was Rodrigue. He needed full control and was prone to impulsive actions. This quality made him a contentious figure throughout Quebec junior hockey as well as in the community. In 1974, he incredibly dismissed his team's head coach during the QMJHL finals and went behind the bench himself. In 1977, he moved the team to Verdun then abruptly pulled it back to Sorel in the middle of the 1979–80 season. In 1979, dabbling as an agent for star defenceman Ray Bourque, he tried to negotiate a financial settlement worth ten times the agreed rate for underage players. He locked horns with Boston Bruins president Harry

Sinden and lost. In 1988, he was reprimanded by the Quebec Bar for insulting and threatening another lawyer. Rodrigue also tried his hand in politics and in the 1989 Quebec provincial election ran as an independent candidate in the riding of Richelieu. He finished a sad third, with less than 5 per cent of the vote.

Nevertheless, I considered Rodrigue a friend and saw good qualities in him. (When I was in hospital he brought the entire Black Hawk team to visit me.) Unfortunately, later in life, he became entrapped by more than one addiction, and he paid dearly for it. He passed away in 1997 at age sixty.

* * *

Christmas Eve, 1975. In the Desmarais family tradition, we were gathered at the home of one of Louise's sisters for the evening. Life was good. Louise and I were happy, Chantal was a joy and I was back coaching — albeit tentatively. Then around 8 p.m. I started to sweat and feel weak. I resisted for a while but eventually I was on my way to the local hospital where tests showed severe internal bleeding. My bowel condition had flared up and walls were falling apart. I was being poisoned from within. Dr. St. Germain, an internist who had become my main doctor, laid a hand softly on my shoulder — it's never a good sign when a doctor does this — and said it was serious. They had to move quickly. He explained that I might end up with a permanent apparatus on my side, and might even become impotent. I told him to do anything he needed, just get rid of the pain. I'd handle the rest.

I was on the operating table for twelve hours, during which they gave me an ileostomy — a surgical opening made by bringing the end of the small intestine out onto the surface of the skin. (Intestinal waste passes through the opening and is collected in an external pouch system, which is stuck to your skin and drained a few times a day.) Near the end of the marathon surgery one of the doctors told Louise it would be a while before they'd know if I was going to make it. "It's up to the guy in the sky now and how badly John wants to live. He's exhausted. Maybe he's tired of the battle . . ."

Tired of the battle? The doctors didn't know that "battle" is this dog's middle name.

There were complications, however. One evening in the hospital during the recovery period, I fell as staff were helping me to the bathroom. As a result I required an emergency operation that lasted another miserable twelve hours, during which I moved in and out of consciousness. I tried to cope by conjuring mental images of Chantal and by focusing on a crucifix and a photograph of Marie-Chantal, both hanging on a nearby wall. At some point in the procedure I began seeing deceased members of my family, including my grandmother and Uncle Freemo, plus a friend from Hantsport, Nova Scotia, who had died in a car accident when we were both in our teens. None of these people spoke, but it was all very comfortable and reassuring. I had never experienced anything like it. It was silent, yet I absorbed their warmth and their love. I felt content, untroubled by anything. I lay still and listened to silence. As the warmth began to leave me I encountered a brighter area. I still felt no pain and I remember not wanting to leave behind such peace. Then . . . a jolt! Suddenly I was looking directly into the faces of nurses and doctors.

I was later told that the doctors said I had clinically died. Today this is more commonly called a NDE (near death experience).

I started to describe what had just happened when one of the nurses said, "Hush, John. We know . . ." Later when I was alone with one of the nurses I recounted what I'd seen. "Don't think I'm crazy," I whispered to her.

"Many people won't believe you, John, but me and the other nurses, we've heard the story before, from others. Now you'll have strength that others don't. Keep it to yourself. When you're better, you'll be amazed at the difference in yourself."

"How do you know this?"

"Think about it."

To this day I'm uncertain exactly what she meant by that.

I was in the intensive care unit for a few days. While there, I was annoyed that several people around me were speaking a gibberish I could not understand. I later learned that gibberish was . . . *English*. My mother tongue had somehow been erased. Oddly, I could still converse adequately in French, the working language of the hospital. This was fine for Louise's family. But it dumbfounded members of my family from Windsor, who had rushed to Montreal to see me. I would garble something incomprehensible in their direction and impatiently wait for their response. It was comical at times.

* * *

It seemed as if I would never leave that damn hospital. Day after day, week after week, I lay gazing at those gloomy tan walls. And those were the *good* days. A few times my condition dipped and the doctors wondered if I'd make it more than a day. But I had a special lifeline: my wife Louise.

Each day she travelled to the hospital — sometimes in the middle of the night — to change my pouch. She was better than any of the staff at applying the adhesive and "the wafer" to which the pouch was attached. In the 1970s this was a tricky process. Louise somehow could do it all without any training. Plus she would wash and bathe me, and even help me breathe when I was having trouble with my lung exercises. When I'd get cramps she'd speak to me softly and the sound of her voice made things easier.

Then one day my Louise reached her limit. She went to the

doctors. "I have to take him out of here. He'll wither and die if he stays." Naturally staff thought this was madness. They pointed out that I was hanging on by a thread, and that at home I would not survive. They said Louise didn't have the ability to care for me. She asked me what I thought. I said if I stayed, I'd die. "Take me home."

The doctors relented only after Louise signed a mountain of legal forms absolving them of responsibility. Wisely, only *after* the papers were signed, did she mention my childhood premonition of this whole situation. Doctors aren't big on premonitions.

I was transported home in an ambulance and carried to my room by my father-in-law, Pa Desmarais. Unfortunately, no one had removed the mirror from the room. I took one look and lost control. "That's not me! That's not me! No, no, no, no, no, no!" I weighed sixty-seven pounds. My bones were practically popping out of my skin. My face was hollowed and misshapen. Some visitors were so affected at my appearance that they were unable to work the next day. Pa later confided to me that he was convinced I was not going to survive. Word got around and people started calling and sending letters of condolence to Louise. A few asked about my funeral. Err, small problem, folks . . .

Meanwhile, it seemed *no one* could resist telling me how lucky I was to be alive. Most counselled that I should accept my physical limitations, and praised a passive life of reading and television. Initially I required twenty-four-hour care. Nurses came to the house daily, but the major burden was carried by Louise and Titou, a true angel who was originally hired as a housekeeper by Ma and Pa, but who over the years had become part of the Desmarais family.

For many weeks even simple things were challenging for me. To get out of bed I had to slide inch by inch. To get from one room to another, I crawled. Sometimes Chantal crawled beside me, giggling and thinking it was all a game, that I was down there on my hands and knees to play with her. The whole scene had a sad, absurd quality. I often wept out of frustration.

One day I was crawling to the bathroom when a voice out of nowhere spoke to me. *"C'mon John, you are not finished. There's much more to do for you. Your daughter . . . your wife . . . Damn it, John, you're not finished . . ."* I stopped. I felt instantly stronger. I remember gritting my teeth and making a personal, silent declaration that I would accept no pity, that I would not be a burden. It was a powerful moment.

I refused to take part in a formal rehabilitation program. My rehabilitation was going to be my mind. Through will and concentration I learned to control different body parts — my arms, my legs, my neck. The left side was harder. It was — and still is — heavier and more cumbersome. My emotions rose and fell, but I battled on. Gradually my body adjusted and movements happened with one sharp, quick thought. I also relearned English, reading every English book I could get my hands on, aided by a dictionary.

I lost a substantial amount of memory from this period. Perhaps three to five months. Maybe more. It has never returned. But when the Lord takes something away, he replaces it with something else. My mind *did* begin to work better. Maybe that's what that nurse meant when she said to "think about it." Indeed, over time I *could* understand things with a new clarity. Hockey became simple to teach. I studied human behaviour and could read people more accurately and better anticipate their reactions. Weird as it seems, evil became *visible* to me. I even gained patience (except with referees).

Slowly, one day at a time, I clawed my way towards a normal life. I consciously tried to get out more. One evening in Sorel my friend Eddie Godding escorted me to a special marketing conference held by a local travel agency. Before leaving the house I had another premonition and announced to Louise and Chantal

I look frail, but coaching minor hockey after my illnesses helped me recover. Note the goalie is wearing a blindfold.

that I was going to win the big door prize of a Caribbean vacation. I also asserted this to several people I knew at the event. Everyone thought my confidence was sweet and amusing — until my number was drawn! I chose Guadeloupe, in the French Antilles. Unfortunately, the day Louise and I arrived in Guadeloupe I had an attack of acute pancreatitis (a sudden and painful inflammation of the pancreas) caused by my surgeries and all the medications I was taking. We flew back to Montreal and I was immediately transported to the hospital. It took a while, but I recovered well.

Over time the required lifestyle adjustments became part of my new reality in what promised to be a relatively active, normal life. Living with a pouch on my side is not fun, but at least it's usually not visible under regular clothing, unless it becomes too full. I also follow a very strict diet. Tough or high-fibre foods (such as raw vegetables) are hard to digest in the small intestine and can block the opening so I have to chew all food extra well. Then there's the odd incidence of gas. A tad socially embarrassing, but manageable.

* * *

As I worked my way back to health and gradually back into the hockey life, I encountered first-hand the intensity of elite minor hockey in Quebec. In that province hockey is approached with fervor unmatched. This is certainly the case at the midget level where fifteen-, sixteen- and seventeen-year-olds are poised for junior A, a stepping-stone to a career as a professional.

- In 1987 in the Colisée Cardin in Sorel, when I was coaching the Riverains du Richelieu AAA midgets, I was hung in effigy. Some idiots with the visiting Magog AAA midgets during warm-ups had strung a dummy from the rafters, with a face painted black and "nigger" and "John Paris" scrawled on it. This was during a playoff game in front of a crowd of more than a thousand. Authorities came and cuffed three guys and carried them out of the rink. They didn't go easily. Officials on the Magog team seemed to have allowed this. At least one player on their team mentioned to me afterwards that their coaches talked about it's being there and were smiling and joking about it.
- Fans once poured *poutine* (French fries covered in gravy and cheese curds) on my wife and daughter, who were sitting in the stands. Chantal was thirteen years old at the time. For the next game, our team supplied me with a six-foot-eight bodyguard. That ended the problem.
- When my team played in Laval we had to provide police protection for my family as they couldn't even go to the washrooms or concession stands alone. In addition, a Laval midget coach had some sort of

representative figure of me in his team's dressing room and whacked it with a stick, screaming, "Nigger Paris. Kill the bastard!" My source: his own players.

- Even The Hell's Angels were part of the Quebec minor hockey fabric — at least in Sorel. The Angels chose Sorel to establish themselves in Canada and soon they were a significant factor in much of the city. While the Angels usually didn't accept blacks, they seemed OK with me. I think this stemmed from my successful intervention with the local hockey association on behalf of a youth who, unknown to me, turned out to be the son of a full-patch Angel. Another possible reason I was in their good books related to the wagering on our games when I coached the local AAA midgets. The bikers would put a few dollars on our team and maybe they deduced we had a better chance of winning with me behind the bench. That meant ensuring I was safe. People saw them at home games and at "away" games and behaved accordingly.

While I never wavered in my commitment to the minor hockey teams I coached, sometimes the chaos made things tough. Encouragement from supportive parents meant a lot, as did a few words from others outside the team. One evening in Cornwall, Ontario, a well-known lawyer came up to me and said hello. I was amazed he knew who I was. Smartly-dressed in an expensive dark suit, he was very polite, but carried an undeniable aura of power about him. Our talk lasted a few minutes and concluded with him urging me to persevere. "You'll be fine," said Alan Eagleson.

Few midget teams in Canada included ballet jazz as part of their formal training, as my Riverains du Richelieu did. That's local teacher Jocylyn Bibeau leading the boys.

* * *

Partway into the 1985–86 season I took the reins of the Riverains du Richelieu, the regional team for Sorel-Tracy, and a member of the seven-team Midget AAA Hockey League. As my energy increased I was gradually able to be more hands-on. By the end of the season I was on the ice handling practices. By the playoffs I was running the bench. I was pushing it a bit, but as I told a worried friend, if I was going to die, it would be *my* way.

After we lost in the finals that season, I immediately began scouting the area and attending tryout camps for next season. My star player, a sixteen-year-old black kid named Reggie Savage, was returning. But I had to rebuild much of the team and went after five very talented fourteen-year-old bantam players. Two of them — Steve Larouche and Christian Campeau — were top-six forwards. However, old fashioned hockey politics complicated things when the Quebec Ice Hockey Federation instituted a series of qualifying skills tests for elite players. After a lot of persuasion the federation president, Mario Deguise, allowed us to use my bantam-aged players, even though both Larouche and Campeau failed the skills tests.

Our local executives were not thrilled with me for pursuing these players. Some thought I was a crazy little black man and predicted we'd be the laughing stock of the league. At an association meeting I retorted that not only would we not be a laughing stock, but we'd win the Air Canada Cup, the national midget championship. A few of them though this was hilarious. One of them looked at me and said, "Let's be serious here, John. The rest of Canada plays with seventeen-year-olds while we play with sixteen-year-olds."

"We're *still* going to win," I insisted.

To ease the tension, someone said that if my team wins the Air Canada Cup I could have anything I wanted. I said I'd take the van given to the winning team. They all agreed.

We played nine exhibition games — and lost them all. No panic. I knew we were in preparation mode and that things would turn around. They did. We won our first game that season and kept on winning, dropping just eight games all year and finishing first. It was no accident. We worked hard and we worked smart. I employed comprehensive, highly specialized off-ice training — cutting-edge stuff for the mid-1980s and certainly far more sophisticated than what I did in junior with Herve Lalonde in the 1960s. We regularly employed sight-vision training, jazz-ballet sessions for balance, and "edge and balance" skating exercises. We held core strength workouts in a local gym.

Dubbed "voodoo stuff" by some skeptics, it also included extensive biomechanical studies and advanced testing on each player. We also used the services — given free of charge — of Dr. Sylvain Guimond, who would go on to work with golfer Tiger

Woods and who for many years has been the sports psychologist of the Montreal Canadiens. This information helped me be even more sensitive to my players' individual personalities and needs. For example, long before it was common to do so, we addressed the issue of attention deficit, appreciating it was a disorder having nothing to do with intelligence. (Today many elements that we incorporated in our training are included in the NHL "combine" testing.)

Trust was our main ingredient as a team. We preached on-ice communication, helping teammates be aware of and support one another. We promptly benched players who didn't communicate.

All this continued to pay dividends in the postseason, when we won the provincial playoffs, earning us the privilege to represent Quebec in the Air Canada Cup.

* * *

Canada's national midget championship used to be called The Wrigley. Now it's the TELUS Cup. For many years in between it was the Air Canada Cup Midget Hockey Championships. Whatever its name, since 1974, the tournament has brought together Canada's top sixteen- and seventeen-year-olds, on teams representing provinces or regions.

In 1987 the tournament was held in Ottawa. We arrived there an underdog — for good reason. Quebec's midget AAA league had reduced its age limit to sixteen, while all other teams in the tournament had an age limit of seventeen. For example, Sudbury was Ontario's representative and carried a dozen seventeen-year-olds. The favoured team was defending champion Notre Dame Hounds, of Wilcox, Saskatchewan, also with many seventeen-year-olds, and boasting a roster featuring future NHL stars Scott Pellerin and Rod Brind'Amour.

"Le Magnifique" Reggie Savage, Quebec's first major black hockey star, seen here with the midget AAA Riverains du Richelieu, 1986. He was a first-round draft pick for the Washington Capitals.

But I knew we had a good chance. We were confident and fast . . . and we had *Le Magnifique.*

* * *

Reggie Savage was being hailed as one of the top midget players in the country, destined for stardom. His statistics were Gretzky-esque. In 1986–87, in just forty-eight games Savage scored eighty-two goals, many of them dazzling. He scored six goals in one game, and at least three times scored four goals in a game. Reggie was also drawing attention because he was black.

"He's going through a war," I told a local reporter. "They hack him, they insult him, they try and do anything they can to slow him down. I've had people — both white and black — tell me they've never seen a player get the treatment he's gotten . . . He's the first real black star we've had in hockey in Quebec. A lot of players wouldn't be able to handle the pressure. He can."

At five-foot-ten and a rock-solid 185 pounds, Reggie had raw speed and power to augment a scorer's touch. I played him almost thirty minutes a game and he carried the load well. Some scouts questioned his toughness, but he showed otherwise against opposition players who ran at him the entire game.

The adopted son of two white parents, Reggie was a nice kid, a silent leader who was well-liked by his teammates. He even showed an interest in my daughter, but Chantal demurred. In Grade 11, he had an average in the high eighties. His father was a scrupulous guardian of his son's athletic career. In fact, one evening Jean-Guy aggressively challenged me on how I was using his son. Things got loud and I kicked him out and told him to take his son with him. Looking back, justified as I may have been, this was huge risk on my part. Luckily Jean-Guy returned a few days later and we talked things through. Today we are good friends.

After midget, Reggie starred for three seasons with the Victoriaville Tigers of the QMJHL, another war zone for him where he averaged almost a goal a game. In 1990 he was picked in the first round by the NHL's Washington Capitals. Although he scored a goal in his first shift in the NHL (on a penalty shot), his NHL career was a huge disappointment: thirty-four games, five goals. Most of the next fifteen seasons were spent with varying success in the AHL and IHL.

Was Reggie Savage handled in the right way? The answer is no. I'm sad that I didn't have Reggie long enough to teach him to be more creative, to better use his linemates. It was so easy for him to dominate in midget that he didn't have to learn these things; he could go end-to-end and control everything. I would have turned him into more of a play-making centreman to help him employ all facets of his game. In junior they gave him ice time, but they never insisted he expand his tool belt. He should have been able to play in the NHL. Reggie was intelligent, so I think he was not well-advised. Certainly the Washington Capitals didn't listen to me and one of their main scouts when we both suggested Reggie attend an intense four-week camp to help him improve his ice "awareness." In the end, Reggie missed out, we missed out, hockey missed out.

* * *

We opened the Air Canada tournament by beating Dartmouth, Nova Scotia, 5–1. Reggie Savage scored four goals. It could have been more one-sided, but I had no interest in humiliating the Nova Scotia representatives. We went undefeated in the round-robin, then topped Sudbury in the semifinal, 7–5. In the final, against Notre Dame, we were nervous at the beginning, but won going away, 6–2. Our bantam players were vital to our success. Larouche and Campeau played against the opposition's best lines, killed penalties and helped on our power play. Campeau brilliantly shut down Brind'Amour in the final. Reggie Savage was the tournament's top scorer and named its most valuable player. Our Patrick Daigneault was named the tournament's best goaltender. Yvon Bourduas, my team manager, should have received an award. A diabetic, he had an attack during the competition and consequently had trouble seeing. But he never missed a beat.

During the postgame ceremonies I stood in a doorway and watched our players celebrate. It was their moment and they deserved it. My goaltending coach, André Lebrun, a college professor, said he was proudest of how the players conducted themselves throughout the year, especially the discipline and respect they showed.

For me, just a few years before, lying in my deathbed, such a thing would have been unthinkable. I was still not fully recovered

Discussing strategy with Danny Chaisson of the national midget champions Riv-erains du Richelieu, 1986.

from my surgeries, but this was a tremendous boost for me. Later that day Steve Larouche told everyone that they had won it for me. Steve and the rest of the team could not have known how much I appreciated those words.

Back in Quebec we won a host of AAA individual awards. I was chosen coach of the year.

I never did get that van.

CHAPTER 7
Strike

Suddenly I was a wanted man.

After the Air Canada Cup offers came from midget AAA clubs in Quebec, from junior teams in Alberta, Ontario and Quebec, and from the pros. Even the Montreal Canadiens organization dangled both scouting and bench positions in front of me. Some teams didn't bother waiting until the Air Canada tournament was over and came to meet with me in Ottawa.

Over the next couple of months I weighed the options. Louise became part of the selection process and grilled teams who courted me. "Are you *really* aware of his health?" she asked one rep from a junior team. "Do you know him as a person? You understand if you harm him, you'll have to deal with me. And you may find that difficult."

Louise would've made one fine agent.

Ultimately I accepted the offer to coach the Trois-Rivières Draveurs of the Quebec Major Junior Hockey League. My friends in Sorel-Tracy cringed. They knew that coaching a major junior team was 24-7 demanding. Three games a week, countless practices, lots of travel, constant administrative requirements, late-night preparations, management expectations, public relations events, media obligations, etc. Two good friends — one a local lawyer and the other a bank president — both bluntly told me that in my condition accepting the Draveurs job was my way of committing suicide. Another friend reasoned that, given my penchant for confrontation, the stress would be too much for me. "John," he grumbled, "I can't afford to buy a new suit for your funeral."

Their concern was compounded because they knew I had already rejected the Quebec government's "legally incapacitated" label and the pension that went with it. I even refused to use the handicap parking sign. For me, it was a symbol of limitations that I was just not willing to accept. I wanted to be able to fly on my own without *any* restrictions. Friends who tried to persuade me to use the safety net eventually gave up. "If John decides he is going to do something," said a close friend, Eddie Godding, "we may as well all just step back and watch. He's not going to stop until he passes away."

Privately, however, I *did* worry about my health. I was stronger but still fragile. Fatigue remained an issue and there was still occasional fever. While I had become more comfortable living with the pouch apparatus on my right side for my regular body functions, I still wasn't confident I knew how to deal with my disability under stress.

In addition to my health considerations, there were also concerns about how the demands of the job would affect family life. Louise had her children's clothing store in town, and Chantal, in her important teen years, was firmly anchored with her friends, school and grandparents. Both had every right to expect my support and my time.

And then there was the matter of the league itself. Teams in "The Q" had this *thing* for coaches: they loved to fire them with ruthless dispatch. Hire 'em, fire 'em. Then hire the guy who has just been fired by another team, then fire *him*. It didn't seem to matter if a coach had a winning record. *Vous êtes renvoyés.* It was rare to have a Q coach last as many as four years with one team. By comparison, both the Western Junior Hockey League and the Ontario Hockey League had lots of coaches go five, ten or even fifteen years with the same team. Brian Kilrea, of the Ottawa 67s, for example, around this time was approaching twenty years behind the bench. Next to the Q, coaching in the WHL or OHL looked like a government job.

* * *

My appointment with the Draveurs made me the first black head coach in the QMJHL and, possibly, the first in major junior hockey in Canada. I didn't realize this until a reporter pointed it out to me. It was still a noteworthy accomplishment, one that helped pave the way for minority head coaches in junior hockey, such as Larry Marson who coached the OHL's Niagara Falls Thunder in 1992–93 and for part of the 1993–94 season.

For me, Trois-Rivières was as good a place as any to break a colour barrier. Partway down Highway 40 between Montreal and Quebec City, Trois-Rivières was once the world's pulp and paper capital, and the working-class nature of this industrial city has long been a source of pride to the hundred thousand or so "Trifluviens." So was its hockey and its most famous native son, Jean Beliveau.

I inherited the Draveurs from Alain Vigneault, now one of the NHL's elite coaches, who in 2013 with the New York Rangers became the highest paid coach in hockey history. Back in 1987 Vigneault left a losing Trois-Rivières team for Hull — where he replaced Pat Burns — and immediately took the Olympiques to the 1987–88 QMJHL championship. Meanwhile I took the reins of a team that had missed the playoffs and which management decided needed to be rebuilt. So that spring we drafted with a two- or three-year plan in mind. Our draftees included goaltender Dominic Roussel, defenceman Eric Charron and, from my Riverains du Richelieu midgets, underage forward Steve Larouche, who we called "La Mouche" (The Fly).

As I looked for a place to live in the area, I stayed for a few weeks with Draveurs general manager Michel Boucher and his family. They were gracious hosts. Michel was a former head coach of the University of Ottawa Gee-Gees and a reasonably capable hockey man, but frankly I thought his strength was as a scout, not a general manager.

As we got down to business at training camp and then rolled into the season, odd things seemed to be happening all around me. In their own way, all spoke to the complex business of hockey. For example, in a harbinger of my relationship with the Draveurs, my assistant coach, a fine young man named Mario Paradis, had a disagreement with management regarding his travel per diem and quit. He told me it was a matter of principle. I hated to see him go, but I admired his resolve.

Then, in Shawinigan, Dean Bergeron, a black eighteen-year-old winger, had his entire life change during a training camp fight with a teammate when his unprotected head hit the ice, snapping his neck and leaving him permanently paralyzed. He subsequently sued the league, his team and his coach. The matter was settled out of court. Over time Dean and I became close. He went on to become one of Canada's most decorated paralympians, competing in wheelchair track and field.

The third oddity involved Jean Perron, then the coach of the Montreal Canadiens, and never a man lacking in opinions. Perron stunned the Quebec hockey world when he told the media that he felt Quebec's francophone junior hockey players were pampered compared to junior players in the rest of the country.

It was quite a statement, made from the most influential hockey pulpit in the province. He blamed Quebec's permissive society. The entire QMJHL was abuzz. Many disagreed with Perron. Me, for one. I chided him in the *Gazette,* the province's largest English-language newspaper, for not doing his homework. It all made for a lively discussion across the province and perhaps did some good in the long run.

The final matter that got my attention around that time concerned hazing. Having tutored maturing young men for two decades, I was fiercely opposed to this activity, which for generations had been treated as "just part of the game." Unfortunately, among coaches my ardent opposition to hazing placed me in a minority. (Imagine me being in a minority!)

Broadly defined, hazing involves rituals and other activities where individuals are humiliated, abused or harassed. Usually this was to "initiate" them into a sports team, gang, fraternity, etc. This can mean physical abuse or psychological abuse or both. Sometimes it includes sexual acts or nudity. Effects on a victim can be devastating and can last a lifetime. Recently both hazing and bullying (which I consider in the same family as hazing) have made the news with many teen suicides linked to this nasty pursuit. Back in the 1980s and 1990s hazing was certainly occurring in the Q.

But not on my watch. Believe it.

When the Draveurs' strength and conditioning coach informed me he suspected hazing on our team I quickly called a team meeting where I glared at the veterans and asserted that hazing, in any form, was not permitted. Period. If it was happening, it was going to stop — *now*. Then I told the whole team — especially the rookies — that if this was occurring to them, they *had* to come to me immediately. I would handle it from there. I didn't give them the choice. Soon a couple younger players approached me and described what was

Steve "La Mouche" Larouche, who I coached in midget, junior and the pros.

taking place. Nothing criminal, but bad enough. I went directly to the culprits. They were less than forthcoming so I warned them that if they even *touched* a younger player I would suspend them immediately — and make public why I did so. You want to humiliate someone? Then game on, boys. We did not have any further hazing issues that year. My message had penetrated. And the players themselves helped eradicate it. Mission accomplished.

* * *

I got the Draveurs off to a good start. After eight games we were 4–3–1, and by the half-way mark of the season we were in second place. However, I knew we were overachieving, temporarily propped up by strategies I employed against stronger teams who tended to overuse their big lines and star players in the first two periods. Our plan was to play tight and hang on until the third period when the opposition's level of play dropped off and we applied a very heavy forecheck. A few memorable comebacks resulted. But our team was small and just too young. I alerted Michel Boucher that we needed to trade for a few bigger, experienced players. We never did. After Christmas we slumped, winning just five of twenty-one games during one stretch.

I was fired in early March. There were seven games left in the season. Michel Boucher took over as coach and the team still missed the playoffs.

I tried to go out gracefully. I publicly acknowledged that the team gave me a chance and I just didn't win. Still, it hurt. Being fired *always* hurts. I was forty-one years old and in my first crack at major junior. I wondered: *Would this be my one and only chance?* When I took the job I understood it to be a two-year rebuild. "I guess in junior hockey there's no such thing as a rebuilding period," I said in the press, just a touch sarcastically. "The name of the game is to win and to win in a hurry."

In the end Michel and I didn't share the same vision. For example, there was the team budget, an issue foreshadowed when Mario Paradis quit during training camp. Management was cheap. They didn't even supply shampoo and tape until our captain personally complained. Nor did they attempt to fashion pride and respect in the players by offering team jackets. When players did something exceptional, they were not rewarded.

I have mixed feelings about my experience with the Draveurs. The players were fine. Our goalie, Dominic Roussel, had "prospect" written all over him. I pushed Philadelphia to draft him, and they did. After his time in the NHL he became a top-notch goaltender trainer. Other memories are less gratifying. These include a local reporter. Although I didn't know him well, I defended him by reprimanding people who made rude remarks about his physical disability. Yet when I left, he found it necessary to roast me. I let it ride. Lesson learned.

* * *

Without a junior team to coach, for the start of the 1988–89 season I returned to midget AAA. "Considering that these coaching jobs in minor hockey are without financial remuneration and demanding in time, you have to wonder about the sanity of the applicants," noted the *Gazette* in a feature article published around this time. Sane or not, I was able to stay in touch while QMJHL jobs opened up . . . as they did with alarming regularity. Until then, it was elite minor hockey and elite minor hockey parents.

Most parents are fine, but some are not and their behaviour could be beyond belief. Enraged fathers or mothers — women can be equally bad — shaming their child by berating game officials, confronting other parents, etc. How many times has a minor hockey player felt he had to apologize to his coach or teammates for his parents' conduct?

Over and over I encountered the same issues:

. . . parents loudly yelling instructions to their child from the stands, thereby confusing and intimidating the child

. . . parents telling the coach how to do his job, but never going behind the bench themselves or teaching at practices

. . . parents assuring the coach at the season's outset that they want their child to be disciplined for not giving maximum effort, yet when a coach does exactly this the parents make excuses for their child and turn on the coach

. . . parents overestimating the abilities of their child, not appreciating that their little star may not be a star as he ages and moves through the competitive levels.

The list could go on. Frankly, there are parents who are not even *conscious* of their behaviour. These parents should see a therapist or, better yet, just stay away from the rink. This would directly benefit the child because frequently coaches, to avoid dealing with an off-the-wall parent, will simply not select the child for the team. I'm against this approach. A player should not pay the price for his parents' ignorant behaviour. I prefer coaches ban parents from the arena.

Naturally some situations aren't in any handbook. When I was coaching in the United States, on another team the mother of one player actually started "dating" one of her son's teammates. All the players on the team knew about it. Awkward, but technically legal. It mercifully didn't last long. On my teams I had my suspicions at least a couple of times that something was amiss, but I never had any proof. Just in case I made certain all parents knew that I had zero tolerance of any player-mother sexual interaction. And if I found out, I would name the parent — no hesitation. Everyone knew I wasn't bluffing. In a similar vein, I knew some coaches in Colorado who were taking advantage of their position with some moms. Highly inappropriate.

* * *

The Granby Bisons were off to a 10–23 start in 1989 and there were rumblings around the QMJHL that their coach, Réal Paiement, was about to be shown the door. Paiement, who was just thirty years old, was in his fourth year with the Bisons, making him a current top survivor among league coaches. As anticipated, a couple weeks before Christmas, Paiement was axed. Team president Yves Proulx cited a bad team attitude and a communication problem. Paiement's departing comments echoed mine in Trois-Rivières. "When we sat down two years ago," he said, "the plan was to go with young players and to rebuild. I told the owners the next two years would be tough, but next season, [the] potential was there. I risked my job, and lost it."

The Bisons offered me the job. I seized the opportunity and accepted. Paiement actually helped me out and briefed me when I arrived. It was a classy thing for him to do, and I appreciated his gesture.

By then I realized I didn't merely *want* to be involved in hockey, I *needed* to be involved. "Hockey is like a drug to me," I told the press. I was not exaggerating. Yet I always found it weird — and maybe even *wrong* — to take another man's position. But I knew that if it was not me, then in a blink of an eye it would be someone else. And eventually someone will do the same to me. That's the sports world.

* * *

It's often better to join a struggling team. In this circumstance a new coach does not have to win right away, only to move things in the right direction (meaning upwards) in the standings.

In Granby I inherited two terrific assets. One was my assistant coach André Ruel. Short like me, André was a bright, dapper fellow with impeccable manners and an astute hockey mind. He became like a brother to me. I gave him plenty of latitude and he never let me down. The second asset was my young team captain, Marc Rodgers. Just five-foot-eight and 172 pounds, Rodgers played like a wrecking ball and took his captain's responsibilities very seriously. I saw in him a talented, pure leader who was also an interesting young man away from the rink. For instance, in a league that emphasized education, Rodgers was a dropout who spent his days cleaning automobile engines for a living, which is not to imply he was unintelligent. Marc just found sitting in a classroom difficult.

André and Marc helped offset some thorny issues in Granby. In addition to what management labeled a "bad" team attitude, I had an inexperienced roster with only five players aged nineteen or twenty. Another matter was that the franchise appeared to have financial issues. The Bisons were tussling with the city of Granby and threatening to sell the team to outside interests who could move the franchise. Finally, there was the matter of the man I was replacing — or at least his ghost.

Réal Paiement, who was also the general manager, was popular with his players . . . as goaltender Boris Rousson made clear: "I don't think a new coach will change the whole thing. The coach was not the problem. For a young team (Paiement) was the best man we could find."

In Granby, we selected future NHLer Phil Boucher as the second overall pick in the 1990 junior draft. That's Yvon Robichaud, one of the Bisons owners, on the left.

Given all of this, it was especially important that I get the team off to a quick start.

After eight games we were 1–6–1.

* * *

In Granby I stayed true to my trusty coaching approach: be fair with the players and demand their best. One night following a loss where I saw little effort, I kept the team on the ice after the game and skated them for twenty minutes. My postgame session made the papers and all I did was skate them. I was called a tyrant. Meanwhile, a coach in Shawinigan put his players in the shower with their equipment on as punishment and there was little said about him. Go figure.

Tyrant or not, I coached the Bisons for the better part of three seasons. My results varied. In the first season, I took over when the team was 10–23. We ended 20–49–1 and missed the playoffs. We lacked experience and talent, but communication improved and we played a spirited game. We also missed the playoffs in my second season, but were among the most improved teams in all Canadian junior hockey, finishing 34–30–6. We actually had a better record than at least one team in the other division that *did* make the playoffs. Frustrating.

I had high hopes for 1991–92, my third season in Granby. We were now a veteran, talented team with top-end players such as Rodgers, goaltender Martin Brochu and defenceman Philippe Boucher, the first-round pick by the Buffalo Sabres in the 1991 NHL entry draft. We also had Hughes "The Doctor" Mongeon, a slick five-eleven, 170-pound centre, who we obtained in the off-season in a trade from the Shawinigan Cataractes. (À la Eric Lindros, Mongeon had demanded a trade from Shawinigan to a QMJHL club with an English environment, which we had in Granby.) Another reason I was so optimistic was that our players now knew my system of tight, disciplined defence. As Olympiques coach Alain Vigneault groused after we had beaten them in Hull: "Granby is a team which is difficult to develop any momentum against. They play *that system* and it's very hard to get into a rhythm."

As I expected, we started the season well (8–4–2) and were in second place in our division. I allowed myself to think that, with a little luck, this might be our year. The players believed it. In a show of togetherness, they all bought pullovers with "Paris Man" on the front.

Then something happened that made news all over the sports world.

And I was at the centre of it.

* * *

Despite our fast start and winning record I had a bad feeling in my bones. Team management was becoming dysfunctional. One owner, Yves Proulx, who was unfailingly respectful and upfront with me, seemed to have his hands full keeping another of the owners sober. Worse, that summer the Bisons had hired a new general manager, René Constantin, who had a limited hockey background. I found his knowledge shallow. (I suspect that Constantin was brought in by Gilles Goyette, a team official who blamed me for getting rid of one of his pals, the head scout. Others were also part of the decision to replace the scout, but it seemed that I alone was taking the heat.)

Right away Constantin and I locked horns. During the midget draft that spring we disagreed about a player he wanted as our first pick and who I wanted nothing to do with. In the end he got his way. (The player turned out to be a dud, as I anticipated.) In training camp our players had picked up on the negative vibes between me and Constantin. I think they felt sorry for what I had to deal with. Our captain, Marc Rodgers, came to me and said that if they were to fire me, he'd quit. I reminded him that he had a bright future, and that coaches come and go. I then assured him and others that as long as we were winning, everything and everybody should be fine.

Wrong.

In late October 1991 I was fired as the head coach of the Granby Bisons. Officially, the Bisons told the media that the firing was the result of "philosophical differences" between me and Constantin. They informed me before practice. I wasn't shocked. I knew Constantin had recently spoken with Luc Boucher and Pierre Cliche, two coaches from the Magog AAA midgets who worked as a tandem. After I was told, I spoke with André Ruel and André Lebrun, my goalie coach. I then met with the team. Several Bison players became upset and wanted to do something to show their disapproval. I never encouraged any action — none. That day I merely thanked them and encouraged them to play hard. I reminded them that hockey has a way of taking care of things in the end.

The team's next game was the following night in Granby against the St-Jean Lynx. The Bison players all showed up at the arena, but to protest my firing they refused to go on the ice. Game time came and went and they just sat there in their Paris Man pullovers, demanding I be reinstated and ignoring their two new coaches. QMJHL president Gilles Courteau, alerted to the situation, told the team that the league would suspend every player and fine the team $10,000 if the game was aborted. Bisons' president Yvon Robichaud stormed into the dressing room and ordered the players to suit up and play or the fine would come out of their pockets — a threat even the players realized he might have had some difficulty enforcing.

I didn't know any of this was happening until I saw it on the television. I immediately tried to reach Marc Rodgers, but I couldn't get through. Finally I got a hold of another player and urged that they end their protest and play the game. They eventually put on their equipment and played, losing 6–5. In a show of support for me, Rodgers refused to play the third period and just sat there quietly on the bench. "I wore the uniform in the first two periods out of respect for my teammates," he said after the game. "For the final twenty minutes, I didn't play because I had promised John Paris that if he was fired I would not play out of respect for him."

Other Bison players also spoke out. Hughes Mongeon told the *Gazette*, "John taught me a lot of things and he was the one who gave me confidence. In one month with him I learned more than I did all of last year. It was very emotional for the players who were with him for three years. John didn't just talk about hockey . . . we learned a lot about life from him."

I never heard of any significant ramifications for the players. Likely the team just wanted the whole episode to go away . . . like the new coaches soon did. The first coaching tandem in league history won only one of its first six games and was replaced before the end of the season. The Bisons finished 25–42–3 and missed the playoffs. A great opportunity squandered.

The Granby players' strike made national news in both Canada and the United States. Some reports carried it as a novelty item, while other coverage portrayed the players as loyal warriors. Truth is, nothing in my hockey life has meant more to me than what Marc Rodgers and the rest of those Bisons players did that evening. Their support is something I treasure. To indirectly thank them, in future years I made certain to court French-Canadian players who were often overlooked by professional teams.

As for Bison management, I lost no sleep over their predicament. Most of them had it coming.

* * *

The same year as the Granby incident, my mother died. She was seventy-four. Her large funeral in Windsor was a testament to how much she was appreciated in the community.

When I was home for a visit that summer Mom had tenderly prepared me for her imminent passing. She told me she realized my life had not been easy, but that's the price when one steps out from the crowd. She said no matter what happens, to always remember she loved me. "I'll always be there, John, even if you think I'm not." We sat in our living room talking until almost 4 a.m. Usually when my visits ended Mom would walk me outside to my car to say good-bye. Not this time. This time she stood in the window slowly waving to me. Somehow we both knew this would be our last time together on this earth.

* * *

I was one of three or four coaches with a winning record to get fired that season in the QMJHL. The most noteworthy execution was that of Gérard Gagnon, of Collège Français de Verdun. His surprise dismissal followed what the press called a "revolt" by his players and their parents. Gagnon, age forty-three, once coached Laval to a 53–17–0 record, aided by his star player Mario Lemieux, and seemed pretty close to untouchable. But not in the Q. His firing prompted several QMJHL coaches to complain that Quebec junior clubs were far too quick to pull the trigger. Alain Vigneault was particularly vocal, calling Gagnon's firing illogical. "It used to be that you had to win if you wanted to keep your job, but that doesn't seem to be the case now." The purge continued into early 1993 when Normand Flynn, an acquaintance of mine at the time, was given the boot by the St-Jean Lynx. Team president Paul Poulin said the Lynx were performing "below expectations."

I replaced Flynn.

Normand understood it was all part of the business. In any case, he landed on his feet remarkably well. He's now a popular, colourful analyst with the French sports network RDS and not hurting financially, I'm sure.

I was forty-seven and the Lynx were my third QMJHL team. I signed for the remainder of the season, with an "escape clause" if the opportunity to move up came about. In addition, for family reasons, I decided to commute the two-hundred-kilometre round trip each day from my home in Sorel-Tracy to St-Jean.

In St-Jean I had a respectable lineup to work with. Future NHL enforcer Georges Laraque was there, as was goaltender José Théodore, a great kid who for a few years would parlay his good looks, pleasant personality and considerable talent to become one of the NHL's most popular players. We were a .500 team, but after a long Christmas break there were signs we were poised for a good stretch run.

Then, a month later, I resigned.

Like every junior coach with aspirations, I had been having casual conversations with well-connected NHL people for some time. One of those conversations was with a fellow named Joe Bucchino who was in the front office of the Atlanta Knights of the International Hockey League. The Knights were the top farm team of the NHL expansion Tampa Bay Lightning. Formerly the assistant GM of the New York Rangers, Bucchino had been receiving information about me from several hockey people. Apparently it was positive. In December, I flew to Atlanta and talked with Bucchino and two members of the Knights management team, president Richard Adler and vice-president Charles Felix. There was no formal offer made, but I went back home with things to think about. Louise was convinced I was going — again. She was not pleased about it.

I returned to Atlanta for a second meeting, this time with Richard Adler and owner David Berkman, who offered me the head coach job. I accepted.

The Lynx supported my decision, both publicly and privately. The players took me out to dinner to celebrate. St-Jean GM Jacques Chaput, a member of the Quebec provincial police, was especially encouraging: "At your age, John, you can't watch the bus go by. Jump on it."

* * *

My overall health was improving and my energy level was up, so I could put in longer hours with only the odd concession. My marriage to Louise, however, was not doing as well. As often happens in a relationship, we had begun to grow apart. Hockey played a major role, as my focus on my career robbed from my home life.

Even when I was there, my mind and my emotions were still at the rink.

Hockey also had other, strange ways of imposing itself in my personal life. For example, the "fan" from the West Island of Montreal. In the early 1980s when I was coaching major junior he somehow got my home phone number and would call anytime of the day or night and ask my opinion of a wide variety of issues: a ref's calls, Canadiens trades, particular players, etc. Sometimes these calls would come at 3 a.m. and were driving Louise crazy. I wasn't even sure who he was. Finally I connected the dots when he approached me at an arena and I recognized his line of questioning.

"You calling me?" I asked.

"Yes, but I don't want to be a nuisance," he said.

"Well you're *more* than a nuisance. So, look, we have two choices here. Either you stop or I'll be calling the police."

He stopped.

Worse yet was my stalker. She'd call all the time and was going around telling people she was my girlfriend or my wife, anything to draw attention to herself. One day she called the house and said to Louise, "I'm with your husband." Luckily I was right there with Louise on our couch. Still, understandably, this created havoc in my marriage. How do you explain to your wife that you really have nothing to do with this person? Most women would think you are lying. I was not. But this episode made for a climate of mistrust in our household. The stalking eventually stopped.

Louise came with me to Atlanta for a while, but soon returned to Sorel-Tracy and that was that. Even during our most difficult period, however, she and I never stopped caring for one another. And while today we have both moved on to other relationships, we are still close. We always will be.

My dad Buster Paris and my first wife, Louise Desmarais, chat in a hockey rink — naturally.

* * *

Louise figured in one of the more peculiar incidents of my years in the QMJHL. It happened one October afternoon in the office of a certain general manager who I will not name to spare his family embarrassment. He and I were casually discussing the team when he abruptly said, "You know that you have a pretty wife. She dresses classy."

The remark was out-of-context and caught me off guard. "Yes . . . thank you," I replied. If she was nice to him, he continued with a little smirk, I would have a job as long as he was there.

I looked across at him. "Nice? What do you mean by *nice*?"

"You know, *nice*. Maybe she and I could meet," he said, awkwardly. I froze while this registered. Was this sleazeball offering to reward me if I would consent to letting him have sex with my wife? I got up from my chair and started to raise my left arm to drop him right there, but luckily remembered my mother's advice to always hold for the perfect moment. This was not it.

"You'd better be joking." I was not smiling.

He mumbled something that I didn't hear. Just as well. I stormed out of his office with my heart beating out of my chest and my fists clenched. I went home and told Louise. Livid, she grabbed her coat and wanted to confront him on the spot. I pointed out that we did not have concrete proof. It was only my word against his. And I was already a bit of a controversial coaching figure in the province, plus there was that "coloured" thing.

We let it go. Bad decision. Looking back we *should* have set him up, or at least reported it. Who knows how many others he put in this position since that day, abusing his power and threatening careers?

So I'll just have to settle for him reading this . . . many years after he thought it was buried.

It's not.

CHAPTER 8
The Blues

It's been said there is no more difficult job in hockey than that of the amateur scout. I've been an amateur scout. I agree.

Officially, I was a part-time scout for the St. Louis Blues of the NHL for four years, overlapping my time as a coach in the Quebec Major Junior Hockey League. But really, in some form or another, with my father as my mentor, I'd been analyzing hockey players from the time my blades first touched Long Pond back in Windsor. It's in my DNA.

Not only was I scouting players, I was also scouting the scouts. It's an intriguing community. Modern scouts are more uniform in personality than back in the 1960s and 1970s when they brought more of their own individual qualities to the job, for better or worse. This point is illustrated by two men I met early in my hockey career.

My first significant exposure to big-time scouting was as a teenager in the early 1960s when I sat in my parent's living room across from Scotty Bowman, then the chief scout of the Montreal Canadiens. On that day, though my haze of excitement, in some elementary way I was actually studying our guest. I watched how Bowman carried himself, what he was wearing, how knowledgeable he seemed, how effectively he conversed with both my parents. I noted the questions he asked and observed his professionalism. Bowman seemed relaxed in this setting, but he never cracked the dignified, confident demeanor befitting the organization he worked for.

At the other end of the scouting spectrum was Doug Harvey.

When I was playing junior in Montreal there were always lots of scouts around who shared my passion for hockey. Feeling this bond, I was never shy about pumping these sanguine hockey men with questions as I watched them do their jobs. Often their opinions about certain players were imparted nonverbally, with a slow shake of the head, a furrowed brow or a derisive snort. They would stand in cold rinks and drink hot coffee and recognize things that the hockey fan misses. It was a remarkable classroom for me.

Of all the scouts I talked with, I enjoyed Harvey the most. Whatever people said about him — snickering behind his back was common — to me he was still the brilliant Canadiens' star I would watch on television with my father. He was the best defenceman of his era, really tough, a great passer, a master stickhandler who controlled games because he controlled time and space. (He was also involved in the NHL players union, a pursuit distained by team owners.)

As a scout, Doug Harvey was typical of the breed: a former player, in the game all his life, who knew little else. Afflicted with bipolar disorder, for years Harvey tried to find a career away from the sport. He sold aluminum siding, did carpentry, co-owned a sports shop, and operated a restaurant. He also had a hockey school that lasted for almost twenty years. Invariably, things fell flat. Later in life he would end up living for several years in a railway car at the entrance of a racetrack outside of Ottawa.

When I met him in the mid-1960s he was still playing, bouncing from team to team and league to league, with time off in between to service his demons, mainly alcoholism. He retired in 1969.

Harvey had a well-honed eye for talent. Over the years he would scout for several organizations, including the Houston Aeros of the World Hockey Association. (He's credited with helping lure Gordie, Mark and Marty Howe to the Aeros in the 1970s.) I'd see him in a corner at the Sorel Coliseum, run up and say hello, then sit down beside him. We'd talk all during the game. Usually I'd go get him a coffee and was thrilled to do it.

Harvey once asked me why I was always around him. "I'm not exactly a great person," he said.

I replied, "For me, you are. You talk to me and I learn a lot from you." He looked at me and grinned a little.

He then told me a story about a former teammate who almost everyone thought was a good person, but was anything but. In other words, a phony. Harvey's tone became wistful. "At least they know who *I* am, and they know about my problems. But I never sold out a teammate. Never."

Harvey was said to be a sloppy record-keeper and disorganized with his files. I don't know if that was the case or not. He certainly didn't always look professional. I don't think I *ever* saw him in a suit. He favoured a hockey jacket, nondescript pants and shoes that were well broken-in. He was not always clean-shaven. Unfortunately his alcoholism was a major ingredient of his life story. Once in a while I could smell booze on his breath, but I never actually saw him drunk. It would trouble me when I heard people make fun of him. He was a decent man who I think deserved more respect than he received.

One evening Harvey and I were sitting way back in the Colisée Cardin in Sorel watching a prospect named Michael Bossy perform for Laval. Another scout, from Laval, working for the New

York Islanders, adored Bossy. All the other scouts laughed at him for this because they'd decided Bossy was too "soft," and that his scoring skills would never bloom in the NHL because of this deficiency. I was about the only one who agreed with the Islanders scout. I felt Bossy *was* going to be good player and I never thought him soft or timid. He was much tougher in the corners than people were acknowledging. When I announced to the group that someday Bossy would score forty or fifty goals in the NHL, someone growled that "you're just as crazy as that guy in Laval." Doug Harvey, I recall, was lukewarm about Bossy, although he was impressed by my reasoning. "You understand the game, don't ya," he said to me. "Ya understand what you're looking at."

I grinned up at him. "I've been listening to *you*, and I talk to people."

"You may be right about Bossy. But I don't know about the fifty goals though . . ." Of course, Bossy had *nine* seasons of fifty goals or more in his Hall-of-Fame career with the Islanders.

I've been told that many years later people still remembered those exchanges in Sorel and my insistence that Bossy was special. They even ragged Harvey that I had seen something he missed.

"That little coloured boy," replied Harvey, "how *did* he know?"

I've always liked that story. I hope it's true.

* * *

One of my first scouting assignments was in 1972 for Rodrigue Lemoyne, owner of the QMJHL's Sorel Black Hawks. Rodrique asked me to look at a seventeen-year-old Quebec Ramparts forward named Pierre Larouche. I didn't know it, but it was actually a test. Rodrigue's head scout, the very competent Roland Salois, had already given his report about Larouche and Rodrigue was looking to see if mine matched. I had no qualms about telling Rodrigue that Larouche was an outstanding talent who worked best when given freedom to improvise outside a system. "He's cocky," I said, "but he's a good kid." My report aligned with Salois's, so Rodrigue traded for Larouche. A very good move. Over the next two seasons, in a Black Hawk uniform, Larouche scored 141 goals in 110 games. He would be an NHL star with both Pittsburgh and Montreal. I also pushed hard for a Sorel kid named Michel Deziel. He would play four years with the Black Hawks, capping his junior career in 1973–74 with an unbelievable 92 goals and 227 points in 69 games.

Sometimes my views went against the tide. In 1980, for example, I had strong opinions about a couple of very high-profile juniors. One was Doug Wickenheiser, a forward from the Regina Pats of the Western Canada Hockey League. While I agreed that Wickenheiser was a stellar young man, I didn't think he had the speed to be a top NHL player. His time-and-space execution was not good. I thought he'd be just a role player in the NHL. Clearly, this was *far* from the conventional wisdom as the Montreal Canadiens drafted him first overall in the 1980 entry draft. After four years in Montreal he was traded to St. Louis and never approached the success so many had predicted for him. I compared Wickenheiser to his contemporary, Denis Savard, who I thought should be the number one pick. I was certain that Savard's quickness, great hands and character would make him a star. Plus he was fearless. Savard was taken third overall by Chicago, where he became the core of their offence for many seasons. He's in the Hockey Hall of Fame.

* * *

My relationship with the St. Louis Blues covered 1987 to 1991. The initial connection was made by agent Bob Perno, who is now associated with the powerful Newport Sports Management, run by super agent Don Meehan. Perno dropped my name to the right people and the next thing I knew The Prof was calling me.

The Prof was Ron Caron, vice-president of the St. Louis Blues, so nicknamed because of his encyclopedic hockey knowledge. He was a Montreal Canadiens alumnus, and I had first met him in 1963 when he was tagging along with Cliff Fletcher at the Montreal train station. "You were with us for a while, weren't you, John?" he asked me when I went to see him in St. Louis. I was flattered that he remembered. The Prof did not forget much. And anyone who met him never forgot The Prof.

Diplomatically stated, The Prof was highly emotive. When he'd get upset, assorted objects would be wildly flung about for a few minutes and then . . . poof! He'd be fine. I witnessed a bit of this, but apparently I never saw his most explosive episodes. There are stories galore.

"Caron stood alone for his famed dual-personality," wrote Toronto journalist Howard Berger, upon Caron's death in 2012. "An engaging, articulate gentleman when his team wasn't in action; a raving, uncontrollable lunatic during games. Though he was universally known as a bright, learned man [Caron] would simply lose his marbles in the immediate moments before, and during, games involving the Canadiens or Blues. All sense of logic, perspective and decorum would abandon him, only to return — somewhat magically — once the final buzzer sounded."

With the Blues I was assigned to work under Teddy Hampson, the highly respected scouting director. Hampson had a long playing career in both the NHL and the WHA, and in 1969 won the Bill Masterton Trophy given to the NHL player who best exemplifies the qualities of perseverance, sportsmanship and dedication to hockey.

During one Blues' game I saw Teddy in the stands and asked why he was not sitting upstairs with The Prof. He explained with a little grin, "Well John, I'll go for a while, but sometimes it's best down here. I'll take you up with Caron, but if you're not used to it . . . well, just don't sit too close." I appreciated the tip. Sure enough, I watched Caron, in a world of his own, become very animated as he glared at the play down below. I was told this was very mild.

Teddy showed me the ropes in other ways, too. Things like how to be more detailed in reading a player, and how to fill out and file the team's scouting forms. (These were the days just before computers and mass databases.)

The normal NHL scouting structure separates professional scouting (where the scout assesses players already in leagues such as the NHL, AHL and ECHL, with an eye for a potential trade or to fill a specific need) and amateur scouting (where the scout evaluates prospects for their long-term potential). Today, every NHL team has a director of professional scouting and a director of amateur scouting, each with a network of full- and part-time staff reporting to them.

I focused on the amateur side, but The Prof and Teddy wanted me to understand the whole picture, so in time I was doing both. My assigned area was ambitious. It included the QMJHL and parts of Ontario, as well as the eastern seaboard of the United States. Slowly my responsibilities expanded to include various tournaments. I got paid for part-time, but the actual hours made it close to full-time.

*　*　*

The scouting life isn't glamorous, but it's not horrible, either.

One thing for sure: time-management skills are an asset. My schedule was especially tight, given my QMJHL coaching demands. For weeks on end, for one job or another, I was always in a rink. I did my best to combine things. For my QMJHL teams

I did my pregame evaluation of our next opponent and at the same time I'd take notes on the potential NHL draft prospects on the ice. It was quite a balancing act and was all-consuming, but I made it work.

Travel can be tedious, but it's central to the job as a scout so it's just accepted. You are gone *a lot*. Sometimes it seems you are *always* on the road. You'd leave on Thursday and be back home again on Sunday night or Monday morning. You are around for maybe a day or two — enough time to say hello to your wife — then, depending the location of your next assignment, you jump back in a rental car and you are gone again. You'd be on the road twenty-some days out of thirty. On the average weekend you'd see four games: Friday night, Saturday night, Sunday afternoon, Sunday evening. Sometimes during the week you'd catch major junior or college games and take in an occasional AHL contest. Home for a scout is often a suitcase and maybe a favourite pillow. At least the long drives would give you solitude and a lot of time to think. Sometimes an assistant coach from one of the junior teams travelled with me, but usually I was alone on those treacherous Quebec winter roads.

Eating well was a challenge, but it's a myth that you eat bad food all the time. You can eat well if you want. Most of the scouts eat poorly because that's their way. I always managed to watch my diet and avoid fast food.

Is there a lot of drinking? In some cases, yes. Less now than in previous decades, but bars are still where many of "the boys" congregate on the road, especially in the smaller towns. Again, one does not have to imbibe. I don't drink and I never felt ostracized because of it. When I was in a bar — and this was rare — I would just order a soft drink or ice water with a piece of lemon. Truth is, I've just never acquired a taste for alcohol. (One night as a teenager I went out and I had a beer — I didn't even drink the full bottle — and got so sick that I thought I was going to die. That was it for me, other than a rare glass of wine or a bit of cognac on special occasions. Besides, it wouldn't take much to get me drunk. I start to feel it right away. I've also seen how ridiculous people get when they are drunk. Not for me.)

There is camaraderie among the scouts. This is a little strange because technically the other guys are your competitors. On occasion I travelled with François Allaire, who is widely credited with revolutionizing the position of goaltender. He was scouting for Montreal at the time and in a few years would become the Canadiens' first-ever goaltending coach. Allaire's "butterfly" technique was a major departure from the day when goaltenders were encouraged to stay on their feet as much as possible. (Patrick Roy was among Francois' early devotees.) Our respective bosses didn't want Francois and me travelling together, so we stopped . . . officially. But we still did it from time to time. While we never exchanged team secrets, we always talked about hockey and enjoyed each other's company.

When I scouted for the Blues I became part of an *almost* all-male scouting fraternity — I recall one or two female scouts — populated by former professional players with a love for the sport and a loyalty to particular teams. (George Armstrong, the former long-time captain of the Toronto Maple Leafs, was typical of this group.)

Most scouts were good guys, but sometimes you overheard things that you didn't like. Once several of us were in Cornwall, Ontario, assessing a hot prospect named Owen Nolan, when I heard an OHL scout mention Edmonton Oilers' star goaltender Grant Fuhr, who is black. The scout said: "We don't need *that*. Leave the niggers out of our game. I wouldn't touch him with a ten-foot pole if he was in a hole." Another scout looked over and saw me, then nudged the scout who was talking. I made a mental note.

* * *

*In the Montreal Forum, 1988, listening to goaltending guru Francois Allaire
(seated below me). Francois and I were traveling companions when I scouted for
the St. Louis Blues.*

Top scouts bring a special intelligence to bear, a combination of
interpretative skills and instinct. Most look for largely the same
things in a prospect, but every scout employs his own lens and
experience that shape his opinions. For the amateur scout, in
a nutshell, it's all about *potential*. Accordingly, one looks at so
many things. My main criteria are: character, hockey "sense,"
skating, size and physical condition.

First, I want to see their **character**. Without good solid character, I would never recommend a player, regardless of how
many evaluation "points" he has. This is because in the NHL
the *difference* is character. By "character" I mean being able to
consistently function through adversity. Good character includes
a mental toughness and a willingness to adapt, adjust and learn.
But here's the twist: a youth cannot have this purposeful, resolute

quality unless he has solid, basic hockey skills. Mental toughness requires a reliable underpinning of these skills. So when I tell a player he's not mentally tough, I reflect upon his former coaches who did not provide him basic skills to do the job.

Second, **hockey sense**. Although there are checklists that try to capture some elements, hockey sense is hard to quantify. Nevertheless a scout knows it when he sees it. It's an intangible *something* — an ability to do the right thing at the right time in the course of play, to watch a play unfold and make the correct decisions. Players with strong hockey sense are usually more poised, and as a result can more effectively adapt to sudden changes in the play. They find openings on offence *and* on defence, and are less likely to drift out of position without a reason. They seem to somehow *feel* the play and know where the puck is going. That acute ability to anticipate is why the puck always appeared to follow Wayne Gretzky and Bobby Orr, and why Nick Lidstrom and Larry Robinson were rarely out of position. Today, players such as Sidney Crosby and Henrik Zetterberg have this gift.

Third, **skating**. Edges, speed, quickness, power, stability.

Fourth, I look for **size**. Not surprisingly, as in all contact sports, bigger hockey players are coveted more than smaller players. (At five-foot-five, I feel this one personally.) It may be cliché, but you can't teach size. It's no longer true that larger players are slow and lumbering. While it's unlikely that a six-foot-five winger will match Sidney Crosby or Claude Giroux for quickness, the gap is closing. Canada and the United States tend to treat a big, fast kid differently in their minor hockey programs. In Canada, if you are sixteen and a big kid, we are more likely to develop you. In the United States, they take the kid who can do the most for them right away. Development becomes secondary. The development ideal has always been a foundation of my coaching philosophy so I think this is a big mistake.

With a young goaltending prospect named Martin Brodeur.

Fifth, **physical conditioning**. I look for this all the time. Are they strong and stable in the corners? Are they able to go all-out for a forty-five-second shift? Do they wilt late in a game? Players frequently don't understand the *why* of physical fitness. Before a player does a specific exercise, he should realize why he is doing that exercise, and know the precise results and benefits to expect. In other words, there is an intellectual side to high-level training. Once players *understand* their training, they have a choice: are they willing to do it? Are they willing to *apply* themselves to a particular exercise and to an effective fitness program? Recently Tampa Bay Lightning star Steve Stamkos agreed to a very-targeted conditioning program aimed at making him bigger and stronger. Understanding the exact purpose, he dedicated himself to this training and it helped him become a sixty-goal scorer.

* * *

Scouting is complex. It's an art, a craft and a science all in one. Plus it's a lot of luck. Books have been written on the subject and I'm sure more will follow. So, for now, some random thoughts on the topic.

The first relates to goal-scoring. It's a huge misconception that the best player is the one who scores the most goals. Although it seems counterintuitive, I usually avoid the goal scorers because it doesn't tell me all that much about their overall potential. When the game is played at a slower pace, some players will score a lot, whereas a better overall player will not have great statistics. However, at the next level when the pace of the game is quicker, often the kid who scored all the goals can't elevate his game. The other player will show better. This is why many players who are exceptional in junior peter out at a higher level. Perhaps they are not used to making extra effort . . . perhaps they are accustomed to over-handling the puck . . . perhaps they habitually overstay their shifts . . . perhaps as pampered "stars" they don't feel compelled to listen. They expect to play their own way. Eventually this catches up with them.

One curious thing I noted about some scouts is that they would leave before a game ended. I rarely did. If I was there alone representing my organization, after the game I made sure I talked to the players I was interested in. My first question: *Did you make your team better tonight?* That's a Teddy Hampson question and a Prof Caron question. I would then ask about specific moments in the game, for example: *Why didn't you drive the net on this play?* Then I would point out positive plays he made. Having a balanced discussion was very important. If I mentioned a negative, I would always give a couple of positives. And I would always end with a positive. I think I was able to explore more deeply than many scouts just because I'd ask more questions and could drill down into the finer points to gauge the player's personality.

Because he is assessing potential, it is imperative that an amateur scout take a longer-term view of every player he assesses. If you are scouting just on the basis of where that kid is *at that time*, then you are not scouting. I always conjectured where he would be in four or five years. Does he understand what he has in front of him? Is he willing and likely to stay with a program? Does he have the desire? That's why character is so important.

Some kids are difficult to reach emotionally and intellectually. Others are easy on both counts. An example of the latter was Sidney Crosby, a fellow Nova Scotian who had scouts drooling over him when he was barely out of the womb. I would have loved to have coached Sidney because he was so easy to teach. He's a fine young man and his ability speaks for itself. I don't know his parents well, but his dad and I have talked a time or two. I recall him asking my opinion on a few people who were actively seeking to become part of his son's life. I was more than happy to offer my views.

Young men mature at different rates. Sometimes a prospect is a prospect only because he matured early. These early bloomers are placed at the top competitive levels, but as their contemporaries mature and catch up, they no longer stand out. Conversely, sometimes we'd stumble on a kid with significant potential playing in a lesser league.

For example, many years ago I saw a kid, who I had coached in minor hockey, was playing junior C. I quickly concluded he was much better than that. I broke him down point-by-point. I saw how his knees were bent . . . how he pivoted . . . noticed how he "saw" the whole ice surface . . . The kid had hockey sense. He ended up playing major junior for three seasons and university hockey as well. The young man was Nichol Cloutier, a defenceman. Today he is my son-in-law. Seems my daughter Chantal was also doing a little scouting.

When they first met each other I saw a flicker — a dad's radar, you understand. So I laid down a few rules. First, I advised everyone that there would be no players around my daughter. She was too young. Second, I told Nic that if in the future he wanted to date my daughter, it had better be when he was in university and serious. Finally, I took Chantal aside and stated: no hockey bums allowed! Not that Nic was ever a bum, but he was also too young. Time passed. Then one evening just after dinner there came a knock on our door. There stood Nic.

"Ahhhh, coach. I'm in college now . . . Concordia . . . for two years . . . can I talk to Chantal, please?"

He mentioned something about going for dinner or for a walk. In any case, I was obviously impressed. I looked at him and smiled. I said to go ask Chantal.

As he went to talk with her, I called out to Chantal that there was someone here to see her. She asked who it was.

"Just some college bum," I said.

* * *

It was no secret in the Quebec hockey community that I was doubling-up: scouting for the Blues and coaching in the Q at the same time. It was mentioned in the press a few times and the QMJHL surely knew. Then, after four years, league president Gilles Courteau told me it was a conflict of interest. Gilles was never rude about it — I think it had to do with a policy change by the league — and I said that I understood his position. In any case, I now had to pick *one* job. I chose to stay in the Q.

Was this a mistake? Maybe, yes.

Teddy Hampson accepted my decision, but he always thought I had a bright future with the Blues. Certainly this was a "crossroads" moment for me. I was ambitious for my hockey career and I still had dreams of coaching in the NHL. I now think that

Signing the register at my daughter Chantal's wedding to Nichol Cloutier (far left), 1994.

leaving the Blues may have been a strategic error: a short-sighted decision. It was a good situation in St. Louis where I was learning from some of the top scouts in the business. If I had remained as a scout I would have advanced up the levels there. I may have even one day had a chance at the GM job. I was accumulating the experience and all the tools: I coached in major junior, I had administration abilities, I could run a draft, I knew how to build teams, I had good people skills, long hours never mattered to me as long as I was learning and I was good with numbers.

Yet I selected to stay in the QMJHL. Because the choice was all mine, I can live with that.

CHAPTER 9
Turner Cup

In February 1994, the Atlanta Knights organization announced that I would coach the Atlanta Fire Ants, a roller hockey team they planned to launch. While I would nominally handle the Ants that summer — and make $35,000 in the process — I was *really* being hired to coach the Knights. The problem: the Knights already had a coach. His name was Gene Ubriaco, and they weren't quite ready to move him at the time of the announcement.

Ubriaco was a good hockey man. He played five seasons in the NHL and coached the Pittsburgh Penguins at one point. With the Knights he seemed to be performing well. The team was leading the Midwest Division with a 36–17–11 record and the previous year finished 52–23–0–7. He was also doing a reasonable job promoting the team around town, and was tight with Lightning general manager Phil Esposito. Nevertheless, in mid-March, with seventeen games left in the 1993–94 regular schedule, Gene got the word. The Lightning made him their pro scout. It was officially called a promotion, but I'm not sure Gene thought so.

Meanwhile, I was named interim coach of the Atlanta Knights.

* * *

From the moment I was announced as Knights' coach, my skin colour was an issue. I received phone calls from across North America, fifteen to twenty a day for a while. Others came from the UK, Finland and Sweden. While I anticipated *some* interest — this *was* a hockey first, after all — the level of attention caught me off guard. In Atlanta, I came to fully appreciate the significance of such a breakthrough, even in a sport few African-Americans knew much about. Over and over, black and white Atlantans would spot me and come up to let me know how proud they were. Very gratifying.

In every media interview I felt it necessary to stress that I was a good coach, that I was there on merit and hard work, that I had earned the chance, that I was ready. "With the background I have a guy would be an idiot to try to hold me back," I told *Atlanta Journal* columnist Steve Hummer, holding nothing back. "I'm not afraid to sit down and talk the game with any-one. That's not being conceited, that's having confidence in the knowledge I've acquired."

As for being "a representative of my community" . . . Please, no! That's an insult. I'm an individual. I don't have to repre-sent *any* community. Same as being "a credit to my race." That smacks of bigotry. Do I tell a Caucasian that he's a credit to his race? C'mon!

* * *

Settling into Atlanta was easy for me. The city felt familiar and I was instantly comfortable with its culture and its rhythms. Maybe a little *too* comfortable. One day soon after I arrived, I decided to park my car and walk around a bit to get to know a few neigh-bourhoods. This one area included "the projects," but it was daylight and I didn't sense an immediate threat, so I thought I was okay. I was standing on a sidewalk when a black man in his early forties approached me.

"You the new hockey coach?"

I was astonished he recognized me, even though my appointment had received pretty heavy local media coverage. "Yes, sir," I replied.

He looked around slowly and furrowed his brow. "Man, you don't know where you are, do you?"

"No, but I'm just looking around and . . ."

"You not afraid, right?"

"Should I be?"

He laughed. "Man, you ain't from the neighbourhood, easy to see."

He squinted at me, then called across the street to a couple of young guys who were hanging around on the other side. They strolled over. Their names were James and Tas. I quickly said hello. "Hey," was their barely audible answer. The older man told them I was the hockey coach and wasn't to be bothered. He ordered them to put the word out. They nodded, but one of them volunteered "there be some messed up motherfuckers out there . . ."

I thanked the older man and started off. Then, astonishing even myself, I stopped and shouted back at James and Tas. "You guys wanna go for a ride and maybe a drink?" Amused at my offer, both young men got in my new luxury-grey Buick Park Avenue and off we went, the hockey coach and his new pals, heading for a nearby mall. Part way I pulled over and asked if James wanted to take the wheel. He happily accepted. At one point he even gave me a phone number and told me to call if I had any problems. Tas remained more wary. He was packing and made certain that I saw.

"Got one?" he asked.

"No."

"Get one, man. You gotta have one."

"I'd be too dangerous," I said, half-joking. "But I *would* use it if I had to . . ."

"That's the idea, bro. Protect you-self."

After our drinks — I had a Sprite — as we were returning to the neighbourhood, another car eerily pulled up alongside my Buick. Seeing this, James yelled, "Get outta here! Run, man!" They both jumped out and sprinted off. I stupidly just sat there as the other car stopped. One of the guys inside thrust his arm out the window. The barrel of a hand gun was now less than a foot from my face. His finger was on the trigger.

"What da fuck you doin' here, nigger? . . . Hey, you the hockey man?"

Strange. At this moment I should have been terrified, but wasn't. Maybe my previous brush with death left me feeling invincible. I don't know. Anyway, I calmly acknowledged I was the hockey man. The young guy with the gun rapidly explained this was *their* territory, and since I was not one of *them* I had better stay the fuck out. He said a bit more, but that was the essence of his message. When he finished, another voice in the car said, "C'mon, man. Forget that motherfucka. Move our asses, man."

Later I was told that people watching all this from nearby buildings were sure I was about to be badly beaten or worse. A week or so later, in a music store, I saw one of the guys who almost blew me away. I went up and cautiously asked him about the incident. He told me that when he recognized me, he decided to give me a pass. It was that simple. It was that close.

A postscript: I did get a gun. Two guns, in fact. One for the car and one for the house. I also got a permit to carry a concealed weapon and took shooting lessons from the Atlanta police. After my first training session I was so stiff and sore after taxing muscles I had never used before that I couldn't get out of bed the next day. I recall thinking, *Why do I have to go through this?* Then I thought of the hate mail and I had my answer.

It didn't take long before letters bearing all manner of slurs and threats began arriving. Surprising to me, most originated from outside Georgia. Wisconsin, for one, seemed a frequent and unexpected location. Also Ohio, Maine, Alabama and Tennessee. A few from Ontario, as well. A lot of the mail was filtered by the team, but some got through to me. The predictable stuff: fuckin' nigger get out of here . . . scum . . . we'll get you, we know where you live . . . we'll get your family, too . . . you're a dead man, etc. Sometimes there'd be artwork, such as me hanging from a tree.

In Atlanta I lived on a secured site. Outside the gates I had to be careful wherever I went. Stuff happened. Like the time I was walking through a busy supermarket parking lot and a pickup truck cut in front of me. The driver looked at me and pointed his index finger to make a gun and said, "You know we're gonna get your ass." He then smirked and drove off. There was another guy in there with him and I thought I saw a rifle hooked on the back of the cab. The entire episode took just a few seconds, but I have no idea how long they were there waiting for me or if was just all spontaneous. Fortunately I was able to get the licence plate number and reported it to the police.

That day I had let my guard down and didn't have my gun on me or even in my car. Perhaps this was a good thing because it's possible I would have used it, if only to protect myself.

* * *

Arriving late in a hockey season requires an adjustment by both coach and players. To ease some anxiety within the Knights' family I quickly laid out my intentions and my approach: no major changes, but always a maximum effort. I chose my words carefully concerning Gene Ubriaco. You walk a fine line because there's always some lingering loyalty to the departing coach. Defenceman Chris LiPuma, for example, considered him a personal friend. He attended Ubriaco's hockey school as a youngster and Ubriaco even served as his agent for time. Gene and I only ever talked twice. Both conversations were brief and congenial, and occurred in the lobby of a Chicago hotel after he left the Lightning to become head coach of the IHL expansion Chicago Wolves.

Luckily, in my coaching travels I had either coached or come to know a number of Knights players. Steve "La Mouche" Larouche, whom I coached in midget and junior, was there. As were Normand Rochefort, Éric Charron, Eric Dubois, Martin Tanguay and Christian Campeau. Several of them told the press I was imaginative, patient and open-minded. Also, I'd done my homework. I saw the team on the road and watched tapes. I had my plan. "From what he says himself," the *Journal* wrote, "Paris will enter his first game [with] a positive, low-key approach."

That's me. Low key.

* * *

March 12, 1994. My first game as Knights' coach. I barely slept the night before. By midmorning I was at the Omni, the Knights' home rink.

Located downtown, the Omni was far from a state-of-the-art facility. It was about twenty-five years old, dated by its 1960s, egg-carton, steel roof. The place had few amenities. There were no club seats or luxury boxes and just one restaurant. It didn't have video or replay boards. Restrooms were inadequate and there were plenty of bugs and rats. However, one plus for me was the designated underground parking spots for the Knights and the Omni's other primary tenant, the NBA's Atlanta Hawks. So, being one of the privileged, that morning I proudly pulled in to my spot. However, once on foot, couldn't get inside the building.

I pulled and banged and pushed buttons but the entrance from the parking lot wouldn't budge. Eventually I headed up and went the long route, through the concourse, hoping that this was not an omen.

Usually I'm calm before a game. Not this one. There were 13,489 fans there that night, including IHL president N. Thomas Berry. Our opponent was the Las Vegas Thunder. With a record of 43–11–8, they were the league's best team, brimming with former and future NHLers. Lyndon Byers, Ken Quinney, Brad Lauer, Marc Habscheid, Jim Kyte, Clint Malarchuk and Peter Ing. Las Vegas's marquee player was Radek Bonk, a six-foot-three, eighteen-year-old Ottawa Senators prodigy who was busy constructing a forty-two-goal season. They were coached by former New York Islanders stalwart Butch Goring.

I was standing near a gate at the far end of the rink as they announced the starting lineups. Finally, they got to me. "And the head coach . . . he's yours . . . John Paris, Jr.!" Then they threw the spotlight on me. I didn't know whether I was going to be cheered or booed. They cheered — loudly. My entire body lightly trembled as rugged Chris LiPuma cupped my elbow and escorted me across the ice to our bench. It seemed like a very long walk that night. Finally, at the bench, I thought to myself, *I made it!* During the national anthem I sweated big time, especially in my armpits. I was wearing a sports jacket so it didn't show, but I had to change my shirt between periods.

We won the game, 6–1, but things got wild. A couple of lengthy melees resulted in eleven game misconducts, 274 penalty minutes, and the referee having to temporarily suspend play in the second period. At one point, as a big show, one of their goons glided to our bench and gestured like he was going to challenge me. I was ready. In the end, I was automatically suspended for two games because one of my players was first to leave the bench to fight. It drove me crazy to watch the rematch the next day up in the broadcast area. I tried to direct things during the game even though a suspended coach can't legally communicate with his bench. We outfitted my assistant coach Joey Bucchino with headphones and from the press box team president Richard Adler relayed instructions from me. But Las Vegas rapidly noticed our ploy and soon the league president personally came down to the Knights bench and made Joey remove the head phones. Still, we won again, 4–3. Three days later we lost to Milwaukee.

I did a tally: I had been officially a pro coach for three games, but was behind the bench for only *one* of them.

Low key, eh.

I finally returned and we marched on. I liked how our players were responding to me and embracing their individual roles. Management also appeared pleased with my work. Yet, the Knights brass fell short of offering me a ringing public endorsement. "He's interim right now, and he's going to stay interim," Richard Adler told the *Journal*. "We'll see how he does the rest of the season. So far, the players like him." But even Adler had to concede, "If we win the Turner Cup, how do we *not* give him the job?"

At least I knew where I stood. I've always liked a challenge.

* * *

Atlanta has a patchwork history when it comes to ice hockey. The sport seems to have had almost no presence in the city until Atlanta's first NHL club, the Flames, arrived via the NHL's 1972 expansion. The Flames lasted eight seasons, until 1980, when they relocated to Calgary. The NHL returned in 1999 with the Atlanta Thrashers. They lasted twelve seasons then relocated to Winnipeg and became the Jets. Squeezed between the Flames and the Thrashers were the Atlanta Knights.

The Knights began play in the International Hockey League in

A Knights tradition: being escorted across the ice by hardrock defenceman Chris LiPuma, one of our leaders.

1992, coinciding with the inaugural season of their parent club, the NHL's Tampa Bay Lightning. Not only would the Knights be a good hockey organization, but an *important* one as well. They were the first professional hockey team to have a woman on their roster — goaltender Manon Rhéaume, who had departed before I arrived — and the first to be coached by a black man. Not bad for a club that would last just four years.

Knights' owners frequently pointed out that the IHL was *not* the NHL, nor should fans expect it to be. The ethos of the IHL, founded in 1946, was summed up beautifully by Richard Adler: "This is a league for the masses and not the classes." Nevertheless, the IHL offered excellent hockey with stable organizations, many of which were farm teams for NHL clubs. And during the 1990s the IHL was better than the American Hockey League, having more veterans. This also meant bigger salaries and higher travel expenses.

The bipolar nature of the farm team makes for a constant test. You are there to develop the talent, but you also must win. Your best players can be ripped from your lineup in a blink of an eye, yet you are expected to adjust and compete. It's a colossal balancing act, but everybody knows the deal going in.

While the Knights' parent club, the Tampa Bay Lightning, wrestled with meddling ownership and conflicting personalities (Phil Esposito's memoir, *Thunder and Lightning*, exposes his frustrations around this time), the Knights' front office was comparatively harmonious. Their owners made no secret they were hoping for a couple of good seasons to better position their bid for an NHL franchise. Mind you, at that time a second group in Atlanta was also thinking seriously about pursuing an NHL franchise. And that second group was rumoured to include Ted Turner, the CNN mogul. Tough competition. Still, the Knights management and front office was a determined, interesting cast.

David Berkman was the main owner. He was a real estate tycoon who built considerable wealth buying apartments in the region during the real estate depression of the 1970s. He loved making deals. A reserved man in his sixties, he once said he'd be perfectly content as a beach bum. He harboured a passion for sports, especially hockey, which he embraced when the NHL's Flames were in town. With the Knights, he stayed mostly in the background. Berkman would occasionally invite me to his house where his staff would treat me very well.

Richard Adler, who grew up in Montreal, was another owner. He was also team president and, for my first year in Atlanta, the general manager as well. Married to a top American figure skater, Richard was intense and highly creative, befitting a former regional vice-president of Ringling Brothers and Barnum and Bailey. One day during a demonstration ball hockey game at a local Boys and Girls Club, he attempted to hit a couple of our players even though we all understood there was to be no body contact. This looked funny, until he laid a huge hit on me when my guard was down. The pain instantly exploded through me, especially around the area of my ileostomy. I briefly paused to recover and then went on the hunt. He wisely didn't come near me the rest of the game. I told him later that he was lucky we were in the auditorium. And I meant it. He never played in another demo game when I was there.

Charles Felix was the chief financial officer and, for a period, team president. He also may have owned part of the team for a while. He and I were close. We'd both arrive at the office early in the morning and he'd always have coffee ready. Then we would talk hockey and all matter of world issues. I came to know his sons and he was at my daughter Chantal's wedding in Sorel-Tracy in 1994. He never interfered with the players or tried to influence my thinking on coaching issues. Charles had flare. One time in a San Diego underground parking lot, he and

I were heading back to our car when Charles spotted a couple of guys attempting to break into another vehicle. Suddenly he whipped out a sheriff's badge — I later learned it was legitimate — and yelled at the two culprits to get on the ground and freeze. Impressive stuff. Unbelievably, the two guys didn't move until the authorities came and took them away. Later Charles confided to me that it was fortunate that the guys didn't have guns. Otherwise we might have had a little problem.

Joe Bucchino was a sensitive, versatile young man. He was a former head trainer and assistant GM for the NHL's New York Rangers. In Atlanta he was assistant coach under Gene Ubriaco and later became the GM. Even so, with the Knights "Joey B," as we called him, didn't always have full say. He frequently had me over to his house where I ate like a king. His wife is a delight and I would spend lots of time with his son, A.J., a fine baseball player, working on his hitting using the back yard apparatus they erected.

* * *

We completed the 1993–94 regular season with a 45–22–0–14 record and finished first in our division. (After I took over, we were 9–5–0–3.) However, the season did not end well for us. After clinching a playoff spot, we lost our intensity and dropped our last four or five games. The psyche of a sports team is fragile and even a confident group can start to doubt itself after just a couple of bad games. But I wasn't too worried. Tampa Bay had temporarily called up a few players and I was also testing individuals in different situations. Still, a slump is a slump, and I could feel management's breath on my neck. Fortunately, we turned things around quickly.

We swept the opening playoff round against the Milwaukee Admirals, winning the first game thanks to a four-goal performance by Cape Breton's Bill McDougall (despite a significant groin problem), and the second game in a double-overtime thriller. The Admirals folded after that. In the Western Conference finals, we blitzed the San Diego Gulls in four games. It was our eighth straight victory in the playoffs. We were completely locked in. Our players had swagger and were clearly there for each other. I could feel it. As Joey Bucchino observed, "John has them looking in the mirror each morning and thinking they're great."

However, on the brink of my biggest triumph, it could have all ended for me right there.

Following the five-hour flight from San Diego I got in my car at the Hartsfield-Jackson airport, by then fatigued by a long day. In the wee hours of the morning I started to drive home but didn't get far before I dozed off behind the wheel, causing my Buick Park Avenue to slip off the wet road into a ditch, near exit 11 on Highway 400 in Alpharetta. I was dazed but unhurt. More embarrassed than anything. In short order a couple of cars pulled over to help me, followed by the cops and a tow truck. While I stood waiting, three young girls from one of the cars recognized me and came over. One of them asked, "Coach, can I touch you?"

"What?"

"Can I *touch* you, please?"

I looked at the cops who grinned at me and shrugged. So there, on the side of the road, as dawn was breaking over the American South, I felt the reality of fame — or at least public recognition — as this young woman squeezed my arm and began to jump around and squeal, "I touched him! Ahhhhh! I touched him!"

The other girls then did the same thing. I'm still unsure how to classify this memorable moment. Except to say that I was touched.

* * *

My coaching philosophy seemed a perfect fit for this group of players on the Atlanta Knights. I conveyed a positive message at

Instructing at Atlanta Knights practice, circa 1995.

every opportunity. When I signed an autograph I added, "Yes! Yes! Yes!" We even had our own battle cry — *Carry the lamp!* — borrowed from the Montreal Canadiens motto of holding the torch high. If a player made a mistake, I didn't scream and yell. I took him aside and pointed out the cause of the error or I would mention something to him on the bench. Frankly, I believe each mistake or bad decision by a player is partly my fault as well. There are two people involved: the teacher and the student. Why should any coach hammer his players without fully evaluating the situation? Everybody makes mistakes. Most times the player knows what happened.

Many players appreciated that I allowed them more freedom than Gene Ubriaco. I never tried to control everything, and I let my offensive players improvise. I encouraged my defencemen, especially Shawn Rivers, to get more involved offensively. Forwards Bill McDougall, Steve Larouche and Jason Ruff blossomed under this style.

Everything should be done with respect. Teaching is a big part of coaching and you have to do it slowly, bit by bit. The key is patience. I believe you can learn from everyone so I took time to ask players' opinions. I often sat with them individually, employing visualization techniques and providing what they needed emotionally and physiologically. One case in point was my goalie, Mike Greenlay.

If we were going to have any sort of playoff run, I knew Mike had to be a big part of it. He was a nice kid — and maybe the only professional hockey goalie ever born in Vitoria, Brazil. (His father was a civil engineer who travelled a lot.) He was also the lone member of our team with a Stanley Cup ring, thanks to his stretch with the Edmonton Oilers in 1990. The previous season he was a co-winner of the James Norris Memorial Trophy, given to the goaltenders of the IHL team with the lowest goals-against average. But as the 1993–94 season ended, Mike was struggling.

Soon after I arrived I talked with Mike about his focus and how important it was to work on the basics. That is, the fundamental things he did *when he was playing his best*. He needed to remember his own formula for success. I constantly reassured him. Before some games I'd take him in my office, turn the lights out and visualize with him. It worked well. I also made it a point to express my support for Mike openly, employing the old Scotty Bowman trick of using the press to get my messages across to my players. "He has all my confidence, and he knows it," I told the *Atlanta Journal*. It all clicked. Mike was one of our playoff stars. (By the way, I don't think that goalies are all somehow *different*, as some contend. I believe they are worriers because they are the last line of defence. So they are often more detailed, more attune to nuance. There is a reason why a disproportionate number of media analysts are former goalies.)

While several players publicly sang my praises — Stan Drulia, Steve Larouche, Shawn Rivers, Chris LiPuma and Normand Rochefort among them — management was still reserved. Richard Adler took pains to remind the media that I was *still* interim, and stressed that the only reason Gene Ubriaco departed was because the Lightning had another assignment for him. "Coaches don't get paid for winning popularity contests with

players, they get paid to win. Gene didn't lose. With John, timing
was everything."

* * *

I was in the middle of a practice during the Western Conference
finals when I looked up and I saw him there watching me, his face
an inch from the Plexiglas in the Omni. My father was at the end
of a two-week visit to see me in Atlanta, and, while he'd been at
the rink before, I knew this would be the last time I would see him
for a while. He was seventy-four, long-retired from the post office,
and still in reasonably good health. But in life, one never knows.
After the practice we embraced and Dad couldn't resist a few
observations. Good ones, too, about getting defencemen to step
up into the play quicker. Before he left town he told the *Journal*,
"Naturally, I'm proud of him. I kinda figured that if John stayed
at it long enough, something would happen."

* * *

Our opponents in the Turner Cup final were the Fort Wayne
Komets, the defending IHL champions. The Komets had a ton of
veterans, some with several years experience in the NHL, including Doug Wickenheiser, a number-one-overall NHL draft pick.
By contrast, many Knights were only in their second or third year
of pro hockey. The media saw the series as dead-even, although
the *Atlanta Journal* wrote we had the edge in coaching. The
Komets coach was a rookie named Bruce Boudreau, now widely
considered one of the best NHL coaches. I wish I would have
saved that newspaper clipping.

It had been decades since Atlanta had won a professional
sports championship of any sort, and the city was anxious to
mute the "Loserville" put-down. While we pursued the Turner

Cup, the Hawks were in the NBA's playoffs against another Indiana team, the Pacers. Granted, the Hawks were getting more ink — but not *that* much more. Frankly, I think the city found our quest more interesting.

We won the first two games of the finals, in the Omni, 7–4 and 1–0 respectively, the latter a masterpiece by Mike Greenlay. The series then shifted to Fort Wayne for the next three games.

Next to the local General Motors truck factory, the Komets were about the biggest thing in Fort Wayne, a city of two hundred thousand. An IHL member since 1953, they had been in eleven Turner Cup finals, winning four times. The Komets regularly packed the 8,003-seat Allen County War Memorial Coliseum, known locally as "The Jungle" (after the popular Guns N' Roses song, "Welcome to the Jungle"). The facility was built in 1952, expanded in the 1980s, and had a seating contour that placed spectators very close to the ice. This resulted in a raucous, intimidating atmosphere for visiting teams. The Turner Cup sat in a trophy case in The Jungle, along with an ornate plaque, the original version of the championship award from 1946, rescued by a local guy at a garage sale.

Fort Wayne was also adept at mind games. Nothing huge, just little things that get under your skin. For example, the owner of a local laundromat, who knew full well who I was, wouldn't give me back my suits that I had dropped off the day before. He said he couldn't find them. I just stared at the guy. "I'm not leaving until I get 'em, so we're going to work this out." The stubborn bugger continued this little charade for thirty or forty minutes as I stood there. At one point I said, "Look, I'm here to take the cup. I'm not leaving without that cup — and I'm not leaving without my suits!" Finally . . . a miracle! Out he came from the back with my suits. He charged me full price, too. I didn't leave a tip. Same sort of silly thing happened with the Komets, who refused to lend us some hockey tape when we ran out — a usual courtesy between teams. Not there.

Nova Scotian Billy McDougall was a major factor in the Knights' 1994 championship run.

We lost the third game of the series 3–1. In the fourth game, we fell behind 5-0 but ultimately won 7-6, in triple overtime, rescued by an incredible team resolve and by a five-goal performance from 'La Mouche' Larouche. They extended the series by beating us 5–3 in the fifth game. Up three games to two, we headed for home. It would have been easy to concede that at least some momentum had moved over to them. But I was not going to let us concede anything of the sort. I was determined to keep things positive and talked only in terms of what we had done well.

* * *

Game six. I arrived at the Omni before noon. More than a hundred fans had already congregated at the main entrance. As game time neared the crowd outside grew and its volume increased. By

5 p.m., two hours before puck-drop, more than a thousand had gathered. From our dressing room we could hear a steady buzz and intermittent chanting.

That afternoon I had a roster issue to address. Defenceman Cory Cross, a top Lightning prospect, was made available to us for game six. Usually it was automatic to insert a player of his quality, but I had promised our other players that I would stick with the lineup that had won our previous games. Otherwise I would have to bump Shawn Rivers. Given the way he was playing, that would have been excruciating. I went to Cory and explained that I was sure he would have a fine NHL career, but for *this* game he would be a healthy scratch. He took it well, never mentioning it to me afterwards. I learned to never put myself in that position again.

The crowd of 14,107 smashed the IHL playoff attendance record. There could have been twenty thousand if the fire chief had not insisted the team close the gates. Understandably, we were tight at the start and Fort Wayne led 1–0 after one period. We tied it early in the second period as the game opened up with good scoring chances both ways.

And then . . . enter Claude the Happy Trumpeter.

Seems Richard Adler, the consummate Barnum and Bailey promoter, had hired a fellow named Claude Scott to be the Knights playoff mascot. Calling himself Claude the Happy Trumpeter, he wore a Knights jersey, blew his horn vigorously (if not altogether musically), and lead cheers for the home team. In the second period, after we tied the game, Claude came scampering down the aisle and, as part of his routine, threw himself up against the Plexiglas. Only this time the panel shattered and Claude the Happy Trumpeter crashed through to the ice below, landing on his head. Out cold, he lay there, trumpet at his side, as the players and the referees tried to process what they just saw. The game was delayed for thirty minutes as arena staff attended to the Happy Trumpeter and replaced the panel. Claude was rushed to the hospital, but heroically returned near the end of the game wearing a neck brace, trumpet in hand. The crowd went wild. Players from both teams had a good laugh.

When play resumed, we took over. Bill McDougall gave us a 2–1 lead, then just sixteen seconds into the third period Stan Drulia put us ahead 3–1. I knew in my gut we had it. The Komets attempted to rally but Mike Greenlay stoned them each time. The Omni rocked as the clock ticked down. With forty-four seconds to go and the play stopped, Greenlay leaned on his crossbar and waved his glove to the crowd. More than fourteen thousand Southerners waved back and counted down the final ten seconds. At the horn, Mike sprinted out of his crease, hands aloft. A tide of screaming teammates greeted him, knocking him to the ice, one after another flying on to a growing heap. On the ice Chris LiPuma snuck up behind me and drenched me with a tub of orange Gatorade. (Luckily, I had another suit in my office.) Fans hugged fans, players hugged players, coaches hugged coaches, owners hugged owners, and Claude blew his happy trumpet for all he was worth.

Our captain, Stan Drulia, was named the playoff MVP. Also key was the performance of Mike Greenlay, who was slumping when I arrived. Graciously, he gave me some credit. "John Paris, this is the guy who stood with me and every player on the team," he told the media. Those words meant the world to me.

After the Turner Cup was presented at centre ice, Joey Bucchino and I took it for a victory lap around the ice. Fans cheered and reached down as we passed by. The unbridled joy moved to our dressing room area where young men, bruised and battered, laughed and sprayed streams of beer and champagne on each other and anyone else within reach. A few guys just sat for a spell, flopped near their lockers wearing goofy grins as the Turner Cup was hoisted and filled and refilled with champagne.

As the players celebrated, I stood in my office, accommodating a sea of cameras and microphones. I was the first stop for most of the reporters as they knew I could be counted on for a good quote. But this time the emotion of the moment got to me and I laboured. I could feel tears at the corner of my eyes. "We are very proud to be Atlanta Knights," I said. "I just wish my mother was alive to see it." I found a quiet spot and called Chantal and Louise, and finally my father in Windsor. They were all very happy for me.

It was a long time before I left the Omni that night. I knew to take my time, to soak it all in. Eventually, however, a few of us went to a restaurant where people came to our table non-stop to offer their congratulations. The Turner Cup itself had a splendid time that night as well. The players escorted the three-foot trophy to their favourite local taverns where they continued until dawn to pass it around and take a swig. The next morning the grand mug was found floating in Shawn Rivers's swimming pool. It needed the rest.

Two days later Atlanta paid tribute with a victory parade through downtown, after which I was invited to David Berkman's mansion. As we chatted he pointed out that history had been written in the Deep South by my team. I corrected him. "Thanks, but you mean by *our* team."

He leaned forward. "John, do you know what you accomplished? Not only on the ice, but off the ice?"

I said that I thought so, and that I was aware of the significance and . . .

He cut me off. "No, the team didn't have to win, but *you* did. *You* had to win. Understand? *You* had to win *here*!"

He felt it was the *context* of the victory — rather than the victory itself — that mattered most. In that region, in that environment, given the history and the politics. (Oddly, an almost identical remark had been made to me by "Wild" Bill Hunter,

Celebrating our Turner Cup triumph, 1994, with GM Joey Bucchino.

the Edmonton-based sport impresario and a chief architect of the World Hockey Association. He called one day shortly after I got the job. I was sitting in my office with our trainer. "You had best win there, John," he said. "I don't see where you have much of a choice.")

Atlanta enjoyed the victory and the dent it made in the Loserville image. The next year, 1995, the Atlanta Braves won the baseball World Series and the city has never looked back. Our Turner Cup triumph was also important for the Knights owners looking to demonstrate to the NHL hierarchy that Atlanta was — and could be again — a major-league hockey town.

CHAPTER 10
Crossroads

Over the summer of 1994, having been informed that the Knights would lift my *interim* coach status, I happily went about exploring Atlanta's cultural endowments. One evening in July this meant taking in Whitney Houston at the Omni. Whitney was on her gigantic *Bodyguard* world concert tour, at the apex of her physical beauty and her popularity, even as the tabloids were feasting on stories about her rocky marriage with singer Bobby Brown and on rumours of drug use. But her true fans, including me, chose only to hear that stupendous voice.

When I arrived for the concert that evening I was told by the receptionist that someone was waiting to meet me near the production room in the far end of the building. Thinking a female cop friend was playing a joke on me, I went along and was escorted by arena staff to the sparsely furnished production room and asked to wait. In a few minutes someone pushed back the door and in walked Whitney Houston.

I gulped.

Whitney had on a long dark outfit and was, frankly, stunning.

She walked over to me and smiled as she extended her hand. "You're the man around here," she said, with a short laugh. "A *black* hockey coach! I'm pleased to meet you."

I replied the pleasure was all mine.

Whitney had a mischievous way of looking at you, a sweet little smile that made you like her right away. And she was playful. "I thought you'd be bigger," she giggled. Ouch. She was three or four inches taller than me, so I sort of anticipated something like that.

"Wait 'til I tell Bobby about this," she said, "he'll be interested . . . How'd you become a coach in hockey?"

I told her about my father and friends and the rest. "You are aware of hockey?"

Whitney laughed again. "Of course I know something about hockey. But damn, a *black* man in that position of power . . ."

"I don't know about the power," I said. "I'm just a coach. But you, you're a superstar known all over the world."

She wagged her index finger. "Uh-uh. You accomplished something big — and a championship. That's something. It's important that people see we can do other things. Bet it's not always easy . . ."

"It's not that bad. At least I have a job." She grinned. I was on a couch along a wall and she sat a few feet away on a small chair. Throughout our conversation she rose and paced, chatting away as if we were old friends.

"Are you always this way to talk with?" she asked.

"I think so, but maybe not when I'm running a practice . . ."

"I wanted to meet you because everyone around here was talkin' 'coach-this' and 'coach-that.' Someone said you speak with all of the staff from the cleaning people to top."

I explained it was my upbringing. I then turned our conversation to how she managed her fame and such an enormous career.

"I manage," said Whitney Houston, wistfully, with a slight rasp in her voice, "but it's not always as some people think. It's not always a great thing."

I told her that in a small way I could relate, with all the sudden attention I was receiving. "But I'm a small fish in the ocean while you're like the entire ocean!"

She looked at me a little sadly and thanked me.

"Coach, how do I reach you?" I wrote my phone number on a slip of paper and handed it to her. I volunteered that I travel a lot so I may be hard to track down. "I'll find you," she said, again with the mischievous grin.

"I best let you go," I said.

"Not yet. I wish my man could meet you. But you and him are in two very different worlds . . ."

Somewhere in our conversation I mentioned that I played keyboard. Her eyes widened and she asked if I would I like to come up with her on stage that night! I stopped breathing. *Me on stage with Whitney?* I thought it over for a couple of seconds and declined. "This is *your* show."

"How 'bout we flash you [spotlight] in the seats? I can find out where you are." I agreed. Sure enough, midway in her first set Whitney mentioned I was in the audience and someone turned the spotlight on me.

In the coming months and years Whitney and I would meet in person only once. It happened over lunch in an international restaurant in Roswell, an affluent suburb in the northern part of Atlanta. We were in a private dining area, again just Whitney and I. She was wearing blue jeans and a baseball cap and was very relaxed. It was nice.

We also talked on the phone several times. One day in the late 1990s she called just to say hello. (She had tracked me down by calling Chantal, but didn't say who she was. Chantal gave her my phone number, thinking it was just a female acquaintance of mine.) When I asked how things were with her, Whitney said not good, but didn't mention Bobby Brown. During another conversation, in 2004, Whitney said that she had learned that another major star — with whom I had a brief, clandestine relationship some time before — had called my apartment and was impolite to Stephanie, then my fiance. Whitney most definitely did not like this other star.

"She can dance, but be careful with that bitch," she said. I explained to Whitney that I talked with the other star and told her not to speak to Stephanie that way. Whitney again warned me to be careful.

"This Stephanie, she must be special," she said. "Hang on to her." I assured her I would.

I heard from Whitney only a couple more times. In 2007, when I was coaching in Campbellton, New Brunswick, she called our team office and left a phone number and the name "Whitney." No last name. A short time later, the call became the subject of some speculation among staff, but I squelched it by claiming the name was taken down incorrectly. A little white lie.

The last time I spoke with her was in 2009. Over the phone she said her life was "messed up." During our talk she faded in and out, speaking in mumbles, going quiet, then suddenly happy and lucid again. The conversation lasted about thirty minutes.

"You and I never did anything wrong, did we," she said.

"No, we didn't Whitney. Not at all." I underlined that we were never involved romantically, and that other than Stephanie and a couple of others, no one had any idea we even knew one another.

"Who'd a thought," said Whitney, "no smut . . . You could've sold me out, coach, or made something up about us, but you didn't." She thanked me for never asking for anything from her, and for being there regardless of when she called.

"I'm messed up," she repeated. "I have to get my act together . . ."

I never heard from her again. After the last call I mentioned to Stephanie that I thought it was not going to end well for Whitney. But I never imagined it ending as it did. When I learned she had passed, I thought of how Whitney, so talented and powerful, in many ways was like a little girl. There was a sweetness about her, but also a sadness. You could feel it.

It was an honour to know her.

* * *

Befriending Whitney was merely the tip of the iceberg when it came to meeting highly successful people during this period of my life. Many others were well-known athletes playing for one of the city's three major sports teams: the NBA Hawks, the NFL Falcons and the National League's Braves.

The Braves were just beginning their fabulous run, led by former Toronto Blue Jay manager, Bobby Cox. The team gave me a press pass with full access to Turner Field and one day Cox invited me into the clubhouse room where — a little star-struck — I made small-talk with guys such as David Justice, Fred McGriff, Greg Maddox, Tom Glavine and John Smoltz. A huge thrill for me was having a short conversation with home run icon Hank Aaron, a childhood hero of mine. Not a boisterous man, you could see Aaron's confident, gentlemanly way. Very classy. One year I was honourary chairperson for the banquet held in his name in Atlanta.

Less genteel were my encounters with the Hawks — with whom the Knights shared the Omni — and with players from several visiting NBA teams. (Our assistant trainer washed the uniforms for the visiting basketball teams so I often got "the skinny" on who was doing what off the court.) One evening I was invited out with a couple of Hawks stars and three members of a visiting team, who I will not name out of respect . . . plus the fact they are a foot-and-a-half taller than I am.

Before leaving that night I discreetly pointed out to them that I really wasn't a drinker and that, as a hockey coach, I was not making the money they were. Money didn't mean as much to those guys, most of them instant millionaires. (Once I witnessed a couple of Hawks lose thousands of dollars on a golf course, engaging in a host of side-bets as they played. But I have always believed it is the business of the individual athlete how they spent their disposable income. So no harm done.)

"Go easy on me," I begged as we set out, only half-joking.

Almost right away one of the guys slipped a huge wad of bills into my hand. I laughed and tried — albeit half-heartedly — to give it back. They insisted I keep it all: about $2,700. We climbed into the limo and off we went into the night. I never had to use the money because everywhere we stopped one of them would quickly pick up the tab. That night we hit several glitzy clubs. The thing I noticed most was the women. All over the place and all over these guys like white — and brown — on rice. Flirting and pawing. All sorts of women. But the players behaved themselves for the most part, and really got in to the music, especially at one incredible blues and jazz place off Highway 400 in Alpharetta.

The next morning at the Omni one of the Hawks coaches came up to me with a huge grin.

"Coach, you're a great guy, a non-drinker and you took care of our players. Hey, somehow you managed to convince them to stay out of the strip club!"

I laughed, but there *was* a little self-interest at play in avoiding the nudie bars. Frankly, I have always felt that women were being exploited in such places. In addition, I didn't want to reduce my tidy windfall by having to stuff bills into some g-string.

"They told me you even offered to put the gas in the limo when they brought it back," the coach added, probing just a bit.

All true. I *offered*, but one of the others actually took care of the gas. I went home with the exact amount of cash given to me. My mother didn't raise a fool.

* * *

Apart from meeting interesting people, there were other fine things happening in my life at this time. My personal relationships were changing, hockey was a joy and I was finally able to declare myself healthy again, albeit with certain very manageable lifestyle adjustments required by my pouching system and my restrictive diet.

Adding to my good run over that spring and summer three NHL teams offered me jobs as an assistant coach. I was at another career crossroad: is it better to be an assistant coach in a higher league, or a head coach in the minors? I decided that the best way to achieve my ultimate goal — to be a *head* coach in the NHL — was to stay with my head coach job in the IHL. I reasoned that, as an assistant coach, I'd get the "assistant" label, and be defined as a second banana and gofer. Once tagged in that way, the image would be hard to shake. I wanted to go in the front door or not go in at all. I knew it was a gamble. My stock was high, but it wouldn't stay there unless I had another strong season with the Knights. With a second Turner Cup on my resume, or even another appearance in the finals, I anticipated that doors would fling open for me. Obviously I was banking on the Knights retaining most of their talent.

There was another factor at play: my agent. His name was Jay Grossman and the Knights management said I didn't need him. In fact they *urged* he not be involved in any way. So around this time Jay and I parted company. In retrospect, this was a huge mistake on my part. A lawyer who is now president of the successful New York–based PuckAgency firm, Jay was an honest, competent agent who talked candidly with me about the problems a minority person would have with specific hockey people. I told him how the Knights felt about him and he never put any pressure on me. He left the decision to me. I made the wrong one. (Some time later I approached Bobby Orr to be my agent. It would have been fantastic for me, but Bobby explained that regulations prohibited him from representing coaches. He said that if he were to try to circumvent the rules, I'd likely lose respect for him. Further confirmation that Bobby's an honest man as well as a good agent.)

In late May, the Knights finally had announced me as their head coach — no more *interim*. I would have liked to think it was a no-brainer, although life has taught me not to count my chickens before they hatched. The deal re-confirmed that I would also coach the Atlanta Fire Ants roller hockey team.

That summer with me behind the bench the Ants finished fourth in their division in the twenty-four-team Roller Hockey International and were swept in the semifinals. The crowds were poor: averaging 3,400 for our eleven home games. This was despite coverage by ESPN, $6 tickets and resourceful efforts by our management. ("This will be a great place to hang out when it's ninety degrees out.") It was my last experience with roller hockey. The next year the Ants left Atlanta for Oklahoma City and became the Coyotes.

(Before I got fully involved with the Ants, I returned to Sorel-Tracy for the wedding of Chantal to Nichol Cloutier, whom I had coached on our Air Canada Cup team. It was beautiful: a hundred and fifty people, Motown music and lots of fun. I walked Chantal down the aisle as a saxophone played the wedding *valse*. The ceremony lasted almost three hours. Charles Felix arrived with the Turner Cup and created quite a commotion. Every man there wanted a picture with it. All in all, a perfect day.)

* * *

The 1994–95 season with the Knights was a jumble from the start.

The NHL's impasse with their players' association was putting its season in jeopardy. One fallout was that legitimate NHL players, seeking a temporary place to play, came to the IHL. I felt it wrong to bring in bona fide NHL players because they took jobs away from our younger players. Fortunately, the IHL, wary that it might be directly drawn into the labour unrest, soon stopped its teams from signing locked-out NHL players. IHL rosters were frozen, but not before some teams had signed Peter Bondra, Michal Pivonka, Curtis Joseph, etc., for a few games.

The lockout burned several Knights players from our Turner Cup squad who were aspiring to crack NHL lineups, players such as Chris LiPuma, Stan Drulia and Jason Ruff. As a consolation they still had the Knights, where, as *Atlanta Journal* columnist Steve Hummer wrote, they could find "a players' coach in John Paris. Big-thinking ownership. Trainers who don't use leeches."

The lockout aside, our main problem in 1994–95 was that our roster was an interminable tsunami of hockey flesh sweeping in and out, a complete hodgepodge. Gone were Larouche, Cummings, Rochefort, Charron, MacDougall, Madill, Rivers, Miller and Cross. I could never count on a stable lineup due to injuries, callups and trades. In total, we had an incredible eighty — yes, eighty! — roster changes that season. The equivalent of four full teams. I was going out of my mind. I never worked harder in my life.

Several noteworthy players passed through our revolving door.

Our most ballyhooed acquisitions were New York Ranger prospects Peter and Chris Ferraro, twenty-one-year-old twins from Long Island, New York. They had played on the US national team and could skate like the wind. "The Ferraros are going to set this league on fire," Richard Adler crowed to the *Journal*. I cringed when I heard this. I never felt the boys were ready. Time proved me right. They had a productive time with us, and I worked hard with them on several aspects of their game, but late in the season the Rangers placed them in the American Hockey League — an environment more suited for their development.

One player Phil Esposito sent down to us as a result of the labour stoppage was highly skilled Russian winger Alexei Selivanov. The idea was to give him some ice time. He played four games with us and it was a memorable stint. Alex had this bad habit of thrusting both arms in the air when he was annoyed, such as when he was not getting the puck or one of his teammates fumbled a pass. I explained to him that he was embarrassing his teammates and irritating the referees with such gestures. "You've got to stop doing it," I said. No luck. He continued this way and I began to get flack from players, referees, fans and opposing coaches. I defended him as best I could, but finally I had enough. "Alex, keep those damn arms down and stop the waving! You know better!" A few days later Alex, looking irritated, came to me and announced: "You disrespected me!" I was flabbergasted. Soon after he returned to Tampa to — so the explanation went — *improve his English*. Sure. (Over time, Alex developed both professionally and personally. He became a top-six forward for Tampa and the Edmonton Oilers, and married Phil Esposito's daughter, Carrie, who tragically died in 2012 of an abdominal aneurysm.)

Among our returnees was centre Brent Gretzky. While not one of the stronger players on our championship team, I felt he was ready to take the next step in 1994–95. But he struggled early, so I was told to sit him. He grumbled, but I continued to work with him and by November he was much better. Brent was a good kid and, in his own way, a respectable hockey player. But that surname had to be an albatross for him. I could only imagine what it was like to have a brother known as The Great One and have to endure the constant comparisons. He went on to have a long career in the minor pros and played thirteen games in the NHL, where he scored once.

Also on our roster was defenceman Chris Nelson, who was African-American and a fifth-round NHL selection in 1988. The child of two UCLA professors, he was passionate about the idea that black children can excel in traditionally "non-black" sports, like hockey and golf (these were the days before P.K. Subban and Tiger Woods). His main message: "You don't want to make excuses for yourself." Music to my ears. Chris was a polite, respectful young man and easy to coach, but after forty-nine games he had just nine assists and no goals. Tampa saw no future for him in their organization and moved him out.

Then there was Rich Sutter. The six Sutter brothers from Viking, Alberta, were all *very* good. Tough as nails. Any coach's dream. Rich was the second youngest of the lot, but was by then thirty-one years old and near the end of a fine NHL career. When he arrived in Atlanta, Rich walked into my office and said he wanted return to "the show" (the NHL) as soon as possible. I told him to play his game, and that I'd try to play him in a way to make this happen *as long as he applied himself.* (Imagine saying this to a Sutter!)

Rich was with us for just four games, before being traded to the Toronto Maple Leafs for future considerations. Before he left he thanked me for keeping my word. I loved having him even for this short period. He made a difference on the ice and in the dressing room and his presence pushed our other players to greater effort. If only every player had the Sutter ethic. When instructing youngsters I still use the Sutter family as my guideline to complete performance.

* * *

We opened the 1994–95 season well, but at the all-star break we were only 20–20–1. The mood was not good: Joey B. went public with his dissatisfaction; our playoff hero from the previous year, goalie Mike Greenlay, was loudly booed; and Tampa Bay general manager Phil Esposito was personally evaluating our situation. We were all feeling the heat. Even our mascots. One of them, Sir Slap Shot, was physically attacked by Cincinnati Cyclones coach

Don Jackson, who Sir Slap had accidentally knocked over during a game. Irate, Jackson climbed over the glass, ran into the stands and pummeled poor Sir Slap Shot. Inside the costume the guy was pretty well defenceless because his arms were taped to his sides. Sir Slap repaired to the dressing room — or wherever injured mascots go for treatment — only to make a glorious return the next period, his head wrapped in bandages. Jackson was questioned by the Atlanta police and suspended by the league over the incident. And Sir Slap Shot got national attention: pure gold in the mascot world.

Throughout the year I was the sounding board for complaints about the endless roster changes. I didn't like it myself as I witnessed what it was doing to players with families. But I knew that my role was to stand up for management. So when someone started to gripe about Joey or Phil, I would automatically shut it down. I tried to keep things positive, rationalizing that as an affiliate team we're always trying to prepare players for the next level. It was a tough sell to hard-core Knights fans who had made an emotional commitment to the team.

We entered the playoffs with a record of 39–37–5, third in the Central Division. Short a few players, we were eliminated by the Las Vegas Thunder in the opening round. Game three, in Atlanta, was vicious, with more than 250 minutes in penalties and a load of game misconducts. The torch was lit when our fans threw beer on a couple of Thunder players in the penalty box, including their goon Kerry Toporowski. Toporowski and other Thunder players then charged into the stands to fight fans. In the melee Vegas coach Bob Strumm swung a stick at spectators from the bench, resulting in a fan pressing an assault charge against him. Strumm and I also shouted and pointed at each other across the ice but it didn't amount to anything.

Our season was over.

* * *

The day after our exit from the playoffs, Joey Bucchino told me he wanted me back next year. The rapid endorsement was a relief for me and my assistant coach Scotty Gordon. Naturally this had the stamp of approval from the Lightning brass as well. A synergy with the parent club was vital. When the Lightning decided they wanted a particular player developed in a certain way, it was my job to ensure it happened. Usually I was able to stitch any requirements into my game strategies.

This said, my direct interaction with Lightning management was not extensive.

Phil Esposito was the flamboyant general manager and still minority-owner when I arrived. A dominant player of the 1970s, he was one of the leaders when the Lightning group was awarded an NHL franchise for the 1992–93 season. My dealings with him were pleasant and he was always supportive. Most of our conversations were by phone and concerned the progress or problems with individual players.

Tony Esposito, Phil's younger brother and himself a Hall-of-Fame goaltender, was the Lightning's vice-president and director of hockey personnel. He was quiet, well-dressed and seemed all business. He never bothered me. Actually, we never had a single conversation. Not one. I can't even speculate why. Come to think of it, I never saw Tony in a long conversation with *anyone*.

Terry Crisp was the coach of the Lightning. He was always professional and cordial with me. His philosophy: hockey is more dictatorship than democracy. This mindset, combined with a strong personality and a propensity to scream and yell on the bench, resulted in well-documented clashes with players during his coaching career. In Tampa, for example, star winger Rob Zamuner approached Phil Esposito claiming Crisp's yelling was making several key players miserable. There were similar complaints in Calgary. Yet in Calgary he won a Stanley Cup. He seemed to doing the job in Tampa, especially given the lack of depth he had there.

I especially enjoyed former NHL tough guy **Wayne Cashman**, then a Lightning assistant coach. Wayne and I spoke frequently about drills or this or that. He was a major force during his playing career with the Boston Bruins, but off the ice he was a softy. But don't get him fired up. Cash had class and I was always happy to see him. He would brief me on specific players and their attitudes. One day he walked into my office just to tell me what an excellent job I was doing with the young players. Coming from him, this was a huge boost and I thanked him for it. Unfortunately, Cash was one of the casualties of the chaos happening with the parent club. New ownership forced Phil to fire him — a gut-wrenching task for Espo. Hockey politics has no heart. Cash later went to Philadelphia as a head coach but was fired after just sixty-one games.

* * *

While I endured a difficult season, one enormous personal highlight came when I met my son. We had not met until then due to complicated personal reasons which will remain private. He had called me in my room at our team hotel in Kansas City, Missouri. We chatted briefly and agreed to meet in Atlanta a short time later. When Robert came into sight at the Hartsfield-Jackson airport that day in March 1995, I knew immediately he was my son. The Paris facial traits were obvious. Age twenty-nine, he was an accountant and fiscal analyst in Montreal. He had known my name for some time and, after much thought, reached out to me. That took courage. I was overwhelmed and instantly proud of him. I introduced Robert to reporters, comparing it all to a movie script. We have continued to stay in touch, although not as much as I would like.

With my son, Robert.

* * *

As the team assembled for the 1995–96 season, I knew it was going to be a difficult year. The reason: talent. We didn't have enough of it. Plus, as with the previous season, there was far too much player movement to coalesce a team.

We started with fifteen new faces on the roster, most of them under contract with the Lightning. We got off to a 4–2 start, but we lacked depth and it caught up with us. Along the way we brought in role players such as Steve Fletcher, thirty-three, a pugilistic legend who had played briefly with Montreal Canadiens. We also signed Reggie "Le Magnifique" Savage, once one of the most highly regarded juniors in hockey. Reggie ended up with twenty-two goals in sixty-six games for us.

It was to be a season of protracted losing streaks, including a long stretch without a home win. Early in 1996, after a five-day layoff, we lost a game 8–2 to the Michigan K-Wings. It was a horrid, listless performance. The loss dropped our record to 17–22–3.

Then the axe fell.

I was removed as head coach. The official reason was a losing record and troubling inconsistency. Joey Bucchino told the *Journal* that he felt a change was needed. "This is a good hockey team. I had done everything in my power to make John stay, but you have to have results." To soften the blow they gave me the title of assistant GM and director of player development.

I had known for some time I was in jeopardy. Things change when you're losing. There are subtle — and not-so-subtle — changes in how people react to you, including management. The intimacies are not there. What were easy, friendly exchanges are suddenly a little forced. As a loner, I didn't have my head in every conversation so maybe there were more whispers about my fate than I realized. I'll never know.

Ironically, my early success was partly responsible for my demise. I had to maintain that level or something very close to it. Otherwise I was in trouble. That's just the law of the jungle. It's business. The guys in management were not going to offer a *mea culpa* and fire themselves. And they couldn't fire twenty-three players, so . . .

I was at the Omni when Joey called from New York. "John," he began, "it's a sad day . . ."

As soon as the news was public I began getting calls, cards and telegrams offering best wishes and comforting words. In a show of pro hockey solidarity, many were from coaches and staff on opposing teams that I didn't know or had ever spoken with.

I was replaced by assistant coach Scotty Gordon for the remainder of the season. I have nothing but good thoughts for Scotty. Until recently an assistant coach with the Toronto

Maple Leafs, he's not a talkative person, but he's knowledge-able and discreet. I came to trust him and we became close. He and his future wife came to my house, and even in social settings Scotty didn't say much. But when he *did* speak, it was worth listening.

Under Scotty, the Knights finished the season at 32–41–9, good for fourth place in the Central Division. They lost in the first round of the playoffs. That season was the last for the team in Atlanta. It all came to an abrupt and angry end, centreing on a dispute over a new arena and propelled by egos. When it was announced that the Olympic Games were coming to Atlanta, public money materialized for new facilities. The Knights made it clear they wanted a piece of the action. Their ultimatum to the city: give us a say in the plans for the new arena or we will leave. They left, relocating to Quebec City.

I had no interest in going to Quebec City. I was apprehensive about the reception the team would get — Quebecers were used to the NHL Nordiques. The Quebec Rafales, as they were to be called, were doomed. They folded after just two seasons.

The next time I saw anyone from the Knights management was in Montreal's Dorval airport a few months later when I bumped in to Richard Adler. He was not part of the old group anymore, but he didn't seem bitter. Like me, he had departed without making waves. He said, "John, they had other ideas." We left it at that. A few years ago I had lunch with Charles Felix in Florida. We picked up right where we left off, as many hockey people do. I'm still in touch with many of the Knights players as well.

My experience with the Knights was mostly positive. In my two and a half seasons there I compiled a 67–60–15 regular-season record and was 14–5 in the playoffs. I also became a better administrator and certainly learned about adjusting to player movement. In short, it made me a better all-round hockey man.

With Scotty Gordon, my assistant coach in Atlanta, who went on to be head coach of the New York Islanders and an assistant coach of the Toronto Maple Leafs.

CHAPTER 11
Macon Whoopee

I was not the first choice of the Macon Whoopee. Actually, for their inaugural season in the Central Hockey League there were at least three coaching candidates ahead of me. Seems Whoopee management didn't think I would be interested. They were wrong.

Having decided I was not moving with the Atlanta Knights to Quebec City, I was looking for another job. One option was with Huntington in the Eastern Hockey League. They were offering a three-year deal: $37,000 a year, plus bonuses and expenses. But the EHL would have been a step backwards, so I passed. I was a bit surprised nothing came from the QMJHL. With my history in that league, combined with my experience with the Knights, I figured to be attractive to several teams. Apparently not. This disappointed me, as well as friends and family in Sorel-Tracy.

Frankly, Georgia was still on my mind. I wanted to stay in the South because I knew the NHL was placing an expansion franchise in Atlanta and I was hoping for an opportunity in that organization. I had had a few casual conversations with Ted Turner, who mentioned a possible role for me with an NHL team if he were to successfully bid. So when the Whoopee eventually called in July of 1996, I listened.

I met in an upscale restaurant near Norfolk, Virginia with the two men responsible for hockey's resurrection in Macon. Pat Nugent, the general manager, used to be director of player development with the New York Yankees. President Richard Ray was a Virginia businessman, a major financial backer of the team and a huge hockey fan. "We don't want to insult you," started Ray, "but we were tossing things around and kept coming back to you. We respect where you've been and what you've accomplished." Both men bluntly stated they needed my help. That was all they needed to say. Honesty works just about every time with me.

Even so, I didn't say yes right away. I had to think it through a bit more. Al MacIsaac, from Antigonish, Nova Scotia, then in management with the Chicago Blackhawks, had recommended me to the Whoopee. Al said it was not an *ideal* job for me, but still a good one. Other people advised me to wait for a better offer. But my health issues — by then largely under control — and the fact that I was almost fifty years old, made me see things another way.

So I accepted the job as Whoopee coach, director of hockey operations and vice-president. (After organizational restructuring, I would also have the title of general manager.) The contract was for three years, at a salary of $60,000 a year, plus a few perks such as housing and use of a new car. I could leave when I wanted. I was introduced to the media at the Edward H. Wilson Convention Center later that summer. Expansion team or not, expectations were high. And it was vital that this whole operation be perceived as credible, especially given the fiasco with the first incarnation of the team in the 1970s.

* * *

The city's first professional hockey team had been the Macon Whoopees (note the plural). The Whoopees played in the Southern Hockey League in 1973 and drew national attention because of the original name: sexual slang made popular in the 1920s jazz song, "Makin' Whoopee." As it turned out, the name was the team's primary asset. The media loved it and went crazy with puns and innuendo. As a lark, NBC aired the Whoopees' scores and highlights on its *NHL Game of The Week,* and years later "Macon Whoopees" topped the All Oblivion Unusual Nicknames list.

The team also became the subject of a book, *Once Upon a Whoopee*, by local writers Bill Buckley and Ed Grisamore.

Inexperience and egos reined the first time around. The owners knew little about hockey or how to operate a hockey team (they had no idea they had to pay for things such as a Zamboni), and were chronically short on cash. The media was also hockey ignorant. Harley Bowers, one of the most experienced sportswriters in Georgia, confessed he didn't have a clue about the sport. (Bowers took solace in knowing that neither did his readers. As a stunt, one day a Whoopees player walked downtown at lunch hour carrying a hockey stick. Few people knew what it was and, once informed, were unsure which end of the stick to use.)

Perhaps the most painful example of inexperience had been the playing coach, KeKe Mortson, my pal from the Quebec Aces training camp in 1967. Mortson, by then in his late thirties, had never coached before. His easy manner and zest for life charmed his players and others associated with the club, but coaching is a demanding craft hard learned. I arrived in 1996 with a reputation as a winner, and I knew how to pick my assistants. KeKe didn't have any such background. Not surprisingly, things didn't go well. The team lost early and often and the fans never did buy in. (Team reports would call crowds of one thousand "partial sellouts," while reporters scoffed that five thousand fans showed up dressed as empty seats.) With poor attendance and the Internal

Revenue Service knocking on the door, the team folded in mid-season in 1974 — on Valentine's Day.

Back then, Macon was just not ready for hockey.

* * *

Macon of the 1990s was more receptive. Located in the middle of Georgia, about eighty-five miles south of Atlanta, it had a population of a hundred thousand, about two-thirds black. While not affluent (about a third of the population was around the poverty line), it was rich in history and culture. Robins Air Force Base, the largest single-site industrial complex in Georgia, was a few miles to the south. While Macon had many things, a conventional hockey climate was not one of them. The area gets only an inch of snow all year, and winter "lows" are in the mid-thirties F. Summers are humid and it rains a fair bit.

Race is a fact of life in Macon. You see it, you feel it. Confederate flags still fly in some white neighbourhoods. Official segregation that divided whites and blacks had been abolished a half century before, but the Macon of the 1990s still bifurcated along skin colour. I went from one side to the other with ease, although not everyone in Macon did. Even so, people got along reasonably well. The races intertwined in the workplace and I witnessed some interracial couples, many of them college students.

An African-American middle class, which existed in every major American city, seemed more prominent in Macon. One thing blacks and whites shared was a passion for education. There's a notion in the South that maintains mediocre education is good enough for the blacks. Wrong! In the black community I saw that education was stressed. Religion was also important to both blacks and whites, but they tended to worship separately. I know some people go to church to experience a quiet reverence.

Some of the out-reach we did to explain hockey in the American South.

That's fine, but I find the quiet a little scary. I go to enjoy the music, to hear the exchange between the minister and his or her congregation. Why would I want to be gloomy? I like a place that makes me happy.

* * *

Building a minor-league professional hockey team from scratch ain't easy. The Macon Whoopee, *circa* 1996, mindful of the sloppy enterprise the first time around, tried to do things by the book: experienced coach, attractive place to play, good players, public relations, solid fiscal management and capable staff.

Having secured my services as coach and having signed a

five-year lease on a modern downtown facility (the 7,900-seat Macon Coliseum) we focused on filling the roster with hungry young guys I had known from Quebec. These talented athletes were on the brink of not being able to continue in their sport, so when I offered them the opportunity I knew they would follow me through fire. Plus, many already knew my systems and had proven they could survive my tough "Paris Island" training camp (not a given, by any means). Younger players were also more likely to stay around for two or three seasons, allowing them to build a profile in the community. We shunned older players because often veteran minor-leaguers were jaded journeymen, looking only for a paycheque and a good time. On opening night our average age was twenty-two and our roster had a distinct French-Canadian flavor.

Promotion was another key part of our building process. We did a lot. We visited scores of schools, where students were charmed by the thick French-Canadian accents of our players; honoured the military with "Operation Ice Storm" and our custom-made camouflage jerseys; and heavily hit the air waves. *Face-off . . . With the Macon Whoopee* was a weekly hour-long show on WMWR-AM 940, plus I did regular radio spots where I explained the rules and pushed upcoming games. I also filmed TV bits, including one with tough guy Jason Renard. In the commercial, Renard is lounging by the pool with a beer when I come up to him with a hockey stick and bark at him to get back on the ice so we can win the CHL championship. Not Oscar-worthy, but still fun.

We weren't shy about using a little sex in our publicity, even in this Bible Belt city: our logo was a fig leaf; we had special evenings called "One Night Stand"; and we sold Whoopee cushions at the concession stand. We even presented President Bill Clinton — pre-Monica Lewinsky scandal — with a Macon Whoopee jersey.

Money mattered, of course. As director of hockey operations I had to stretch every dollar, a skill I cultivated at Quebec Iron & Titanium. The CHL had a team limit on veteran players, as well as a $10,000-a-week salary cap, although several teams circumvented the cap by allowing players to sign personal appearance deals. As a result, some teams attracted more talent. We paid most of our players $400–$600 a week, with a couple of our top guys in the $700–$800 range. Each player was provided a respectable apartment, plus a small per diem on the road. It would have been nice to go out and get that star player, but we worked with what we had.

Finally, I knew I needed a capable staff, something that KeKe Mortson had clearly lacked during his truncated tenure twenty years before. In Macon I hit the jackpot with two people who became very dear to me. We were likely the only black-Jewish-Korean troika in professional hockey history.

David Starman was my assistant general manager and then my associate coach. A good-looking, confident young man with a media background, Dave had a quick mind and was very enthusiastic. I liked how he walked with his head high, straddling that midpoint between confidence and arrogance, probably a trait indigenous to young guys from Rockaway Beach, Queens. He understood hockey and would watch games and study video and bring me back all kinds of helpful tidbits. Dave also had grit and one day at a practice stood up to big Jason Renard after Renard poked him with his stick. I moved to intervene, but Dave waved me away. He handled it. Dave went on to become the youngest head coach in Central Hockey League history when he briefly took over behind the bench with the Memphis RiverKings in 2000. He's now with CBS Sports Network and a scout for the Toronto Maple Leafs.

My other pillar in Macon was Lisa Peppin. Officially, Lisa was our public relations director and ran our office. But she was much more. Of Korean heritage, Lisa was adopted by a white family in Minnesota, where she came to love hockey. She started with us as a college intern. I hired her immediately. She had an astute eye for hockey talent and could dissect a game like a veteran coach. If Lisa had a suggestion concerning a player or his role, I listened carefully.

Like Dave Starman, Lisa was protective of me. And I was similarly protective of her. She was pretty and when she dressed up, she looked *fine*. But people knew my rule: you don't touch Lisa. Still, Lisa was a fireball and she and I did have "discussions." I didn't always win. With some people, that strong-willed personality was an issue. If she would have soft-pedalled her emotions, I think she would have been the first female president of a professional hockey team. But she was young and Whoopee ownership didn't fully understand what an asset they had in her. It's possible they were even intimidated by her. After I left Macon she took a front-office job with another team. It didn't last long. She's now married with children and is in another line of work. Hockey's loss.

Largely because of this methodical approach to building an organization, over the regular season we had adeptly re-introduced hockey to Macon. We held top spot until late in the season when our young players wilted, unaccustomed to playing a sixty-eight-game schedule. I rejuvenated the roster by bringing in a few experienced players in the last week or so, adding toughness with additions of two Quebecers, rambunctious Sebastien Parent (he would be suspended for two games for biting a Huntsville Channel Cat in the last game of the season) and a 240-pound moose named Francois Chaput. Attendance was good, our team had talent, and the future looked promising. Then came the playoffs and an incident that could have scuttled everything.

* * *

Our first-round opponents in the playoffs were the Memphis RiverKings. They were coached by forty-nine-year-old Michigan-native Herb Boxer, who was the first American-born player ever drafted to the NHL when he was picked in the second round by Detroit in 1968. Herb and I were acquaintances, but not close. Under Boxer, Memphis played on the edge and sometimes it got to me. In one early season game I lost my temper and tossed a few things on the ice: twenty-five sticks, four pucks, a water bottle, a cooler and a folder. I was ejected, deservedly so. (Granted, my "tantrum" was premeditated, done to attract more public interest. It worked. My meltdown made the television news and the next game we sold out.)

We won game one at the Macon Coliseum — the first profes-sional playoff hockey game ever played in Macon. It was a tough affair. Three players were ejected: Memphis's winger Ryan Pisiak and defenceman Dan Brown, and our centre Thomas Stewart. The next day before the RiverKings' practice at the Coliseum, things got even nastier. The following account appeared in the *Macon Telegraph*:

> *According to Doug Hill, the Zamboni operator at the Coliseum, the incident started when at least one Memphis player took the ice for the 2 p.m. workout and began gesturing toward Whoopee equipment manager Stephen James.*

> *The RiverKings had accused James of tampering with two pairs of Memphis skates before Wednesday's game. Ryan Pisiak, one of the players whose skates were allegedly sabotaged, apparently brought up the allegation again to*

James, who was sitting in the stands with Hill and Whoopee public relations director Lisa Peppin.

Hill, who is black, allegedly became involved in the conversation between Pisiak and James. Then, according to Hill, Pisiak directed a racial epithet toward Hill. Pisiak later denied making the comment, but admitted to calling Hill an 'idiot.'

"(Hill) was yelling at me and the only thing I said was, 'You're an (expletive) idiot,'" Pisiak said. "They're just trying to put the light on me after what they pulled last night (with the tampering allegations)."

"I'm not deaf," Hill said. "He knows he said it."

Word of the situation quickly reached Paris, who went to the edge of the rink and engaged in a yelling match with Boxer and several RiverKings. No punches were thrown, but several Coliseum employees allegedly had to step between Paris and the Memphis team, according to witnesses.

I was actually in my office and came running out when I heard the commotion. True, I got into it pretty good with Boxer and we were close to blows. Boxer apparently thought so as well. He told the Memphis *Commercial Appeal* that anything could have happened because I was "out of control."

Out of control? Me? Hardly. But upon reflection it's a damn good thing Boxer didn't take the first swing. I was very upset and lectured him that using the "n" word — especially here in the Deep South — could trigger a race riot.

Amid the turmoil we tried to calm Doug Hill, nicknamed "Sticks" because he was so thin. Sticks was ranting about getting a gun and taking care of business. (Lisa later told me she heard what Pisiak had said, and that she too had been the subject of racial slurs during the same incident. She let it slide, however.)

All this was great drama and the press was skillfully setting the bait. Two Memphis players, Derek Grant and Jamie Cooke, the following day told the Macon paper that the whole incident was a ploy by me to fire up my team. "There were all sorts of guys around in the arena and nobody heard anything," Cooke said. "John's going to do what he can off the ice to get us off our games."

I blamed Boxer. "He's supposed to explain (to his players) what respect is all about."

The very idea of our equipment manager Stephen James somehow tampering with their skates was silly. What the press quickly dubbed "Skategate" went nowhere, even after the RiverKings made a show of shipping those skates belonging to Pisiak and Grant to the CHL's head office in Tulsa for review. In addition, Memphis put a new lock on its dressing room door and had their general manager Jim Riggs sit in the stands in "an unofficial watchdog capacity." Goofy.

But this whole thing was now about much more than altered skates. Things had elevated. The consensus around Macon was that Pisiak had crossed the line and called Sticks a nigger. In the Deep South that's not the word one wants on the street.

Pisiak, twenty-two, six-foot-three and 215 pounds, from Saskatchewan, was mainly an enforcer with 327 penalty minutes in just thirty-two games the previous season. A late-round draft pick in 1992 by the Los Angeles Kings, he would play with an ocean of teams before retiring in 2006. It would be many years before Pisiak fully realized the hornets' nest he stirred with that remark and how close he came to paying the ultimate price.

* * *

Two days after the Sticks incident I was in the arena parking lot chatting with a couple of employees when a low-riding car pulled up. A black man in his thirties leaned out of the driver's side window.

"Coach?"

"Yes . . ."

He came right to the point. "We gonna handle this."

I immediately knew what he was referring to. And I realized that if that car pulled away, Ryan Pisiak would die. I had to do something right there.

"We need to talk," I told him.

I jumped in my car with one of the employees I was talking with, and we followed the low-rider for fifteen minutes to Riverside Drive where we pulled into a parking lot near a Comfort Inn. I got out and told my friend to go off for a while. The driver of the car also got out. In less than a minute another car pulled up. There were three men in the second car. The two guys in the front got out, but a third man, in the back seat, stayed put. I could barely see him. This was not good. I knew that if anyone there was going to shoot me it was likely him. From where he was sitting, no witness could identify him. I had to assume that a loaded gun was aimed at me. Why else would he be in the back seat?

So, there were three of them out in the open, plus one guy in the back seat and me. We began to talk.

"You can't do this," I said.

They laughed. "The fuck we can't," one said.

"I mean that you don't need to retaliate." They looked at me blankly.

I was sensitive to the fact that I was there on *their* terms, and there's a protocol to follow in these circumstances. They brought me there because *they* wanted to talk. And they sensed

I appreciated their gesture. While they were allegedly doing all this for Sticks, they were indirectly doing it for me as well. It was a black thing. So there was a sort of mutual respect at play and I had to be very careful not to have that change. And I certainly had to be cautious not to say or even imply that I would go to the cops. Dead coach.

The guy from the lead car finally spoke. "We gonna handle it. That motherfucka ain't gonna get away with that. We gonna fix it." One of the others nodded in agreement.

Now these guys were packin' major heat and didn't hide it. So when I was telling them that they *couldn't* do this, it was clear to all of us that they technically had the ability to carry out a hit. They had done their homework. They knew who Pisiak was, what he looked like and where he was going to be. The moment of truth was close.

I couldn't afford to have the hit take place. First, it was just wrong. Second, it wouldn't change what was said to Sticks. Third, it would have been the end of hockey in Macon. All the work by all those people — bang! Gone.

"Look, if this happens we're all gonna lose," I said, trying some logic. "There's gonna be no gain here. That's just ignorant, stupid, dumb. That guy's not worth it."

I felt progress as they digested that thought. Up to this point I was talking to them as a group, making deliberate eye contact with each of them in turn. One of them was a listener, not an influencer. He was hard to read. The second was a mean mother badass itching for action. I was closely watching his body language. The dude didn't want to listen and he thought this whole fuckin' meeting was a waste of time. He wanted to move. The third guy was getting annoyed and barked at him. "Cool it, man."

So now I knew the third guy was the leader. I began to talk directly to him, asking him to please consider what this would do to me *personally*.

"C'mon man, I'll be out of work and you guys'll be in jail. Hey, I'm black like you so they're gonna fry my ass, the same as yours. So don't put me in that position. Don't put me in that position! Instead of helping me, you're gonna fry me. Who's gonna believe me when I say I had nothin' to do with it? You know what they do to us here. It doesn't matter where you go — north, south, east, west. If they want to get ya, they're gonna get ya. So don't put me — don't put *us* — in a position where we're *all* gonna get fried. Leave it alone, man . . . Let *me* handle it."

In effect, I was cashing in whatever credibility I had with them and leveraging whatever brotherhood they were willing to grant. They all stared at me, but my gaze stayed fixed on the leader. Several seconds passed before he reacted. Finally, he nodded okay. They pulled back. There would not be a hit . . . as long as such an incident didn't happen again. A second time? It's done. Over. And they won't bother talking to me.

I'm still not sure why they even talked to me the first time. But I'm grateful they did. And Ryan Pisiak should be, too.

* * *

Our playoff series with Memphis continued. Things didn't get much calmer.

In the final moments of game two, Boxer stormed onto the ice and had a meltdown over a time-clock issue. For game three, the crowd at the Mid-South Coliseum in Memphis booed me most of the night. The press had reported that I was going to bring security from Macon, but this was not completely accurate. Let's just say I had some *companionship*. So when a fan threw beer in my face between periods, he was caught by my companion — a massive brother who worked security for the Memphis police. The culprit *may* have ended up with a bruise or two. He certainly didn't throw another beer on me that night. There were also a couple of Macon cops there, but they came as fans. Unfortunately, they were seen on TV and got in trouble with their department anyway.

At the end of game four, our backup goalie, sitting on our bench, earned a suspension for using his mask to strike a Memphis defenceman in the face, cutting his nose. The defenceman retaliated by swinging his stick at him. He missed.

Ultimately we lost the series in five games. The RiverKings would come within a game of winning the CHL championship. (Herb Boxer was fired the next season after getting off to a 9–23 start.)

Following the final game, played in Macon, I took the microphone at the timer's bench and thanked our fans. I also could have thanked four angry guys in a hotel parking lot for their restraint, but some things were best left unsaid.

* * *

In 2004 I briefly coached Ryan Pisiak with the Laval Chiefs in the Ligue nord-americaine de hockey. He walked into my office in the arena one day — he was ill with the flu — and as we talked the topic of the Sticks incident came up. With no pressure from me, Ryan volunteered that he had indeed uttered the racial slur. I told him I always knew it because Lisa Peppin never lied, and I also highly doubted Sticks would make up such a thing. I told him about the confrontation with the gang. He was astounded.

"I saved your life," I said. "I'm certain that you were dead meat."

He thanked me and said he was surprised that, given our history, I had taken him on the Chiefs. I said I was willing to let things rest and move on. Truth is, I didn't find him to be a bad kid. He just did something very stupid and I hope he learned a lesson.

We never discussed it again.

CHAPTER 12
One Night in Huntsville

The Von Braun Center arena in Huntsville, Alabama, always made me uneasy. Games against the Channel Cats were chippy and the fans were more belligerent than in other cities. Minorities such as our David Starman and Joe Suk certainly felt the attitude. Nothing major, just small things. Therefore it was not a complete shock when one evening, a short time before a game, a fan I didn't know approached me and advised me to be cautious because, he said, the arena supervisor was a die-hard racist and out to get me. I thanked him and mentally filed it away. I wasn't sure what to expect. Certainly I was not prepared for what happened that night, October 23, 1997.

* * *

Huntsville had a tough team with some talent. Their coach was Larry Floyd, whose playing career included stints in the American Hockey League and the International Hockey League. He and I were okay, mainly because we both had been around for some time and — unlike in major junior — pro coaches are inclined to respect one another.

This game, we were up 3–0 with just four seconds remaining in the first period when several of their players jumped our guys and then attacked our bench. Their bench began to clear. Our players quickly responded in kind and the battle was joined. Punches landed and sticks waved with bad intentions. In the middle of this havoc a Plexiglas panel shattered, raining shards on nearby patrons. We had a mess on our hands.

At our bench I quickly wedged myself between the attacking Huntsville players and our guys, essentially blocking my players and restraining them as best I could. In the process I was absorbing blows from all angles, but still managing to hold my ground and keep most Whoopee players in tow. The crowd behind us was growing louder and more hostile. Arena staff, rather than coming to help deal with this chaos, stood a few feet away and started to yell at *me*. The referee, a paramedic from Atlanta named Chip Tyson, screamed at them to back off, telling them I was helping him by trying to control my bench.

Around this time a black arena employee beckoned me towards him. I couldn't leave my bench so he moved close and warned me that "they" were out to get me. This was a lot to process amid catcalls, jostling and roundhouse rights. Less than a minute later, I clearly heard: "Get the nigger now!" This came from either the arena supervisor or another man near him. (I'm unsure which one it was.) Both men were white.

I could feel my body brace for the worst. A black Huntsville cop — seems a black man is always used in a situation like this — pushed his way to the bench. Referee Chip Tyson yelled at him to leave me alone. "He hasn't done anything. I'm not throwing him out of the game. He's helping me!" Too late. I was already being escorted out.

The cops said I shoved the police sergeant who had approached me. This was untrue, but when someone grabbed my arm I *did* jerk it hard to break free. The Huntsville police later told the press that I was asked to calm down by the arena's head of security. They said I refused and that I called the head of security racial slurs. Again, untrue. I'm black and he's black. Unfortunately some blacks allow themselves to be used.

The police also said that three times I was asked by a uniformed cop to leave. They said when I refused, I was put in handcuffs. Well, they got the handcuffs part right. They slapped the cuffs on me so hard that they hurt my wrists. I wasn't going to give those buggers the satisfaction of letting them know how painful they were, so I just gritted my teeth and said nothing. A year later my wrists were still sore from those cuffs.

The cops then began escorting me out of the arena, being none too gentle about it. David Starman, who had darted from the bench and caught up to us, was now shrieking at the cops. "Take *me*, you bastards! I'm white. Take *me!* Take *me!*" I looked back at him. "Dave, shut up! Or we'll both be hanging from a tree!"

A small army of people chased along as we snaked through the hallways to an arena exit where a cruiser was parked. Suddenly a white man ran up and said, "I saw him hit you officer, and kick you, too! I saw the black nigger do it!" This prompted a white lady to holler at the man, "You're lying! He didn't touch him, and officer you know he didn't touch you! You want him bad, don't you . . ."

A cop shoved me into the back seat of the cruiser. We pulled away, with two cops sitting up front. I was not about to make this a pleasant trip for them. "You're wrong and you know it . . . You're a liar! What a poor excuse for a policeman . . . Lying about *me* touching *you* . . ." The ride lasted about ten minutes. I didn't shut up the entire time. They didn't say a word or turn around once. When we arrived at the police station they took me upstairs where a female officer was sitting at a desk. Macon was her hometown and she recognized me. Showing a little mercy, she made them remove the handcuffs.

From there I was deposited in a side room where I sat in a corner as a white cop involved in my arrest stood near the door. In a minute or so a female cop who looked to be in her thirties entered the room and snuggled real close to him. She tenderly touched his forehead. I couldn't believe what I was seeing. "Did they hurt you, honey? Oh, there's blood on you. Are you OK? Oooooooh honey . . ." As she pulled him tighter he slowly turned his head and looked across at me. Suddenly she noticed me sitting there. Ooops!

I grinned. "Well, well, well, well. Isn't this just sweet. My, my . . ."

"Shut the fuck up!" she snapped. She also said something else, which I missed. It didn't seem all that sympathetic.

The male cop then demanded my social identification number.

"I'm from Canada," I said, "and I'm not sure of my American number . . ."

"You don't know it? What? You don't even know your number? You stupid?"

I turned on him. "Not as stupid as you are. Look at you! Runnin' a number with another man's woman, and you're probably married yourself . . . and all this is on the job. You sonofabitch, you'd love to just take me out and hang me. Or have me just disappear, like back in the day. But you can't, you sonofabitch, because there's already people here lookin' for me. And the press probably, too."

He grabbed me by my sports jacket, yanked me up from my chair and off we went.

I caught a small break when on the way we encountered an Asian officer. I quickly perceived him as a *real* police officer; competent, but wary. Under his breath he told me not to worry. The other Huntsville cop wanted to throw me into this "bullpen" cell. The Asian cop said no. I was thinking that if they threw me in there I might not come out alive. But if I die, someone else in there dies, too. I'm *not* going to let them bang on me. Hell no.

Fortunately they took me to another cell. There was just one other prisoner in there, a white man. I'd never seen him in my life yet he looked at me and immediately started yelling, "They got the coach in here, man! This place is fucked up! They got the coach in here! They got the coach in here! They got the coach in here!" Over and over. It was crazy. He introduced himself and told me that no one in the lockup would bother me. I found that oddly reassuring as other prisoners in other cells began banging on their doors proclaiming, "The coach is here!" Positively surreal.

"You're the man," said my cellmate. "They set you up."

They set me up? How did this guy in a jail cell know *that*? Did *everyone* in Huntsville know they were laying a trap for me? We talked for a few minutes. At one point he asked me to call his girlfriend when I got out and to let her know where he was. I agreed and he passed me a small piece of paper with a number and name on it. Unfortunately, I lost that paper a short time later when they came to get me. Too bad. It may have been an interesting phone call.

On my way out, this big, white cop sidled up to me in the hall near the cell and squinted down at me. In a cold Clint Eastwood voice he delivered this gem: "I know you're not gonna holler police brutality, are ya boy? Y'know your place and y'know the consequences. Hear me, boy?"

I looked up at him and responded thusly: "Screw you! You sorry excuse for a human being . . ."

He did not take my retort particularly well.

Luckily we were at the staircase, at the top of which stood a handsome young black man with an earnest expression. His name was Condredge Holloway, Jr., a former University of

Tennessee football star, who in the 1980s was a first-rate quarter-back with the Ottawa Rough Riders and Toronto Argonauts in the Canadian Football League. He was now the Channel Cats' vice-president of public relations. But at that very moment Condredge Holloway, Jr. was my angel. Along with a white lady, who I later learned was the head of the Huntsville Booster Club, he hustled me out of the side door to avoid the media. The Channel Cats had already paid my $500 bond. It was close to midnight.

In Huntsville Magistrate's Court the next morning, I was offi-cially charged with third-degree criminal trespass and resisting arrest. I pleaded not guilty to both charges and told the judge, a black woman named Lynn Sherrod, that I was being railroaded. The case was put over and they let me return to Macon. A month later, on November 21, Judge Sherrod dismissed all charges against me. Videotapes of the incident cleared me of any wrong-doing, compelling Huntsville city attorneys to drop the charges. I later heard through a reliable source that the cops had tried to destroy the tapes. I have no proof of this. But I believe it.

In court I was represented *pro bono* by Mark McDaniel, a prominent Huntsville defence attorney whose clients had included two former Alabama governors, notably George Wallace, the reformed segregationist.

It was a relief to have it all end. At the time of the dismissal I hinted that I might file a civil suit. My musing must have caused a few people some concern. I seriously thought about it, then elected not to file. I didn't want money or anything else, only that my name be cleared. I also didn't want to damage my chances to coach again, especially at a higher level. In addition, I feared the publicity would block an opportunity for another black head coach. My purpose had always been to open doors, and I was nervous that filing a suit would surreptitiously close doors for my peers. Finally, I wanted to protect the league and its image. Without question all this hurt the league and damaged the reputation of the sport in the Deep South, a region drawing much of its perception of the sport from the movie *Slap Shot*. The CHL had been acquired by a new ownership group in the off-season and had moved its headquarters from Tulsa, Oklahoma to Indianapolis, Indiana. It was looking for a fresh start. This affair was not it. "It's certainly not the way we wanted to have the CHL promoted in the national media," understated David Blume, the league's assistant director of marketing and communications.

Still, the media pounced. It was treating this incident as confirmation that hockey was the World Wrestling Federation on skates. ESPN analyst Barry Melrose, a former NHL coach, rather than seeing that there was something fundamentally wrong underlying the episode, dismissed it as simply life in the minor pros. It was lazy, superficial analysis and very disappointing. ESPN's popular SportsCenter and Fox News showed clips of the melee. The *Macon Telegraph* also piled on. This "witty" offering from columnist Joe Kovac, Jr., appeared a couple of days after the Huntsville incident:

> *You knew this would happen when hockey hit the Deep South. You knew the Alabama police would get involved. Yeah, see, they've taken to arresting cheap-league hockey coaches. Thursday night's Macon Whoopee–Punksville Channel Cats tilt apparently overwhelmed arena security. Word is, police there hadn't seen such a frenzy since the new Family Dollar opened. Whoopee coach John Paris Jr. crossed their thin blue line. Dude got shipped to the county penalty box after he was told to leave and apparently told the cops to, um, go patrol a tractor pull . . .*

Striding to our bench with the Macon Whoopee, 1996.

The passing years have given me more perspective on the incident. While I *thought* I was walking away from this mess to protect the league and to avoid jettisoning my career, this may not have been the case. While the league took a hit, I now believe I did as well. The Huntsville incident clung to me. After I left the Whoopee I didn't get offers from another team in the CHL. Somehow within the industry I was seen as culpable and a risk. Forget my win-loss percentage and the overall development and performance of the team. I was tainted.

If I had to do it over again — being older and understanding more — I would have handled things differently. First, I would have filed suit. I had the necessary proof and witnesses, one being referee Chip Tyson and his insistence that I had not done anything wrong. Maybe by filing a lawsuit I would have helped clean up that police station and other police stations like it. Second, I would *not* have come out of that jail that night. If I had refused to leave it would have become a national scandal and kept the spotlight where it belonged. It would have at least put them on notice: *Now you have to deal with this miserable thing you created because this is going to get big. I'm not moving. I want a lawyer . . .*

A postscript: the next night we played the Huntsville Channel Cats again, this time in Macon. With both teams emotionally spent and missing several players due to suspension, it was a calm affair in front of a huge crowd. We lost, but I got a great reception.

* * *

Life in the Central Hockey League was not always as perilous as my experience in Huntsville. However, it's fair to say that the CHL did not offer the niceties of the NHL or even the International Hockey League. Salaries were much lower. Road trips were often protracted to save costs — one lasted twenty-six days. We didn't stay in five-star hotels. We travelled by bus.

However, for a sleeper bus, ours wasn't too bad. I was told it was similar to what a touring rock band would use. It had two satellite TVs (front and back), two living room areas (middle and back), two sofas, a fridge, a bathroom and bunks in the middle. The coaches sat up front. Dave and I liked to read, and the players preferred TV. Despite some tedium, we generally enjoyed the trips because of the camaraderie.

These expeditions gave me time to think. When I had an idea, I couldn't wait to share it. So I'd rouse Starman — frequently in the middle of the night. All the players knew that I'd do this and it was a running joke. Luckily David was a patient fellow and he wouldn't complain — much — because he knew I *needed* to talk. In truth, it was rarely anything urgent. But this could go on all night. Woozy and droopy-eyed, David would sit up in his bunk and listen. After I was finished he'd fall back to sleep for an hour or so until I had another idea.

We had a bus driver called Ned (not his real name), a nice middle-aged fellow whose services we contracted through a local business. Ned took care of us and was always on time, so we soon considered him part of the Whoopee family. A Vietnam veteran,

Ned even provided us with a measure of security and was armed, just in case.

One rainy night returning from Lafayette, David and I were yakking away when we heard Ned yell, "Everybody down. We are goin' in!"

David and I walked up to the front of the bus and saw that Ned was sitting erect and gripping the wheel like a vise, wild eyes fixed straight ahead as we barrelled down the highway. "It's gonna be rough! We may not come out of this alive!"

Huh?

Ned was really worked up. "We have to get *down*! They're out there. It's going to be rough, coach."

Ned was having a Vietnam flashback, and to him — at that moment — the danger was real. I stood next to Ned as the bus picked up speed.

"Stay down! Don't make a noise! We're goin' in! Everybody *down*!"

David joined me beside Ned. We didn't have a clue how to handle this.

"Coach," Ned growled, "there's something wrong here . . ."

Another minute passed as we continued to blast down the highway. Finally Ned announced it was safe to put our heads up. He stopped the bus on the side of the road and soon rejoined the real world. Unlike some teams, we wouldn't fry a member of the family over such a thing. Ned continued to drive for us and didn't have any more flashbacks . . . that we knew about.

For the players, I had my bus rules. One of them was no pornography, either through satellite or VCR. One night we were in the middle of nowhere and I looked up at the screen and saw porn. I ordered the bus stopped immediately. I knew the guilty party and I barked at him to remove the tape. "Take it out or I'll tear it up and throw it in the garbage. Or you can get off the bus — now!"

"Coach, I just bought this . . ."

I pointed at the bus door. "OK, off! And whether or not some-one ever finds you, I don't care . . ." He knew I wasn't kidding. I actually would have tossed him and driven on. He wisely pulled out the tape and put it away.

Nor did I allow beer on the bus. Despite this, a few players would smuggle brew onboard, including Jason Renard, who was a bit of a discipline problem. One night I caught him and con-fronted him. When he continued to deny it I *really* went off on him. The beer was chucked.

* * *

As a coach you are many things to your players: friend, psychologist, advisor, trainer, etc. On occasion you are also a babysitter. This seems as true in the professional ranks as it is in junior or even minor hockey.

Take for example the Whoopee's Alexei Diev, a nifty centre-man from Siberia, Russia. Alexei was an interesting case because of the cultural challenges he faced. Some of those challenges had to do with women, which he seemed to have no trouble meet-ing. One incident involved his Macon girlfriend breaking down his apartment door with a sledge hammer. Seems she had been locked out by his Russian girlfriend, who had arrived from the old country to pay Alexei a surprise — and very intimate — visit. We ended up having to mediate.

One time with the Knights, a talented rookie named Glen Metropolit was staying at a hotel near the Greyhound bus station in downtown Atlanta, an area full of nasty surprises. Now Glen was from Toronto, hardly a small city, but he was no man of the streets. One night when he went out for food he met a girl who said her friend was hurt, back in an alley, and asked for Glen's help. Being a nice young man he followed her into the alley, and behind some building he was rolled and robbed of his wallet.

Glen was embarrassed about the whole thing, but we scolded him anyway for disregarding our team warnings.

Another time I was at a hotel in Atlanta when a white man in his thirties barged into the lobby looking for one of my players. Looking in his eyes I knew this was not going to be a rational conversation.

"Why are you looking for him?" I asked.

"He was with my wife and I caught them and the bastard got away . . ."

I tried to cover for my player and told the husband that the player could not *possibly* have done such a thing because he was with me an hour ago.

"An hour?" he said. "This just happened a few minutes ago."

Oh. "Where do you live?"

"Marietta," he said.

I did some quick arithmetic. "Then there's no way. That's still a long way out and . . ." Blah, blah, blah. Obviously I was lying. Trying to defuse the situation. My ruse ended abruptly when he pulled out a handgun. "Get him down here!"

So there we stood, in the lobby, just the two of us . . . and the terrified receptionist twenty feet away. Hotel security was nowhere around.

"Think about it," I offered, stalling for time. "Ask yourself if it's worth it. If he was with your wife, then this means she's not for you, and you can do better than that."

"She's a fuckin' bitch and I'm gonna kill both of 'em."

"No man is worth life in prison. C'mon, let me handle this, please. I *promise* it will be handled."

Just then a security guard showed up. The husband quickly shoved his gun back in his jacket. I gently waved the guard back. He retreated slightly, but he kept his eyes glued on us.

The husband spoke softly. "Thanks, man. You're okay."

I advised him to go home, pack his bags and get out of there.

Get a lawyer, divorce her. "If you need a witness, I will make the player available. You know where to find me."

We talked for another fifteen minutes, then he left. I took a deep breath. Afterwards the guard came over to me and asked what it was all about. The receptionist volunteered the player was "out making a booty call and got caught by the husband." A good summary, I thought. I followed-up with the player in question and never heard any more about it.

* * *

During my three years in Macon, at various points I had the title of coach, director of hockey operations, vice-president and general manager. My overall record was 111 wins, 75 losses and 20 ties. Few CHL coaches in that era had a better record. We made the playoffs each year. Also during that span the Whoopee drew 126,000 fans to the Macon Coliseum, an average of 3,600 per game. We often cracked the six-thousand mark. As general manager I came in under budget, and corporate sponsorship steadily increased. The bottom line is that we had a healthy bottom line and turned a profit all three years I was there.

Unfortunately, Whoopee ownership and management were in constant flux — hardly astounding, as leagues such as the CHL were not known for their stability. Richard Ray and Pat Nugent, the duo primarily responsible for building the team and who had convinced me to come to Macon, were both ousted. In 1997 Ray, who I always considered a really good man, was forced out when another group bought the team. He became part of a pro hockey team in Louisiana. In 1998 the team fired Nugent, then the executive vice-president, following a restructuring that saw another fellow run the front office and I become the new general manager. Although it was barely mentioned at the time, this restructuring made me the first black man to hold the combined position of head coach/ general manager of a professional hockey club.

At my last press conference I said that coming to Macon had turned out to be the best move I ever made. One good thing about leaving a job on your own terms is the opportunity to influence who succeeds you. The Whoopee's primary criteria for a coach were an ability to recruit players and to be a presence in the community. Two black men seemed great candidates. One was Billy Riley, a fellow Nova Scotian. I would have advanced him for both the coach and GM jobs if I knew he was interested. The other candidate was Graham Townsend, a native of Jamaica raised in Toronto, who played parts of five seasons in the NHL. Graham was a nice person and well-qualified. He had recently been in Louisiana and encountered a few racial problems down there, so he knew the situation in the South. He got the job.

While talk circulated about me staying on, I never seriously considered it. I felt there was nothing more for me to do in Macon. I had developed as a coach and a general manager and had honoured my agreement with the team. I needed to move up. I was looking for something in the International Hockey League or maybe in Europe, but I was honestly hoping for a job in the NHL. Several professional clubs contacted me as the season ended, but none were the right fit.

* * *

One coaching job that *seemed* a natural fit for me would have been with the Halifax Mooseheads of the QMJHL. Actually I did interview for the Halifax job, following my second season in Macon. It was to replace former NHL star Danny Grant who had moved elsewhere in the organization. The Mooseheads, the first QMJHL team outside the borders of Quebec, were just four years old, but were already one of the more successful franchises in the league.

They had great community support and were backed by big money in Moosehead Breweries president and CEO Derek Oland.

The open position was for head coach and general manager, and I was being mentioned in the Halifax media along with "name" candidates such as Claude Julien, André Savard and Paulin Bordeleau. In a column in the *Daily News*, local sports reporter Carl Fleming lamented the attention focused on the high-profile types "who seem to find a new address every couple of years" and "disappear as soon as a better offer comes along, leaving a pack of teenagers to spend another half-season getting used to the next replacement . . ." Fleming said that the Mooseheads should consider the long term and select someone who would stay for a while and put his stamp on the team. "I hope they realize that where a coach has been often counts for much more than where he's going. And if they are looking for a consistent standard of excellence, all they have to do is check the records. Given that framework, is there any other choice but native son John Paris?"

So there was public pressure on the team to at least go through the motions with me.

Similarly, there was pressure on me to take part in the process. The hockey world is small and I preferred to avoid any nasty whispers that could materialize if I didn't at least try for the hometown job. I was obviously qualified: experience coaching in the QMJHL and the pros, experience as a general manager, a professional championship, knowledge of the city and region, skilled in media relations, etc.

Frankly, I had little interest in the position. I was happy in Macon. In fact, Whoopee ownership was puzzled why I was even bothering, given that the QMJHL would have been a step backwards from the Central Hockey League. In addition, being from the Maritimes, I sensed there could be very little margin of error for me in Halifax. And while Nova Scotia weather can be lovely, it was hard to forego Georgia's gentle climate.

Nevertheless, I decided to interview, knowing that teams usually have determined who they want even before the interview process begins. Sometimes the winning candidate has already been informed. I felt this was the case with the Mooseheads.

Dad and my brother Percy drove me to downtown Halifax for the interview. I entered the suite and sat down with Mooseheads president Ken Mounce and team owner Derek Oland. There were the standard questions about my hockey philosophy and my long-term career aspirations, and then came more pointed questions about what happened at my other coaching jobs, especially in the QMJHL. I answered honestly, but tried not to point fingers.

Then, in the middle of the session, Derek Oland asked, "Do you ever listen?"

Pow!

I took a deep breath. I found the remark offensive, especially given all that I had just carefully explained to them. I'm thinking, *Hey, that's the question you should be asking yourself.* At this point I knew they had already made up their minds — at least about me. Nonetheless, I tried to reply diplomatically. In finishing, I told them I was happy in Macon, but I was open to helping them in non-coaching areas, if they wanted.

The process took place just before former NHL star Bobby Smith bought the team, and before another NHLer, Cam Russell, got involved. With Smith and Russell across the table my interview may have gone differently.

But I likely still would have returned to Macon.

* * *

Sometimes the best career choices are the ones that you *don't* make. One example was the Vancouver Seals. The Vancouver Seals? Exactly.

The Seals were part of a start-up minor pro league called the Federal Hockey League. Originally it was slated to be a ten-team circuit and begin in September 2003. Then plans were abruptly scaled back to six teams and a twenty-four-game schedule to be played during the spring of 2004. At one point the league apparently held some haphazard tryouts, with players paying $1,000 each to show their stuff in a couple of "organized" games in front of some coaches. Transportation and accommodation all came out of the players' pockets. They were told to rationalize these costs as an investment on the $500-a-game they *could* earn when things got rolling.

The whole thing was the brainchild of Vancouver business man John Larsen. Larsen, who ran things out of an office in Coquitlam, British Columbia, insisted his league was looking to attract fans who felt disenfranchised with pro hockey. (To complicate things for Larsen, at that same time retired superstar Bobby Hull was trying to resuscitate the World Hockey Association.)

When he called me, Larsen was still looking for team owners. Larsen himself owned the Vancouver franchise and asked me about being his coach and general manager. I tried to keep an open mind. I thought if this gets off the ground and the cheques don't bounce, then why not? They laughed at the WHA in the 1970s, didn't they?

Before my only interview with Larsen he had already taken the liberty to announce in the press that I was on board. Not so. During that interview I got few firm answers to my questions. I recall Larsen saying, "Coach, if all the cities get their act together, then the league will fly." Not exactly the expression of a confident visionary. I told Larsen to call me if things progressed. Of course no call ever came. And the FHL never played a game.

CHAPTER 13
Marc-André

I'm a romantic. I don't know if this is strength or a weakness, but it's a fact. While most of the charming women I met during my time in the American South became only friends, several relationships around this time developed further, often with women in the public eye.

I had relationships with two major music stars, both considerably younger than me; neither relationship lasted. The first began when I was at her concert in Houston, Texas. Intrigued by the idea of a black hockey coach, she sent staff out into the audience to ask me if I'd like to meet her after the performance. I happily agreed. I found her to be a very sweet person and we clicked right away. We saw each other for almost a year without the media finding out, but we knew it was just not going to work because we were both always out of town. Strange to say, she was just too famous, too big in the entertainment world. We are both now married and no longer keep in touch. But she's still a major star and I'm still a big fan.

The second relationship with a popular young singer did not last as long or develop as deeply. (This is the girl that Whitney

Houston did not like and warned me about.) At the time she was on her way to greater heights and, while we had some very nice times, things did not end well. One day, after I'd moved on and had fallen in love with current wife Stephanie, she called my apartment and was very rude to Stephanie. When I took the phone and insisted that she not speak to Stephanie in this way, she hung up on me. We've not talked since. All water under the bridge.

I also came to know an Academy Award–nominated actress who I met one summer in Los Angeles when I was there working at a hockey school. She was engaging, bright and very political. Things heated up quickly between us. But she was already with someone, so our liaison never progressed.

Another time I was with several others signing autographs near a posh gym in Buckhead, an upscale, preppy area of Atlanta. From nowhere we heard, "I love you! I love you!" We all looked up and saw this beautiful lady in front of us — a well-known, top model. I thought she was speaking to football star Buck Buchanan or one of the others. But she came over to me! (Her adolescent daughter, who was at her side, shyly confirmed her mother's John Paris, Jr. obsession.) "Do you know who I am?" she asked, standing there all tall, sleek and eloquent. I just gaped at her and smiled. After a few words she handed me her phone number on a slip of paper. I reached out and took it, leisurely, trying not to show my excitement. I never did follow-up, however, and she never contacted me. Likely just as well.

However, one relationship evolved all the way to the altar.

We met at a Macon carwash. I was sitting there in the waiting area when I saw this beautiful, long-haired woman walk in and mesmerize the room. Tall, classy, African-American. We politely exchanged greetings and she sat down and began to read her book. Luckily, both of our cars were finished at the same time and as we walked out I asked if she happened to like hockey.

"Yes, a little."

"Married?"

"No," she said. "Divorced."

"Boyfriend?"

"No boyfriend."

I asked her name so I could write it on the envelope with the tickets: Miriam. She even agreed to go out and get something to eat with me after the game.

Turns out that Miriam, a realtor, was more than just beautiful. She was also a community leader who in the future would become president of the Macon city council and then, in 2010, a Georgia state senator, representing District 26 (Macon) — the first black woman ever to represent that area of the state in the senate.

We exchanged vows in Macon in 1999 at a tasteful ceremony that she had arranged with a wedding planner. Chantal was there, so were my dad and a few other members of my family. However, early on I became apprehensive about our marriage and even had a premonition it might not work. We divorced in 2004. Miriam and I were from different worlds. She had eight children from her previous marriage — four girls and four boys — and when we were together two of her children were causing her considerable problems. To her credit, she was a wonderful mother and today all her children have graduated either high school or college.

Maybe under different circumstances, at other points in our lives, this could have been a winner. We'll never know. But I *do* know the state of Georgia is lucky to have a champion like Miriam Paris.

* * *

In 2003, still looking to take the next major step in my career, I had agreed to go to Boise, Idaho to help out the local minor hockey program. I think it was fate. Otherwise I wouldn't have been standing in that arena the day *she* walked in.

She was lugging a big hockey bag behind her, clearly intent on getting to the dressing room, so I just watched her go. She was tall and looked in her mid-twenties. A ball cap covered much of her long, blonde hair. The rest of the day I couldn't get her out of my mind. Not long after I was visiting a friend's rental house and — by chance — she happened to be there. I found out her name was Stephanie and we talked a bit. I learned that she was employed in maximum-security and worked the night shift just so she could skate in the mornings and play hockey in the evenings. The next time I saw her I was sitting on a bench in front of the arena enjoying the warm weather. I engaged her in a little polite conversation and found out it was her birthday. So I asked her out. I immediately cut all existing romantic interests in my life and we started to date. One evening at dinner I blurted out, "I'm going to marry you!" She just looked at me and smiled. Stephanie doesn't say much. It's part of her make-up. She's direct. No head games.

Stephanie may look like a beauty queen, but she's also a natural athlete. In high school she was ranked as the seventeenth-best shot putter in the USA. She can hit a golf ball and a baseball further than most men, and can really shoot a puck. She now works with the City of Irving police department.

We were married in 2007 in a civil ceremony in Campbellton, New Brunswick, where I was coaching at the time. We are still like two young lovers and our age difference has never been an issue. I call her my Oregon sweetheart. You rarely see one of us without the other.

* * *

I was determined that after Macon my next position had to help me move forward and have a purpose in my career. And

For an all-American girl, my wife Stephanie looks magnificent in Canada's colors. The photo was taken in Boise, Idaho in 2004. We were dating at the time.

so, in 2004, I signed to coach the Laval Chiefs in the Ligue Nord-Americaine de Hockey, where I could learn first-hand what it was like to coach in an environment where toughness was more important than skill. I found out.

Not to be confused with the North American Hockey League (an American junior league and a completely separate entity) the Ligue Nord-Americaine de Hockey was selling violence — plain and simple. It owned the legitimate reputation as the world's toughest hockey league, with about five times more fights per game than the NHL. Many brawls were epic. Battles went the limit and beyond. Bench-clearing wars like those in the 1950s and 1960s. Often scraps would commence before the puck was dropped to start the game. Mayhem and blood.

The league under one name or another had been around for a few years. I'm no shrinking violet, and frankly I have used the element of intimidation at times myself. But even I was surprised how bad this league was. Maybe I should have clued-in with the name "Chiefs." Or that our uniform was modelled after the Johnstown Chiefs, infamous from the movie *Slap Shot*. Or when I heard our players talk about the fights they planned to have during the *next* game. Or when I saw our guys grease their arms before games to make themselves more elusive in battle.

In 2004–05 the LNAH had ten teams, most based in small Quebec communities. Teams conducted their business largely in French, a significant attraction for French-Canadian players, although English was spoken to accommodate players from the United States and the rest of Canada. Attendance was good. Many teams routinely pulled in four thousand to six thousand fans, with larger crowds for games in arenas such as Montreal's Bell Centre.

All teams courted goons. Many featured discarded NHL enforcers, literally fighting to stay in the sport. Most players made about $200–$300 a game and held down other jobs. Thoughts of making it back to the NHL were not realistic. And it showed. Players lacked commitment. They were seldom in top shape and practices, as infrequent as they were, were not well-attended. Tough guys were coming and going, leaping from one team to another. (Legend has it that the league once suspended ex-NHL brawler Link "The Missing Link" Gaetz for leaving the bench during a game to go to a concession stand for a hamburger.)

The Laval Chiefs were considered the league's flagship franchise, a title earned, as one newspaper article put it, for playing "a style more suitable for a pirate ship than a hockey arena."

The Chiefs were owned by Bob Berger, who once coached the team himself and loved to boast that we had the LNAH heavyweight champion in Patrick Côté, a six-foot-four, 260-pound forward, a former Dallas Star and Nashville Predator. Like the other owners, Berger relished that fans came to see fights — with perhaps bit of hockey in between the brawls. It was easy to get swept away with all the shenanigans.

In one game against our rival Verdun Dragons at the Bell Center in front of twenty thousand fans, Patrick Côté caught his skate in a rut in the warm-up and injured his back and shoulder. We were already undermanned and Verdun took advantage and beat us up pretty good. I objected and was ejected from the game, in the process dramatically whipping off my sports jacket, twirling it over my head and tossing it on the ice. (I was relieved when someone retrieved the jacket and gave it back to me. It was pretty expensive, I recall.) Earlier that day my two top scorers, Denis Chalifoux and Dominic Perna, told me they were going to play in Italy. Neither liked the craziness. They left with my blessing.

While the LNAH managed to attract some talent — our lineup featured former NHL draft picks — it was never a good fit for me. I'm the type of coach who has to establish a system, who has to teach and prepare a team. Any attempt I made to put in a system proved futile with the Laval Chiefs. Strategy? Forget about it. It's nearly impossible to run a bench in a situation like that. (One lesson I discovered: the trick is to get *your* fighters out there first.)

I resigned with a quarter of the season remaining. I got what I came for and escaped with my sanity. Apparently the league is a bit calmer today. Although still tough, it has stopped airlifting one-dimensional enforcers from across North America and is now going with mainly Quebec-based players. This means that the league operates all in French and has attracted more skill, including veterans such as my friend Steve 'La Mouche' Larouche.

* * *

I'm not especially good at this whole networking thing, as many people have told me over the years. I'm naturally shy and have a touch of loner in me. So self-promotion is a forced art for me. If I was better at it, maybe I would have had more opportunities, because remaining employed in a peripatetic hockey life requires staying in touch with people through phone calls, emails, casual conversations at conferences and in arenas, etc.

One such conversation happened in a Nashville, Tennessee, arena shortly after I left the Laval Chiefs. A couple of hockey scouts I knew said they heard I was heading to the Philadelphia Flyer organization. I paused. "No, unless you've heard something I didn't." I laughed it off and forgot about it. Some months later, when I was in Switzerland, Stephanie called to say I had a letter from the Flyers. It explained that they were not planning on making any major changes in the near future, but acknowledged I was well-qualified and thanked me for sending them my resume.

My mind quickly leapt back to Nashville. Now I was curious. I had not sent the Flyers my resume or application or even had a phone call with them. A strange coincidence? I'm not big on coincidences. This worried me. In the past I would get a letter saying that this team or that team had no openings and I didn't really think too much about it. But for this one I started digging. Stephanie did a back trail — it helps to have a wife with a law enforcement background. It took some time, but in 2006 or 2007 we eventually learned there was a "challenged" person out there who actually thought he was me. A John Paris, Jr. impersonator! (He was not exactly a look-a-like. He was six-foot-two and white; I am five-foot-five and black.) He was sending out cover letters and resumes to teams asking about possible positions. Stephanie reached out and managed to put a little scare in him so he backed off. Otherwise, we found out, there was not much we could do about it.

It's quite possible that over the years most applications or resumes sent under my name to various NHL teams were actually not from me. So, in some perverse way, I guess I was networking without knowing it.

* * *

I was fifty-nine years old and labeling myself semi-retired. Frankly, I wasn't sure exactly what that meant but it paved the way for a move to one of the most beautiful spots in North America — San Diego, California. The climate is flawless year-round and the topography unmatched with the ocean and the mountains. Golf? Endless, on courses hard to believe. But a hockey man is a hockey man, semi-retired or otherwise. So when the *National Post* arrived to do a feature on me on Boxing Day 2005, they found me in the Centennial Twin Arenas, happily behind the bench at a midget AAA tournament.

All this and a beautiful young wife. What more could any man want?

The answer came on June 6, 2006, with the birth of Jocya Alexis Paris — my third daughter and fourth child. Beautiful and healthy and joyous.

I was lucky to have another child. Sort of a second chance, in my case. I was around Chantal a lot when she was very young, but mostly because I was ill and housebound. I couldn't do much with her, but at least I was there. When I started to recover, I allowed

Stephanie, Jocya and a very lucky man, Christmas 2009.

hockey to take over my life and was gone most of the time. While I made sure my family never lacked for the material things, my absence exacted a high price, especially on my first marriage. This will not be the case with Stephanie, Jocya and I. I have learned from past mistakes. Certainly my sense of priority has changed.

This said, a hockey career and a good family life are not mutually exclusive. Therefore, when the chance came to get back into hockey full-time, I accepted — even though it meant leaving idyllic, warm, cosmopolitan San Diego for small-town Campbellton, New Brunswick, where there are no big theatres, winters can freeze human flesh, and forestry is the big industry. Many young women would have balked at the idea of such a move. Not Stephanie. At least not much. So off we went to the Great White North and the hidden jewel of Campbellton with two-month-old Jocya in tow.

I accepted the job as coach and general manager of the Restigouche Tigers of the Maritime Junior A Hockey League. I was enticed by a good salary and a chance to apply my development program, as well as the close proximity to my father, who was then in his mid-eighties and not in great health. Windsor was only a six-hour drive from Campbellton so I could visit him and other members of the Paris clan when we played nearby teams or during the off-season.

In my first season in Campbellton, 2006–07, we earned fifty-six points in fifty-eight games and were a respectable fourth place in our division. I brought in a few additional players and we made it to the second round of the playoffs. It would be the high point of my three seasons there. Also during that year the Tigers had shifted to private ownership. Previously the team had been owned by the city of Campbellton, which poured an exorbitant amount of money into the team's operations. The Tigers thought they had to be generous to attract older players to a more remote region that offered fewer postsecondary education options than other centres across the league. As a result, some players were accustomed to annual living allowances of $7000–$12,000 or more. When I slashed the budget by 60 per cent and set up better accounting processes that season, a few players went elsewhere.

* * *

Before my second season in Campbellton my father passed away. He was eighty-seven. A piece of me died that day, June 6, 2007 (also Jocya's first birthday). I got the call when I was with Stephanie and Jocya vacationing in Sarasota, Florida. I knew he was ill, but when I heard the news I still went numb. That evening I sat in front of my computer and began to tap out a stream of thoughts and emotions . . .

The Paris family will never be the same.
Hopefully we all will be more aware of life issues
and have learned from this painful experience. I
am presently in a world of my own and awaiting
the difficult reality that he will not be there in
his physical form anymore . . . Our father made
certain to avoid any form of confusion in regard
to his condition. He did not want to be brought
back if his heart stopped, nor did he want to be
in a lesser state of mind or physical condition.
Dad had dignity and pride . . . He had a knack
of drawing people to him. He was not only liked,
but admired by many. If you were in any place in
the world, under any situation I am certain that
my father would find friends and be invited back.
In areas where people of colour were not easily
accepted, my dad would end up in their homes at
their table. Unbelievable . . . He was also one who
refused to accept injustice in any form.

At the funeral home and again during the service at the
Baptist church in Windsor — where his own grandfather had
been a deacon — I have never seen so many grown men with
tears in their eyes. During the service, black and white mourned
together, told stories or just stood silently. His passing left a big
hole in the community.

* * *

In my second season in Campbellton I had selected a young roster
that I was hoping to develop. Consequently we were off to a poor
start. While I understood why we were losing, it is still better to
win and it was hard not to become discouraged. The kids were

trying, but the talent was lacking. So I began to look for some experienced players to at least get us to the playoffs.

One day I got a call from a contact about a kid from Eastern Quebec who'd recently been cut from the Rimouski Oceanic of the QMJHL. Discouraged, the kid had returned home and began playing in an intermediate league. I had never heard of this player so I was skeptical. But I was on the hunt and the season was marching on, so I checked with some scouts I knew and they told me he should never have been cut by Rimouski. Thinking it was worth a shot, I invited Marc-André Déraspe to Campbellton for a tryout.

"Be patient with me coach, will you?" he said at our first meeting. "It'll take me a little while to get myself back to where I should be. Give me a little time and I'll carry the mail for you."

I laughed. "You are *really* going to carry it?"

"And I'll deliver it too, coach." Then he smiled. Marc-André was always smiling.

Within a few games I knew I had just won the lottery. Marc-André was not just a good player; he was the best player in the Maritime league. Fast, smart, strong, potent. Remarkably, every week he seemed to get better. The team was galvanizing off his energy and we were starting to win. Game after game people pointed out what a find I had.

Regardless of what coaches say, we do get attached to some players. How are you not going to? A good person is a good person. Coaches turn a switch off when we start games or practices, but we are still just people. So Marc-André soon became very close to me. He was like my shadow, always around me, sticking to me like glue, always so up-beat. He'd tell me about his dreams, his family life and his girlfriend. And he'd ask endless questions about hockey. Barely twenty years old, Marc-André had his life mapped out.

By December we were on a roll, winning consecutive games and energized by Marc-André. Then in January, in a game in

Truro, Marc-André fell into the boards and injured vertebrae in his back. His season was over and, with it, so was the Tigers'. It was devastating.

He went home for a short time then came back to see me. He tried, but he couldn't play and he cried when the reality finally hit. Our team changed. We'd lost our leader and went into a nosedive. At the time of the injury I had him set up for tryouts the following year with a couple of pro teams. I kept reminding him he'd recover, and that I'd help him in his career. I assured him that the lowest level he'd play the following year would be in the East Coast League. With some luck, maybe it'd be the American Hockey League. I told him not to worry, that I had it handled. I was going to work with him on a training program that would put him in the best condition of his life. I'd already designed it in my head. Marc-André thanked me often for all this. We were both excited about his future.

One day in late March I called his house to say hello. His mother told me that he was not there, that he was getting ready to go fishing. When he called me back Marc-André said he was going out on a fishing boat to earn money for his training camp that summer. I assured him his costs would be picked up, but Marc-André said he'd rather pay his own way. That's what a healthy young man does, he insisted. In another conversation a short time later, he mentioned that he'd decided to go sealing. He had never gone sealing before.

There were six crew members aboard *l'Acadien II*, a twelve-metre trawler, when it radioed for help after losing its rudder amid the ice floes in the North Atlantic. What should have been a routine rescue operation turned into disaster when *l'Acadien II* swerved into a large cake of ice and flipped over while it was being towed by a Canadian Coast Guard icebreaker. Two of the *l'Acadien II* crewmen were plucked alive from the icy waters by sealers on a third boat that was following behind. The other four crewmen lost their lives. One of them was Marc-André. He had been sleeping below at the time of the accident and drowned.

I was stunned. Pat Belliveau, my hockey operations guy in Campbellton, couldn't stop crying. The media was all over us. Cameras in our faces. The same questions, the same answers. "He was a great kid . . . he was our best player . . . he was destined for a great future . . ."

At Îles-de-la-Madeleine, Quebec, under a grey sky, hundreds jammed into a church for the funeral of the lost sealers. Marc-André's casket was carried by his hockey teammates, who wore jerseys with "Déraspe" on the back. When the casket was taken from the church after the service, in a sign of respect, they held their hockey sticks aloft. A cousin remembered Marc-André as the exceptional son every parent dreams of having, a young man always ready to help people and to smile and express his love.

Looking back, Marc-André was almost too good to be true. Just when we needed it, he arrived, with his skills and his smile. He seemed to come out of nowhere and left us just as suddenly. He was special. I'll never forget him.

* * *

We finished the 2007–08 season with a cloud over the team, playing under .500 and missing the playoffs. But before the season was over there was yet other event that I wished I had avoided. In the last week in April I suffered a mild heart attack. They transferred me from Campbellton to the Saint John Regional Hospital where tests showed something about water in my heart, apparently called pericardial effusion. You can die from it, because it impedes the heart's ability to provide the body with enough blood. Near the end of the season I had caught a virus and was not feeling well. But I stubbornly pushed on and ended up almost paying a horrible price. I recovered well, but the lesson learned was to heed the small signs and take the right action.

While the records for my second and third seasons were not good, I remained true to my philosophy that building a foundation through developing young talent was the best thing for the team long-term. Although not everyone in Campbellton understood or agreed with this approach, this was how I managed. I never made an issue — either publicly or privately — about having a greatly reduced budget. Nevertheless, I did try to change the thinking of both the city and the Tigers organization. In situations where money was scarce, as it was at that time in Campbellton, a prudent long-term vision is best. The goal is stability, both in players and in financial management.

After the 2008–09 season the club changed its name to the Campbellton Tigers, but struggled to find its footing on and off the ice. With new ownership came lots of infighting and the new coach, a former pro named John Leblanc, quickly found out that coaching without the open budget formerly available from the city made things much more difficult. He soon clashed with ownership and quit.

CHAPTER 14
Rocky Mountain

One Sunday evening in late September 2011 two hockey moms from the minor team I was coaching in Denver, Colorado, knocked on my apartment door. As I invited them in I saw the distressed expression on their faces and I knew instantly what it was all about. So did Stephanie, who was sitting nearby. "Well, you're in it now, John," she said. "I'm going to start to pack . . ."

The mothers both had sons on my U16 (under age sixteen) team in the Rocky Mountain RoughRiders Hockey Club and were extremely concerned about a matter that had surfaced recently involving the behaviour of one of the minor hockey coaches in nearby Boulder. They had come to tell me what they knew and to ask for my advice. Before we began, one them quizzed Stephanie about her "packing" remark.

Although seldom emotional, this hit a nerve with Stephanie. "Do you *really* think they're going to leave my husband alone? Because now he has to go to the police, now that you brought this to him. He has no choice. You know John. He's not going to hold back. You *know* there's going to be damage control. And they'll use anything they can get to get at him."

"We can trust your husband because he'll know what to do," said one of the moms, who was now crying. "We've nowhere else to go . . ."

It was not a nice scene.

Monday morning, less than twenty-four hours later, I was on the telephone to the FBI telling them what I knew and what I had just learned from the parents. It was a call I didn't enjoy, but one that I didn't hesitate to make.

* * *

I knew Denver a bit, mainly from when I travelled there with the Atlanta Knights and also through summer hockey camps at the University of Denver and the University of Colorado. Stephanie liked the city and we thought the dry environment may be good for my health. So with Jocya nearing school age, the Paris family moved to Denver. The idea was for me to settle into retirement — as if that would ever actually happen.

Once there I became involved with the elite minor hockey program. Yes, I was compensated, and the money always helps, but mainly it was to give back to the sport and to do something I loved. And the Rocky Mountain RoughRiders seemed like a good fit for me. The organization was formed in 2009 with the alliance of four smaller clubs in the area, including the Boulder Hockey Club. The concept was to develop top-level players to compete against the other three large hockey associations in the state, all with an eye to national competitions. As it was, however, the RoughRiders were the weak sister of the four Colorado super-organizations. (An aside: I thought there should have been only two or three such organizations if Colorado wanted to be nationally competitive. There were not enough highly skilled players in the state, so having four organizations diluted the talent.)

By the fall of 2011 I was preparing for my third season as coach within the Rocky Mountain association. To that point it had been a good experience. The association had allowed me to run my team program properly and most parents were extremely supportive. And we were seeing the results. Every year my teams were the most successful in the RoughRiders association. Using my continuous development approach, I had taken them from bottom-finishers to near the top in their age classifications. The first year we made it to the state competition and did well, and the second year we won fifty-four games and again went to state. We lost a chance to go to nationals when we were edged out in the semifinals. I was anticipating even more success as I began my third year there.

Among the younger coaches in the Rocky Mountain system was a fellow named Zachary Meints. He had been involved in the minor hockey program for a while and was also an assistant on a local junior team. I had concerns about him for some time. During my first season with Rocky Mountain I was in an arena in Boulder and overheard him say that he talked personally to the players all the time. I approached him right there and said he shouldn't be doing that. Witnesses heard me. I said, "Look, I'm a coach and I don't do that. *Ever*. When you're dealing with youth you should go through the parents. There're rules and guidelines. And *certainly* don't call them at night! You should know this."

He looked at me and gave a weak response. Our conversation essentially ended there.

For the 2011–12 season the Rocky Mountain association was considering Meints for an assistant coach position. As usual, the association director sought input from other coaches and officials in the association before he made a decision to hire personnel. So at a meeting I made it clear — and I stated it on the record — that

I did not favour hiring Meints. A couple of coaches, the hockey director and a board member all tried to convince me to change my mind. I forcefully held my ground. I explained that most people who coach minor hockey think they know more than they actually do, and most don't really adhere well to the player-development scale. I stressed that both of those faults applied to Meints. More importantly, I said, I was concerned because he talked inappropriately to youths via text messages and the internet. "I told him to stop and he's continuing to do it. And you need to investigate." A couple executive members speculated that Meints was gay and it was merely "a homosexual thing." I asserted there is a difference between homosexual orientation and sexual exploitation.

In taking this stance, I reminded them of my credentials. I had more overall experience than anyone in the association and over the years had attended seminars and conferences where pedophilia was comprehensively discussed, especially how it applied to minor sports. Once at a meeting in Calgary, Alberta, I sat one-on-one with a local judge, asking question after question to ensure I understood the subject thoroughly. I also took college courses on sexual abuse and attended lectures on misuse of electronic and social media. In Canada, the hockey culture had become highly sensitized to the issue with the high-profile sexual exploitation cases of NHL stars Sheldon Kennedy and Theo Fleury, both who had been repeatedly sexually abused by a former coach. Pedophilia in minor sports did not seem as well understood in the United States where guidelines and policies were either less stringent or not as widely known.

Shortly after stating my opposition to the hiring of Meints, I went out of town to check out a camp in Anaheim, California for the Victoria Royals of the Western Hockey Junior Hockey League. When I came back, Zachery Meints had been hired for the 2011–12 season as an assistant coach for the U15 team. I had lost the battle.

I felt the attitude towards me change after that. Clearly the association did not think my arguments were compelling enough. The Rocky Mountain executives had two choices: listen to me or not listen to me. Some people like to be in denial. I'm not one of them. I knew that where there's smoke, there's fire. I saw the signs. But I did not run the program.

While not everything was yet clear to me, certainly my antennae had been raised. Indeed, they had been for a while. The year before, during the middle of the 2010–11 season, I had called a meeting with the parents to alert them to what I thought might be a problem. I told them that they should verify the cell phones and laptops of their children and know who their child was talking to and when these conversations were happening. I said they needed to know what was going on. I couldn't provide details, but I shared my feelings that *something* was amiss. I reminded the parents how I take away my players' phones and laptops when we are on the road. I gave the devices back briefly during the day, but the kids did not have them at night when they are in their rooms alone.

Nevertheless, as the 2011–12 season neared, all I knew was that Zachery Meints was having conversations with players at odd times of the day or night, and that my gut feeling — supported by my training — had red flags popping up in my head. But I had nothing firm.

That was about to change.

* * *

Kids talk. They also joke and tease and have a fascinating way of banding together in a common cause, especially given the "brotherhood" that forms on competitive sports teams. One day before a practice I was sitting in the dressing room with my U16 team when I heard one youngster whisper to another, "You got a text . . . What did he ask you?"

"Text from who?" I asked, careful to keep my tone casual. "When?"

I learned it happened the night before, at one or two in the morning. Now, I'm not computer-savvy — I only recently sent my first text message — but communication at that hour is seldom a good thing. That dressing room exchange between these kids raised my curiosity. Why would they be doing this? Who was texting them? Again, I suspected it may have been Meints. But I still didn't know for sure.

Normally you don't push things with kids. If you push, you will not get your answers. Parents will tell you that I am demanding with their kids. But their kids trust me. They know I will not lie to them and they know if they get in a jam, I'm there. And if they tell me something, they know that I am not going to report them. I don't pressure them because I know sooner or later they're going to tell me. They'll come to me one-on-one and open up. That's how I build trust. And I've never broken it. (I've found that over the years I've known more about what was going on than many of the parents could even imagine!)

One day I was with one of the players and he mentioned to me that he just shut off his phone to block the texts, and that he also blocked them on Facebook.

"Block who?" I asked.

He hesitated. "I don't want to say anything . . ."

"Fine," I said. "You've got a bit of a problem. You've dealt with it. You've blocked it, you're fine. Thanks for telling me the truth."

In a low-key manner I asked other players on the team who they were talking to. Similarly, respectfully, they said I really didn't need to know. They were circling the wagons. I thought, *That's it! Now I know it's something bad.* I just didn't know who was communicating with them, but I knew I was getting closer to finding out.

More uneasy than ever, I persevered and I went back to the association hoping this time they would share my concerns and act. Once again I didn't get the response I was hoping for. The members of the executive were all younger than me and didn't grasp that the integrity and reputation of their association — and perhaps its entire hockey program — were at issue. I explained if someone in our ranks was not clean, and we did not take appropriate action, then we were all guilty to some degree. I said that in the pedophilia world perpetrators don't act right away, they start out by infiltrating, making that single contact, talking nice, then becoming a little more intimate with sexual innuendo. Once they get their prey where they want them, only then does it start to become physical. Aggression doesn't happen right away. They are intelligent and devious and slowly work their way in.

I pointed out to the executive that this was the situation we were in. Again I stressed that I didn't have solid proof. "If I'm wrong, I'm wrong," I said. "I'm willing to take the hit."

In effect, I was putting my head on the block to get them to act, but I was getting very frustrated. "Gentlemen, we're not sitting on warm coals, we're right in the fire."

* * *

The anxious parents who came to my apartment to talk with me that Sunday evening in September provided ample evidence of wrongdoing. They also gave me a name. As I suspected, it was Zachery Meints.

After my phone call the FBI wasted little time. The file was moved to the Boulder police and by October 3, 2011, the investigation was on. The list of victims immediately started to grow. Exactly how many kids were involved is hard to determine, as is often the case with pedophilia. Clearly, there were multiple victims. When the police contacted the association, the executives went into damage control. They reacted in two ways. Neither of them honourable.

The first reaction, as this scandal broke, was incredibly foolhardy. The association cited legal advice and a concern for the *rights of the accused* to justify not giving police the requested contact information of the alleged victims. In fact, the association sent emails instructing others not to co-operate — communication that recklessly named some of the victims. (Incredibly, I was actually copied on the email. I promptly sent it to the police.)

Ultimately the association was criticized for these actions. Among other things, it needlessly made the police work a lot harder and lengthened the time of the investigation. The authorities eventually got what they needed, however.

The association's second reaction was predictable: discredit the whistleblower. In other words, divert the focus back on me. Stephanie and I were anticipating this. We knew that, whether I was right or wrong, they would come after me in some way. (I actually had already shared this certainty with one of the Rocky Mountain directors I respected.) They attacked my credibility and tried to make me resign. Specifically, they claimed I did not follow association procedures and tell them the name of the individual first, before going to the authorities. This was absurd. I had been *highly* vocal in my opposition to hiring Meints and had clearly explained why. I had been outspoken with my concerns for *more than a year*, but the association chose not to take action and vigorously investigate. In addition, seeking petty vengeance, they tried to make my workload more difficult. They went to parent meetings and said there was some issue with my cutting a kid. Stuff like that. Nonsense. They nitpicked and attempted to find people to speak against me.

The most bizarre attack, however, was that someone from within the hockey community filed a charge of reverse discrimination against me. They said I was anti-white. Anti-white?

Perhaps my first wife (white) or my third wife (white) or the majority of my close friends (white) or 99 per cent of the players that I coached over the years (white) would take issue with this. This nutty charge went nowhere.

Life was made uncomfortable for my family as well. During this period I was accosted in an arena parking lot by a couple of hoodlums who warned that I was going to get hurt if I didn't keep my mouth shut and mind by own business. They tried to intimate me. They were damn lucky I didn't have a hockey stick in my hand. I reported the incident to the police and to the Rocky Mountain association. It may have been merely bluster, but Stephanie and I ensured Jocya was protected at school.

Naturally, all of these attempts to make me back off failed. Desperate to make me pay, in mid-November 2011 the association suspended me. In his communication to parents, Randy Kanai, president of the Rocky Mountain RoughRiders, wrote: "The Rocky Mountain Roughriders Board of Directors met earlier this week. After much debate and careful consideration, the Board of Directors have made the difficult decision to suspend Coach Paris from his duties effective immediately for code of conduct violations . . ."

The news of my suspension quickly spread across the Colorado minor sports community and drew a sharp response from the parents of players on my team. "John you have all our support," wrote one parent online. Another parent stated, "JPJ has built this team to exude character, hard work, and discipline. Until his return the U16 Roughriders will continue to play The Paris Way!" And still another replied, "A lot of players and parents on your side John. Hang in there. [My son] came out to [Colorado] to play for you, anything less is unacceptable."

Parents were ready to raise hell and put heat on the association. They began demanding refunds and asking for releases to allow their sons to go play elsewhere if I was not coaching. No doubt this pressure from parents was a big reason why the association about a week later said it would lift my suspension and reinstate me — with certain conditions. The conditions were petty, childish things meant to demean and curtail me. I would not acquiesce to such crap. I refused to play their game. I had a lawyer compose a letter to the RoughRiders stating that I would return only if I was able to coach in exactly the manner as before the suspension. (It likely didn't hurt my cause that the lawyer was one of Denver's best and was working *pro bono* thanks to a request from the president of Oprah Winfrey's Harpo organization.)

The association relented and I returned, functioning as always under USA hockey rules. I departed after the end of the hockey season. They didn't ask me back despite the fact that mine was the most successful development program they had. Apparently that didn't matter. In any case, Stephanie and I were ready for a change. Denver's altitude was affecting both Jocya and me. It was time for the Paris family to take some deep breaths someplace else. We moved to Omaha, Nebraska, as a sort of temporary measure, where I coached the city's elite U18 team. Several Colorado players followed me there, leaving their friends and family behind and changing schools just so I could continue to be their hockey coach. Quite a compliment.

* * *

On May 30, 2012, Zachary Meints, twenty-four, pled guilty to one count of felony Internet sexual exploitation. He had been originally charged, in December 2011, with five counts, but the prosecution dropped the other charges in exchange for pleading guilty to the single count.

On August 3, 2012, Meints was sentenced to ten years of sex offender intensive supervised probation. This included close monitoring of his personal relationships and regular polygraph tests to ensure he did not act "in a hypersexual way." In addition, he was required to register as a sex offender for ten years beyond his probation. Finally, he was also sentenced to perform 150 hours of community service and encouraged to help investigators as they probed for other issues in local minor hockey.

It could have been much worse for Meints. Internet exploitation of a child — a class-four felony — has a presumptive sentence of two to six years in prison. In a request for a more lenient sentence, his attorney told the court that Meints had been abducted and sexually assaulted at gunpoint when he was in sixth grade. Meints's abductor warned him he would kill his family if he ever told anyone, so he kept it secret until after his arrest in Boulder. Court was also told he suffered severe post-traumatic stress disorder because of his ordeal, which had stunted his emotional maturity to the point he did not know he was harming the boys on his team with his behaviour. Meints's parents said they didn't think he would survive prison because, given his resulting fear of confinement, he might kill himself.

The details of his activity with the young hockey players were revealed in court and rocked the entire Colorado sports community. Meints had sent thousands of explicit text messages and Internet messages to children during the two years he worked as a coach with the Boulder hockey club. The prosecution stated that it was not a "one-time mistake or error [but rather] years of contact with many, many children. This is a serious case that involves a long pattern of behaviour."

According to a warrant affidavit, Boulder police began their investigation into Meints in September 2011 after a fellow coach — actually, me — alerted the FBI to suspicious behaviour. Boulder detectives interviewed thirteen teenagers, who in turn led investigators to other possible victims. Five of them were under the age of fifteen when Meints sent inappropriate messages. Those children were the basis for the original five felony counts.

In the interviews, the victims said Meints would begin by texting or Facebook chatting with them about hockey, but he would soon turn the conversation toward sexual topics. The victims said Meints would ask them questions about the size of their penis and how often they masturbated. They also said Meints would talk to them about watching pornography and using sex toys. Several of the victims also said Meints asked them to masturbate while communicating with them online and requested pictures of them naked. Most of the victims say they either deleted their Facebook accounts or just stopped answering Meints. It appeared, from the affidavit, that only one of the victims had sent a picture to Meints. At least one of the victims said Meints instructed him how to delete the messages. Police also believe Meints hacked into a family member's Facebook account to continue his conversation with the victims after some of them stopped answering his messages.

However, no player said Meints had made physical advances or sent pictures of himself.

The affidavit said Meints told investigators he engaged in some "locker room talk," and that it was common to do so. He said he occasionally asked players, "How big are you?" or "Are you big?" and that he twice jokingly challenged players to "masturbation races" and to send him pictures once they were done as proof.

Sickening stuff.

Four parents of Meints's victims spoke during the court procedures. They focused on how the former coach violated their trust and the trust of their children. The judge took this into account when passing sentence and spoke about a coach's delicate relationship with his young players. "[Your players] see you at the rink and you're friendly, you're their coach; they look up to you, and then at night they're getting these very graphic Facebook messages about sexual conduct. You just mixed a lot of good and bad things for them."

Echoing exactly what I had been telling parents from the outset of this mess, the deputy district attorney told the court that "the message here is parents talk to their kids and report things."

* * *

This regrettable incident has two noteworthy postscripts.

The first is that the parents of the perpetrator were also victims. I didn't know the Meints family well, although I was close to the younger Meints son, a very nice young man who I coached in hockey schools for four or five summers. I knew the parents only well enough to say hello when I saw them. Nevertheless, I found Mike and Marcia Meints to be good people, respected in the community, helpful and giving. They had always been there for sports in the region — some board members were close acquaintances — and I believe it was the association's responsibility to reach out to them early on to let them know what it *appeared* their son was doing. At least it would have given the Meints a chance to react. I think they deserved the opportunity. Instead, the Meints, like everyone involved in this mess, were left to pick up the pieces at the end.

In court, Marcia Meints said her son was not a hardened criminal, and tearfully explained she was "trying to save the life of my child." When it was his turn Mike Meints looked over at the victims' parents and expressed how sorry he and the other members of his family were for the damage inflicted by his son. He offered to help the victims in any way he could. To this offer, one of the victims' parents gently said, "Thank you."

The second postscript is actually good news.

In March 2013, Colorado Governor John Hickenlooper signed Senate Bill 13-012, which addresses the reporting of suspected child abuse and neglect by youth sports organizations. It expanded and strengthened existing legislation. The bill's preamble said it was "vital that persons employed by sports organizations or programs have a legal duty to report any suspicion of or observation of child abuse or neglect, including unlawful sexual behaviour, on the part of an employee of the organization or program or a participant in the program." As a result of this bill there is now less ambiguity within minor sports programs — all suspicions of child abuse must be brought forward. It's the law.

It was a bumpy road for many people, including me. But seeing this bill passed was extremely gratifying. I am proud of any part I may have had in it.

CHAPTER 15
Reflections

I used to play this game of rating coaches. It was in the 1970s and early 1980s when I was sick and recovering, by then reconciled with the fact that if I was going to make my life in hockey it would be as a coach, not a player.

On the wall in my bedroom I had tacked a huge, multi-coloured grid where I listed the names of current and past NHL coaches. Bowman, Arbour, Blake, Abel, Imlach, Shero and the like, along with lesser-known coaches. I constantly added to the list as I studied these men and hunted for a tiny secret or a small gem of knowledge. Drawing on my experience as a cost analyst, every coach received a grade in a variety of categories. For example, I gave Bowman a high grade in "using the media" for how effectively he used the press to indirectly get his messages across to his players. There were more than a dozen categories, including line-matching, line-changing, inserting players, teaching ability and so on. Frankly, one way or another, on paper or mentally, I had been doing a similar exercise since my minor hockey days in Windsor. And this continued even as I met, coached against and befriended some of the best in the sport. Here are some random thoughts on some of the very best:

Jacques "Coco" Lemaire

I knew Jacques Lemaire as a junior and then watched him perform as one of the more complete players of the Montreal Canadiens dynasty in the 1970s. Defensively, he would skillfully reduce the ice surface and remove options for attacking teams. On offence, he had an overpowering slapshot and for several seasons centred the best line in hockey with Steve Shutt and Guy Lafleur. Jacques walked away from his playing career early and became one of the most successful coaches of his generation. I would run into him all the time when he was with the Canadiens organization in the 1980s. It was impossible not to. He would be at a midget or junior game every night, it seemed. Jacques is poised and smart, but a little nervous inside and still uncomfortable in the media glare. Unless you know him, he can be dry, but he appreciates a good joke and I would enjoy watching him sometimes toy with people a little. Behind the bench he quickly adjusts to game situations and in a dressing room he gets immediate respect. Down deep he is actually offence-minded, but with the Minnesota Wild and the New Jersey Devils he was criticized for being boring and obsessed with defence. Still, I doubt any other coach would have extracted more from those teams. Jacques teaches for constant improvement and to win. He holds his players responsible and no lazy player has ever been happy under him. He also selects excellent supporting staff. Some day his detractors may come to appreciate his brilliance.

Mike Keenan

It was the summer of 1988. I was at a Roger Neilson hockey seminar at University of Windsor, standing out in a hallway taking a break when I noticed Mike Keenan walk in through the side door.

He had just recently been fired by the Philadelphia Flyers, and as I watched him interact with others I noted he lacked his usual self-assurance. Something happens to you the first time you are fired, especially at the major junior or pro levels. It's a bit humiliating and you feel as if everyone has eyes on you. That day at the seminar I was relating to what Mike was feeling and wanted to give him a pat on the back. I started to walk over. He saw me coming and I could see him thinking: *Who's this short black guy coming my way?* I shook his hand. "You did a great job in Philly," I said. "You'll bounce back. Another job will come up. And remember, you're the man!" He looked at me a little quizzically and nodded. He didn't say much but I'm certain he appreciated the encouragement. Keenan indeed bounced back quickly and signed to coach the Chicago Blackhawks a few weeks later. And then many other teams over the years. Eight times hired, eight times fired. Likely an NHL record. He was a very demanding coach and as a result always had a short shelf life. Still, for a time at least, Mike Keenan improved every team he touched.

Pat Burns

Pat Burns was a good guy — period. An ex-cop who could curse like a pirate, Pat was a stern coach. But he was fair. If you were honest and tried your best, he'd be your biggest supporter. He was with the Hull Olympics of the QMJHL when I met him in the mid-1980s. The very first words I ever heard him say were directed at a player during an Olympics practice: "Get your fuckin' butt movin'!" I was standing by the boards. He nodded at me and then continued skating by. After Hull, he moved to the American Hockey League and then to the NHL as head coach in Montreal, Toronto, Boston and New Jersey, where he won the Stanley Cup in 2003.

I ran into him in many places over the years and always enjoyed spending time with him, especially at conferences and courses. Pat thought the mandatory certification courses we took together were a problem for aspiring coaches. "This sort of thing may influence people to make the wrong decision in the heat of the moment," he once told me. "Stuff happens quickly on the ice and a coach has to react quickly. You can't say, 'Wait a minute, I have to think about this seminar I took.'" (He had a point, but I liked seminars and conferences because they helped share knowledge and occasionally changed attitudes.)

One time Pat and I were having a casual conversation when he volunteered, "You know John, I said some things I likely shouldn't have about different people and different races. You know what it's like when people are talkin' . . ."

I admired Pat for this. We talked about it a bit. He could be gruff, but he was also bright and sensitive. How many people come out and tell you that they said something racist?

Pat died in 2010 after a long battle with cancer. It was an enormous loss for the sport.

Bob Hartley

I first saw Bob Hartley when I was working as a scout for the St. Louis Blues and he was behind the bench of the tier-2 junior team in Hawkesbury, Ontario. A firm, hands-on coach, and you just knew he was going places. Today he has a resume that includes a QMJHL title (Laval Titan, 1993) and a Stanley Cup (Colorado Avalanche, 2001). His time in the Q overlapped mine and we slowly came to know one another by visiting for a few minutes before our games. (While this happens from time to time in the pros, it's rare that junior coaches share this courtesy.) Bob and I roomed together for a couple of summers when travelling with Mario Lemieux's hockey school. He was very easy-going and a great guy to chum around with. Goofy things seemed to happen when we were together. We went golfing and ended up searching for our balls in a snake pit; after a Dodgers game in Los Angeles we traipsed all over a huge parking lot for more than an hour looking for our car and finally found it only after the entire lot had cleared out; and outside of LA we were conned by a guy at a gas station claiming his car was broken down and his children were starving. Angry about being conned? Not Bob. He never sweats the small stuff. I think that's one reason he's been so successful.

Ken Hitchcock / Jacques Martin

I would have loved to have been a fly on the wall to hear the conversations when Ken Hitchcock and Jacques Martin roomed together during the 2010 Olympics. Two such different personalities: Hitch the extrovert, Jacques the stoic.

Hitchcock is always well-prepared and a workhorse. He's certainly one of the most successful and interesting coaches around. During his Stanley Cup years in Dallas he had a tense and very public relationship with superstar Brett Hull. Hull was a lot to handle, but I always knew he would never get the best of Hitch. Hitch's weight problem is no secret and it has been used against him in the past. I've heard ignorant jokes about it and once I almost got into a fight over it. (It happened — again — at a seminar where some guys were loudly cutting up Ken. I told one of them that I'd knock the hell out of him if he said another word. "Why don't you say something to Hitchcock's face? Aren't you the same guys kissin' up to him earlier this morning?" Embarrassed, they slithered away.)

A final note about Hitch: when he was coaching the Dallas Stars I called him and left a message asking for his opinion about something, hoping he'd get back to me sometime when he wasn't busy. He called back right away, even though he was in the middle of the Stanley Cup finals and had a game in a few hours. That's Hitch.

Jacques Martin is a wonderful coach who takes care of those around him. Over his nine seasons in Ottawa he skillfully directed a potent, young team and a new franchise to a higher level, while driving the local media crazy with his flat, cautious answers. I worked with Jacques at Mario Lemieux's hockey school, and even babysat his kids on occasion. He's a very neat and orderly person and I never once saw a crease in his clothes, a speck of dust on his shoes or a single hair out of place. His teams tended to reflect this type of orderliness and preparation. When he was with the Senators, Jacques once mentioned he had a position for me, but for some reason it never materialized. Too bad. I would have liked working with him.

Mike Babcock

Mike Babcock's status as one of the top coaches in the game was confirmed when he was selected to coach Canada's 2010 and 2014 Olympic hockey teams. Mike is one intense individual. He's as straightforward as they come. He's also loyal to his friends and a very adaptable coach, as he demonstrated when he moved from Anaheim to Detroit. Mike and I talked mostly during seminars, especially when he was coaching university and major junior. One time we had just barely said hello when he looked me in the eye and said, "I am friends with Réal Paiement, the coach you were hired to replace in Granby." I looked right back at him. "That's nice, Mike, I am too." He smiled. It was the perfect response and showed him that I'm as no-BS as he is.

Michel Bergeron

Michel Bergeron was fiery and intense when he played and he was fiery and intense when he coached. We played junior hockey in Quebec at the same time and there was no doubt why he was called *Le Tigre* (The Tiger). On the ice we battled and hacked each other almost every shift, but *Le Tigre* never once called me a name. He's a little guy, an in-your-face type of person and I doubt they fully appreciated or completely

With superstar Mario Lemieux at one of Mario's hockey schools, in the 1990s.

understood his strong personality in New York. Joey Bucchino, then the Rangers assistant general manager, had a tiff or two with him. A little secret: despite appearances, Michel would never *completely* lose it behind the bench. He could be a wild man but there'd be a strategic purpose for his antics. I learned a lot about Michel's coaching style and tactics when I was scouting for the Sorel Black Hawks in the 1970s. His Trois-Rivières teams were well-prepared and hard to play against because he found ways to ignite his players. In the 1980s he enjoyed an excellent stretch coaching the Quebec Nordiques and I often wondered what might have happened if the Canadiens had given him a chance. Few dull moments, I'm sure.

* * *

Over the years I have spoken at many conferences and worked in more hockey schools than I can count, including schools for Mario Lemieux and former Canadiens star Pierre Mondou. I've also consulted or coached with hockey federations in Switzerland, Sweden, Finland, France and England, as well as in the United States and Canada. Some of this has paid well, some I've done for free. Without exception, I've always learned from the experience.

Especially educational was my time with IMG (International Management Group), an American-based global sports and media enterprise. IMG is divided into several divisions, one being IMG Academy, a multi-sport training institute in Florida mainly for younger athletes. Clients have included baseball, football and basketball elite, plus tennis stars such as the Williams sisters and Maria Sharapova. The IMG campus featured more than a hundred tennis courts, two large cafeterias, a baseball field, soccer fields, a football field, a golf course, a sports psychology unit and a state-of-the-art training institute. In addition there was a modern medical facility, condos and apartments, and a private school called Pendleton Academy.

IMG added hockey to its list of sports in 2000 and that year I accepted an offer to help build the program along with hockey director Chip McCarthy and a handful of other well-qualified instructors. In my role as assistant director of the hockey school I was exposed to disciplines such as sales, admissions and marketing, and even watched how vacations were planned. Although this was all a wonderful classroom for me, IMG didn't have a hockey arena on site and we had to bus each day to a rink a few miles away.

To build the prestige of the hockey program I suggested that IMG reach out to a sure-fire future star. And it just so happened I had someone in mind: a fellow Nova Scotian named Sidney Crosby, then about thirteen years old.

Sidney and his parents agreed to come down and take a look at the IMG program. They arrived along with Pat Brisson, who was then acting as an unofficial advisor to the family. We were having a nice tour of the site until outside the training centre one of the trainers — a zealous fellow named Pete Bommatario — began ranting about the merits of the program. At one point Bommatario screamed, "We train monsters here!" A real hard-core pitch. This sort of thing seldom goes over well with folks from "down east" and I cringed as I watched the Crosbys quietly absorb all this. Fortunately, Sidney's dad, Troy, who also played junior in the Montreal Canadiens organization, was comfortable enough with me to ask — under his breath — if I could have a few private words with his son. So after the tour I walked over and sat down with Sidney, an extraordinarily nice kid who was serious and detailed about everything he did. His brow was furrowed.

"I'm worried, Coach," he said in a low voice.

"What about?"

"Well, I don't want to be muscle-bound or lose my smoothness or my balance. Coach, I don't want to be a *monster*."

I chuckled a little and assured him that no one there was going to transform him into the Incredible Hulk. I explained to him how he needed to get stronger, and that Pete Bommatario was merely tossing out a term more common to football. Sidney seemed to relax a bit after our chat. (What I didn't say was that I was not perfectly happy with the training for hockey players at IMG. I wanted more game-situation agility, balance and quickness combined with strength training. In addition, I was suggesting that things such as peripheral vision instruction and on-ice verbal communication be included, along with an individual biomechanical analysis for each player.)

Also during this visit Troy Crosby asked for my thoughts on Pat Brisson, whom the Crosbys were considering as Sidney's agent. I was unequivocal. I told them they would not find anybody better. I had known Pat since he was very young, when he played in the minor hockey system in Quebec. I knew his background. Nothing came to Pat for free. He had to earn everything he had and he wasn't ashamed to get his hands dirty. I told the Crosbys that he could be trusted and he'll take great care of their son. They eventually selected Pat and its been a very successful relationship. Brisson is now one of the most powerful agents in professional sports, as co-head of the hockey division of Creative Artists Agency with partner J.P. Barry.

IMG Academy suspended its hockey program in 2003.

* * *

I'm proud to be a hockey coach. Unfortunately, the designation of "coach" is too easily bestowed on wannabes and amateurs who have not paid the price or made the sacrifices required of the professional hockey coach. The professional is easy to identify.

It's how he talks about the game, how he dissects a situation, how he carries himself, how he addresses a fellow professional. A true professional rarely denigrates another coach because he knows what it's like on the inside. Fans can pretend they are coaches when they go to a game — they paid their money. But unless you've been in a pro dressing room as a coach, unless you've *lived* it, you are a fool to assume you know better.

I'm also proud to be black, but even if I wasn't it wouldn't matter. Nature made the call. When I began, a black man in hockey was a novelty. Of the six teams in the NHL in the 1960s, none had a black player on its roster. That fact alone prepared me for a bumpy road ahead. I've tried to never let race factor in my hockey life, although when others made it an issue I had little choice but to respond.

I'll never really know if the colour of my skin was the main reason I never coached in the NHL. It's reasonable to guess that my race did not help. But there were other reasons, too. I made strategic mistakes. A few times I zigged when I should have zagged.

Perhaps my biggest error was not remaining as a scout with the St. Louis Blues, choosing instead to continue on as a coach in the QMJHL. I was really in a great position with the Blues, learning from top scouts and soaking in an enormous amount about the business of hockey. I was almost certain to move up within the Blues' organization, and that could have led to something big.

Another factor not operating in my favour was something intrinsic to my personality: I was not much of a self-promoter. I have a hard time blowing my own horn. Maybe that's the Maritimer in me. When I was coaching I assumed that my performance would be recognized and automatically lead to other openings. I assumed wrong. I've since realized how important it is to market yourself and to maintain a presence. After even a short time away from the action, you can be forgotten. You need to maintain contacts and let it be known to a wide circle of people that you are still out there, still enthusiastic, still able. Doing that sort of thing is an effort for me.

Looking back, I should have cultivated more political skills and paid homage to the reality of the "old-boy network." Or even had a posse, a small group of friends to methodically spread the word and put the bug into the ear of key people. Lots of coaches do this, and it works. I trusted the system too much and maybe trusted people too much. I tend to believe people rather than listen to my intuition. It's a personal weakness and I've been burned plenty over the years because of it.

Another impediment to me coaching in the NHL was how I was categorized. The late coaching icon Roger Nielson once told me, "John, never say that you are a *defensive* coach. Anything but that, especially when you're looking for a coaching job."

"Roger," I replied, "maybe I can also say that I'm not really black."

He laughed. "One-nothing for you."

Roger was right, however. I was recognized for my defensive systems and this may not have helped my case in the eyes of NHL general managers. Even more, I was known as a player's coach. I couldn't imagine doing the job any other way. I relate best to coaches like Don Cherry and Ted Nolan. Both were NHL coaches of the year, both engendered enormous loyalty from their players, both clashed with management, both lost their jobs.

I never closed my door to a player. I always had time for them and I always sought to know them as individuals, outside of hockey. My players trusted me and — regardless of what transpired between us — I would not betray that trust. I never went to management when a player missed curfew or had personal problems. Instead, I'd sit down with the player. Unless it was something very serious that I couldn't directly help with, we kept it in-house. Many of my former players are still in touch with me and I'm sure that's a big reason why.

* * *

Today, race is less an issue in hockey, although there are still closed minds and pockets of bigotry in the sport. Thanks to trail-blazers like Willie O'Ree and Herb Carnegie, and more recent stars such as Grant Fuhr and Jarome Iginla, a wave of excellent young black players has emerged, led by Norris Trophy winner P.K. Subban and the American-born 2013 first-round draft choice Seth Jones. The number of NHL players of colour is steadily increasing as more black youth get a chance to play minor hockey. This growth will continue as the NHL markets black stars, and blacks — such as Hockey Night in Canada's erudite analyst Kevin Weekes — become more prominent in the hockey media.

Over the years I've coached and mentored many black players. Some people suggest I favoured black players. Absolutely untrue. I treated all my players the same, judging them only by their ability, character and willingness to work. (Proof of this was Marc Tardif, a tough winger I inherited in Atlanta. The Knights and the Tampa Bay Lightning had concluded that Tardif was never going to be a viable NHL player — an assessment I agreed with. Yet I kept him around and got him as much playing time as situations would allow. Otherwise he would have been watching most games from the press box. The next season he was sent down to the East Coast Hockey League where he had a few good seasons. At the end of his playing career, Tardif told a reporter that he blamed me for his lack of progress, implying that as a black man he should have been treated better by a black coach. This upset me. Not only did Tardif overlook the fact that coaches do not make such decisions alone, but he should have known that skin colour merits no special treatment with this coach. Never.)

However, due to my life experience I was in the unique position to talk truthfully — often bluntly — to black players about special challenges that loomed for them. Mike Ribeiro, who has had a long NHL career, was a case in point. During the NHL lockout in 2004, when I was in Laval, Mike, who is of Portuguese descent with light-brown skin, would come around and skate with us. In those days he was exhibiting a lot of the flash and self-assuredness that successful young men often display, especially in how he dressed and with his open, confident mannerisms. I told him that while there was nothing inherently wrong in all this, it's not exactly what his team, the Montreal Canadiens, would embrace given the traditional nature of that organization. I also explained that other players, including his teammates, would give him a hard time. "Walk softly," I advised. "Your talent alone isn't going to be enough. No matter what you do, you're going to be judged. *Really* judged."

Fortunately, in the NHL today players are given more freedom to be themselves and to reflect their racial and national heritages. This is a change for the better, but the responsibility still rests with individuals to show respect for others. There was also something else I conveyed to the young black men I talked with: never turn away from something you know is wrong. Stand up and confront it. Persevere. Will you pay a price? Maybe. But wrong is never right, and you'll sleep well at night. I hope most of them heeded this advice.

* * *

I feel privileged. Hockey has provided me with an education, travel, a good income and great memories. Regrets? Sure. We all have them.

I'm disappointed that I was never a head coach in the NHL, but it was a dream, not a priority. I fell just short of making it, although I had chances to be an NHL assistant coach. I also regret that I never played a regular season NHL game, either with the Montreal Canadiens, Chicago Blackhawks or Philadelphia Flyers.

I am also sorry I continued to play when I was ill. Bad, bad decision. I was sick for years, yet I pushed aside the dizziness, the weakness, the fatigue, the bleeding, the diarrhea and the stabbing pain and allowed ambition and pride to override common sense.

However, my biggest regret is personal in nature. It relates to my family. Specifically, that in giving so much to hockey, sometimes Louise and Chantal were neglected. As a young, aspiring coach I didn't manage my time well, and the imbalance always seemed to favour hockey, with its demanding schedule and long hours. It was the only way I knew how to progress in my career. Given the chance, I would do things differently. I now advise young men to take care of their wives and children, to avoid the temptations and the distractions, and to seek a healthy balance in their lives.

Today, the most precious thing I have are my children, Jocya, Chantal and Robert, and my wife, Stephanie. Sometimes I daydream about one day having all of my children and grandchildren on a beach somewhere in the Caribbean for a big family reunion. I'd be cooking on a barbeque, while music blares and kids play. And all day long no one would utter a single word about hockey.

* * *

I am proud of my hockey career. I was the first black professional hockey coach and honoured to have been the one. Likewise the first black professional general manager, the first black professional director of hockey operations and the first black professional team vice-president. Winning the Turner Cup and the Air Canada Cup were major highlights for me, certainly. I'd love to do it all over again. Not so for my intestinal trouble, my Hodgkin's disease and my heart attack. Once is enough, thank you very much. But even if life should throw more my way, be it hardship or illness or bigotry, I would stand up and battle back. That's me.

With my father, Buster Paris, at my induction into the Nova Scotia Sport Hall of Fame, 2005. A proud moment for both of us.

As I move into the next phase of my life, I feel great. I continue to do occasional motivational and anti-drug speeches using my training as a certified sports psychologist. My passion for hockey remains. I'm still in the game because, frankly, I've still *got* game. I know more about hockey and more about coaching than ever. I'm even developing my own brand, which I'm calling The Paris Way. Simply stated, it's a series of products and philosophies that reflect my approach to the sport. It's exciting for me to share what I have learned.

As I said, ain't no quit in this dog.

APPENDIX 1
First-, Second- and Third-Rounders

Over the years I have coached many players who were drafted in the first, second or third round of the NHL entry draft. Several went on to have excellent professional careers. A few became NHL stars.

Player	Year / Round	Overall Pick	Position	Team	Relationship
Reggie Savage	1988 / 1	15th	F	Washington	Midget AAA (Richelieu)
Éric Charron	1988 / 1	20th	D	Montreal	QMJHL (Trois-Rivières)
Martin Lapointe	1991 / 1	10th	F	Detroit	Midget AAA (Lac St-Louis)
Philippe Boucher	1991 / 1	13th	D	Buffalo	QMJHL (Granby)
Stéphane Fiset	1988 / 2	24th	G	Quebec	Midget AAA (Richelieu)
Steve Larouche	1989 / 2	41st	F	Montreal	Midget AAA (Richelieu) / QMJHL (Trois-Rivières)
Ryan Hughes	1990 /2	22nd	F	Quebec	Midget AAA (Lake St. Louis)
Etienne Belzile	1990 /2	41st	D	Calgary	Midget AAA (Lake St. Louis)
Paul Brousseau	1992 / 2	28th	F	Quebec	Midget AAA (Lake St. Louis)
José Théodore	1994 / 2	44th	G	Montreal	QMJHL (St-Jean)
Georges Laraque	1995 / 2	31st	F	Edmonton	QMJHL (St-Jean)

Player	Year / Round	Overall Pick	Position	Team	Relationship
Jason Doig	1995 / 2	34th	D	Winnipeg	QMJHL (St-Jean)
Steve Veilleux	1987 / 3	45th	D	Vancouver	QMJHL (Trois-Rivières)
Stéphane Beaureguard	1988 / 3	52nd	G	Winnipeg	Midget AAA (Richelieu)
Dominic Roussel	1988 / 3	63rd	G	Philadelphia	QMJHL (Trois-Rivières)
Robert Guillet	1990 / 3	60th	F	Montreal	Midget AAA (Richelieu)
Yves Sarault	1991 / 3	61st	F	Montreal	QMJHL (St-Jean)
Patrick Traverse	1992 / 3	50th	D	Ottawa	QMJHL (St-Jean)

Other notable players I have coached, trained or advised over the years include (listed with their draft team):

- Sidney Crosby, F (Pittsburgh)
- Pierre Larouche, F (Pittsburgh)
- Pierre Mondou, F (Montreal)
- Marc-André Fleury, G (Pittsburgh)
- Daniel Brière, F (Phoenix)
- Alex Steen, F (Toronto)
- Dainius Zubrus, F (Philadelphia)
- Lucien DeBlois, F (NY Rangers)
- Cory Cross, D (Tampa Bay)
- Jesse Bélanger, F (Montreal)
- Boris Rousson, G (NY Rangers)
- Jason Marshall, D (St. Louis)
- Eric Dubois, D (Quebec)
- J. F. Quintin, F (Minnesota)
- Andre Brassard, D (NY Islanders)
- Stan Drulia, F (Tampa Bay)
- Claude Barthe, D (Detroit)
- Michel Picard, F (Hartford)
- Marc Rodgers, F (Detroit)
- Jeff Toms, F (New Jersey)

APPENDIX 2
Ten Commandments for Coaching Success

These commandments are general principles and important qualities for coaching success. There are many such lists. This one is mine. These are things I have learned over my career and that have worked well for me. The "commandments" listed here apply whether you are a professional coach or are behind the bench in minor hockey.

- **Behave with integrity.** Your most precious asset is your reputation. Be honest with others — and yourself.
- **Always be positive.** Keep that positive vision. Positive thoughts usually result in positive outcomes. Remember that your most effective instrument is your smile.
- **Ensure your personal life is in order.** Continually strive to balance career and family.
- **Avoid vanity.** Do not constantly compare yourself to coaches at a higher level. This leads to resentment and wastes mental energy.
- **Make player development your main focus.** If this is not your overriding goal, then re-examine your reasons for wanting to be a coach.
- **Have a strategy.** Especially for player development, this is a must. One comprehensive performance tool for players is "The Wheel of Excellence," by Terry Orlick, a professor of human kinetics at

the University of Ottawa. Abide by it. It's close to foolproof.

- **Be resourceful.** Not all problems are simple. Become creative, do research and welcome others who have expertise.
- **Understand that nothing is more important than a player's attitude.** Openly encourage the virtues of being an unselfish teammate and a disciplined, responsible athlete.
- **Treat the media with courtesy** (mainly for junior, college and professional hockey coaches). Always be clear and polite. Stand behind your words.
- **Help parents keep things in perspective** (mainly for minor hockey coaches). Mostly, this means their child's hockey abilities. Encourage parents to enjoy the moment and be positive with their child — and with his or her coach.

Posing with the Turner Cup.

ACKNOWLEDGEMENTS

Many extraordinary people have helped me during my coaching career and my time as a player; others have been there for me during difficult periods in my life. Some of these people are already named in this book. Unfortunately, to thank everyone, especially all my wonderful family members and all the great folks in my two homes — Windsor, Nova Scotia, and Sorel-Tracy, Quebec — would take another book. Nevertheless, I'd like to express special gratitude to the following people (in no particular order):

To my sister Faye and my brothers Percy, Mike and Cecil as well as Carol-Ann, Marvin (Pop) and Lorne who became like siblings to me, for youthful days and the fun we had as a family.

To Polly and Roy Redden, for opening their home to me as a youth and for providing a protective blanket when needed.

To Howard Dill and family, for allowing my dad and I to skate on "the pond," and for always taking time to spend time with me.

To Jack Dill and family, for keeping in touch and making certain that I made a few after-school or summer dollars, even if there was no real work to be done.

To Uncle Junior and family, who allowed me to live with them for awhile, and to Aunt Mindy (Vivian) Hamilton, who has always been there for me. Also to uncles, aunts and cousins on both sides of the family: Edith, Viola, Dorothy, Maude, Sarah, Mable, Janey, Evelyn, Louise and Florence for making my youth full of love, laughter and joy.

To friends Ellis Redden, Brian Redden, Jackie Payne, Billy Boyd, Joe Robertson, Kenny Rafuse, Rusty Leighton, Delbert Caldwell and Terry Guptel for much-appreciated friendships.

To Charles and Jenny Haley, for making certain that I never was in need of anything, for those envelopes with surprises in them, and for the words, "John, come on in. We were just sitting down to eat."

To cousins Brian Johnson, Lonnie, Garnet, Harrison, Ruby, Missy, Elroy, Phil, David (Skip), Gayle, Sandra, Ricky, Tammy, Debbie, Lillian and Andre for being themselves.

To Mrs. Barb Cochran, for never backing away when there was a need for someone to stand up and speak the truth, and to her husband Red, with apologies for sometimes eating more than him.

To Mrs. Terris, her son Harry and grandson Murray, for allowing me the run of the house and always looking out for me.

To Dr. Garth Vaughan, for his support and expertise.

To Dr. Robert Leland and family, John Schick and family, Mike Gempeler and family, George Gruber and family, the Hillis family, Bob Bloomquist, Mr. and Mrs. Chuck Daugherty, and Zachary, Hanna and Mike Desjardins.

To Wayne Brown, for his computer-like sports mind.

To Norman, John and Ethel Campbell, who owned the corner store in Curry's Corner, for not minding that they never made much profit off me.

To the Harvey and the Payne families, for their friendship and kindness.

To life-long friend Bonnie Doran and her family, who always kept me out of trouble.

To Doc Rogers, arena manager in Windsor, who allowed me and others to be rink rats and not have to pay for skating sessions or to watch intermediate or senior hockey games, and to Carey Ross, for ensuring I had extra ice at the Windsor arena and for his kind words of encouragement.

To fellow Nova Scotian Al MacIsaac, vice-president and special assistant to president of the Chicago Blackhawks, for being there for me.

To Scotty Bowman, perhaps the greatest coach the game has known, and a man who speaks the truth, for fortifying what my parents had told me about life.

To Lucette (Desmarais) Tellier, who is like another sister to me, for being there through good and bad times; and to the entire Desmarais family, for whom "thank you" will never be enough.

To Michel Péloquin and Marc Guevremont, of the Sorel-Tracy sports and recreation department, for their trust and respect, and for always standing beside me.

To Charlemagne Péloquin, director of the St-Joseph-de-Sorel sports and recreation department, for giving me my first head-coaching job and for always having my back.

To Mr. and Mrs. Lequin, parents of Daniel (a fine sports reporter and marathon runner), for their incredible hospitality when I was extremely ill.

To Max Goudreau a junior hockey teammate and close friend, for his deep and well-timed support; and to his wife Rolande and daughter Josée, to whom I am still Uncle John.

To Réal Lemieux, my friend and business partner, who passed far too soon.

To Marc and Nathalie Tellier, who never missed showing me their love and their care.

To Lucien Labine, of Hoey Limited, the plumbing contractor who hired me as paymaster and office clerk, for allowing me to pursue my studies at the same time.

To Yves Proulx, of Granby, for his integrity and friendship.

To Mario Deguise, president of Quebec Ice Hockey Federation, for convincing me to join his midget hockey program and then helping me pursue hockey studies.

To Jean Patenaude and family, for allowing me to live with them in Granby.

To Rodrigue Lemoyne, for always being in the background for me and allowing me to do player evaluation.

To Lucie, Jocya and Byanka Tremblay, just for being wonderful people.

To Marc, Lise, Benoit and Alain Guevremont; Gilles Côté, Gaëtan Picard, Robert Cartier, Jean Guy "Ti-Gus" Cournoyer, Pierre Desaillières and family, for all the good times.

To friends Claude St. Germain and Remi Raymond, for convincing me that I would be able to coach midget AAA despite my precarious health at the time.

To Ben and Nancy Walthall for their continuous support.

To Jay Jarvis, a friend in the true sense, for never requesting anything other than to know how I was.

To good friends the Rodiques family and to John and Irene Vlahos.

To assistant coaches Scotty Gordon and David Starman, for their honesty and competency.

Playing recreation hockey in Sorel-Tracy.

To Atlanta Knights colleagues Charles Felix, for being my friend, and Richard Adler and Joe Bucchino, for never looking at the hours when it came to helping me out. And also to Iris Bucchino (Joe's wife and an excellent cook), for her intelligence and honesty, and for never closing a door.

To Mr. and Mrs. Javors Lucas, for always having time for me.

To Mrs. Regina Middleton-McDuffie, manager of the Macon Centerplex and her wonderful staff.

To Lisa Peppin, my right-hand and hockey assistant general manager, who never counted her hours.

To Eddie Godding, my friend of fifty years, for just always being there, and to Henry Godding, for his joyfulness.

To Pat Manno and family, for their friendship.

To Mike Gempeler, of the United States Junior Development Program, for hiring me on a handshake basis only, no contract needed.

To Bryan Smith, of Rocky Mountain Hockey Schools, for his support when it counted.

To Rick, Renée, Nicole and Josh Ferreri, part of our extended family, for being who they are.

To Dr. James Fretwell and his wife Karen, true family friends, for so effectively looking out for my health.

To Todd Jones, outstanding teacher of hockey in Omaha, for being a friend and with no hidden agenda.

INDEX

Adler, Richard, 12–13, 124, 151, 154, 158, 162, 182
Allaire, François, 136, *137*
Atlanta Fire Ants, 144, 173
Atlanta Knights, 144, 149–65, *152, 157, 161,* 173–81, *183,* 209–11
  management team, 12–13, 124, 153–55, 158, 162, 164–65, 182
  racial issues, 145, 148, 164–65
  Turner Cup, 11–13, 159–65
  See also coaching positions
Babcock, Mike, 251
Barthe, Claude, 263
Beaureguard, Stéphane, 263
Bélanger, Jesse, 263
Beliveau, Jean, 43, 44
Belzile, Etienne, 262
Bergeron, Dean, 111
Bergeron, Michel, 43, 251–53
Berkman, David, 124, 154, 164
Blake, Toe (Hector), 44–45
Bossy, Michael, 130–31
Boucher, Michel, 111, 113–14
Boucher, Phillipe, *118*, 262
Bowman, Scott, 32–35, *34,* 128–29, 158, 246
Brassard, Andre, 263
Brière, Daniel, 263
Brisson, Pat, 254, 255
Brodeur, Martin, *139*
Brousseau, Paul, 262
Bucchino, Joe, 124, 155, 156, 163, *165,* 178, 180, 253
Burns, Pat, 248–49

Campeau, Christian, 101–2, 106, 149
career
  career decisions, 142–43, 172, 212–15, 225–26, 256–57
  career regrets, 259–60
  fans, 125, 156, 217
  health problems, 108–9, 260
  racial issues, 204–5, 256
  self-promotion, 223, 256
  See also coaching positions; scouting
career (as player)
  Knoxville Knights, 75–84
  Maisonneuve Braves, 40–55
  minor league hockey, 30–32
  Quebec Junior Aces, 64–67, 69
  scouted by Canadiens, 32–35
  Sorel Black Hawkes, 56–63, 67–68
  Thetford Mine Aces, 63–64
  training camps, 35–39, 69–75
Caron, Ron, 36, 133–34, 140
Cashman, Wayne, 179
Central Hockey League, 206–7
character, 137–38
Charles, Ray, 55
Charron, Éric, 149, 174, 262
child abuse, 232–45
"Chocolate Rocket", 41–42
Choyce, John, 57, 60
Cloutier, Gene, 49, 53, 53–54
Cloutier, Nichol, 141–42, *143,* 173
coaching
  bus rules, 208–9
  coaching philosophy, 156–58, 222, 261

combine testing, 103
development ideal, 138, 189, 227–28, 231
hazing, 112–13
media use, 158, 246
off-ice training, 101–2, 157–58
role of coach, 209–11, 255–57
roster issues, 162, 177
coaching positions
  Atlanta Fire Ants, 144, 173
  career decisions, 142–43, 172, 184–85
  Granby Bisons, 116–22
  hockey schools, 252–55
  IMG (International Management Group), 253–55
  Laval Chiefs, 198, 220–22
  midget AAA, 114–16
  Retigouche Tigers, 226–31
  Richelieu AAA midgets, 99–100
  Riverains du Richelieu, 101–7
  Rocky Mountains RoughRiders Hockey Club, 232–44
  Saint-Joseph-de-Sorel hockey association, 86
  Sorel Black Hawks, 86
  St-Jean Lynx, 123–24
  suggestion of, 45
  Trois-Rivières Draveurs, 108–14
  See also Atlanta Knights; Macon Whoopee
Corriveau, Len, 64–67
Corteau, Gilles, 142
Crisp, Terry, 178–79
Crosby, Sidney, 141, 254–55, 263
Cross, Cory, 162, 263

DeBlois, Lucien, 263
Déraspe, Marc-André,
  228–30
Desmarais, Louise, 62–63,
  87–88, 91, 95–98, 124–27
Doig, Jason, 263
Drulia, Stan, 163, 263
Dubois, Eric, 149, 263
Dumont, Paul, 66, 67

Eastern Hockey League,
  76–77
Egan, Pat "Boxcar", 77–78
Esposito, Phil, 144, 153,
  178, 179
Esposito, Tony, 178

family. *See* Paris family
Favell, Doug, 70, 74
Felix, Charles, 124, 154–55,
  173, 182
Ferguson, John, 44
Ferrano, Chris, 174
Ferrano, Peter, 174
Fiset, Stéphane, 262
Fletcher, Cliff, 36, 38
Fleury, Marc-André, 263

Gilbert, Ronald, 79–80, 82
goal scoring, 140
Gordon, Scotty, 181–82,
  183
Goudreau, Max, 59, 62, 86
Granby Bisons, 116–22,
  262
Greenlay, Mike, 158, 160,
  163
Gretzky, Brent, 175
Grossman, Jay, 172
Guillet, Robert, 263

Halifax Junior Canadiens,
  58–61
Halifax Mooseheads,
  212–14
Hampson, Teddy, 133–34,
  140, 142
Hanna, John "Junior", 70
Hartley, Bob, 249–50
Harvey, Doug, 129–31
hazing, 112–13
health problems
    career decisions, 108–9,
    260

Hodgkin's lymphoma,
  89–91
Knoxville Knights, 84
Maisonneuve Braves,
  47–50, 55
Quebec Junior Aces,
  65, 67
Retigouche Tigers, 230
Sorel Black Hawkes, 57,
  59, 68
Thetford Mine Aces,
  63–64
training camps, 39,
  69, 75
ulcerative colitis, 91,
  93–98
Hitchcock, Ken, 250
hockey, 10, 13–14, 116
  growing up, 28–39
hockey sense, 138, 141
Hodgkin's lymphoma,
  89–91
Holloway, Condredge, Jr.,
  203–4
Houston, Whitney, 166–70,
  216–17
Hughes, Ryan, 262

IMG (International
  Management Group),
  253–55
International Hockey
  League, 151–53

Keenan, Mike, 247–48
Knoxville Knights, 75–84

Lafleur, Guy, 64–65
Lalonde, Herve, 40–41,
  49–50
Lapointe, Martin, 262
Laraque, Georges, 123, 262
Larouche, Pierre, 131–32,
  263
Larouche, Steve, 101–2,
  106, 107, 113, 149, 161,
  262
Laval Chiefs, 198, 220–22,
  259
Lavigueur, René, 66–67
Lemaire, Jacques "Coco",
  247
Lemieux, Mario, *252*
Lemoyne, Rodrigue, 62,
  92–93, 131–32

Ligue Nord-Americaine du
  Hockey, 220–23
LiPuma, Chris, 149, 150,
  151, *152*, 163

Macon Whoopee, 184–98,
  206, 207–9, 211–12
  promotion, 187–88,
  189, 191
  racial issues, 193–97,
  199–205
  staff, 190–91
  See also coaching
  positions
Maisonneuve Braves,
  40–55
Marchand, Butch, 56
Marshall, Jason, 263
Martin, Jacques, 250–51
McDougall, Bill, 155, *161*,
  163
Meints, Zachary, 234–39,
  241–44
Mondou, Pierre, 263
Mongeon, Hughes, 119,
  121
Montreal Canadiens, 36,
  38, 41–44, 45–48, 50, 103
Montreal Jr. Canadiens, *34*
Mortson, Cleland "Keke",
  70–72, 186, 190
music, 52–55

near death experience,
  94–95
Nelson, Chris, 175–76
nicknames, 41–42
Nielson, Roger, 257
Nugent, Pat, 185, 211

off-ice training, 101–2,
  157–58
organized crime, 53–54,
  100

Paiement, Réal, 116, 117
Parent, Bernie, 70, 74
parental conduct, 115–16
Paris family, *19*, 20–24,
  22, 32
    birth of John Paris
    Jr., 13
    son Robert, 179–80
Paris, Annie, 19, 23–25,
  59–60, 122

Paris, Buster (John), 19, 24, 25–27, 34, 59–60, 126, 159, 226–27, *261*

Paris, Chantal, 91, 96–97, 142, *143*, 173

Paris, Joyca, 224–25, *225*

Paris, Marie-Chantal, 87–88

Paris, Miriam, 218

Paris, Stephanie, 219, *220*, 223, 225, *225*, 232–33

Paris Way, The, 261

Pelletier, Marcel, 74, 75

Peppin, Lisa, 190–91

Perron, Jean, 111–12

persistence, 10, 32, 59–60, 260–61

Philadelphia Flyers, 69–75, 223–24

physical conditioning, 139

Picard, Michel, 263

Pisiak, Ryan, 192–98

Plante, Jacques, 44

potential, 137–40

precognition, 19–20, 96, 97–98

Provost, Claude, 43

Quebec Junior Aces, 64–67, 69

Quintin, J.F., 263

racial issues
    Atlanta Knights, 145, 148, 164–65
    career, 204–5, 256
    growing up, 15–19, 23–25, 31–32, 51–52
    Knoxville Knights, 76, 78–83
    Macon Whoopee, 187, 193–97, 199–205
    professional hockey, 136, 249, 256, 258–59
    Richelieu AAA midgets, 99–100, 104
    Rocky Mountains RoughRiders Hockey Club, 239–40
    Sorel Black Hawkes, 58–62

Ray, Richard, 185, 211

Retigouche Tigers, 226–31

Ribeiro, Mike, 258–59

Richard, Henri "The Pocket Rocket", 43, 44

Richard, Maurice "The Rocket", 41, 45–48, 50

Riverains du Richelieu, 99–100, 101–7, 262–63

Rocky Mountains RoughRiders Hockey Club, 232–44

Rodgers, Marc, 117, 120, 121, 122, 263

Rondeau, Claude, 79–80, 82

Roussel, Dominic, 114, 263

Rousson, Boris, 117, 263

Ruel, André, 117, 120

Saint-Joseph-de-Sorel hockey association, 86

Salois, Roland, 131–32

Sarault, Yves, 263

Savage, Reggie, 101, 104–6, 180, 262

Savard, Denis, 132

scouting, 128–31, 134–36
    assessing potential, 137–41
    NHL scouting structure, 134
    other scouts, 32–36, 38, 92–93, 129–32
    position offers, 75, 142–43
    St. Louis Blues, 128, 132–34, 256
    See also career (as scout)

Selivanov, Alexei, 175

size, 138

Skategate, 192–98

Slap Shot (movie), 76, 205, 221

Smith, Murray "Moe", 30–31, 32

Sorel Black Hawkes, 56–63, 67–68, 86

St. Louis Blues, 128, 132–34, 256

Stamkos, Steve, 139

Starman, David, 190–91, 201, 207

Steen, Alex, 263

Stoyko, Bob, 79

Sutter, Rich, 176

Tampa Bay Lightening, 13, 178–79

Tardif, Marc, 258

Théodore, José, 123, 262

Thetford Mine Aces, 63–64

Toms, Jeff, 263

training camps, 38–39, 69–75

Traverse, Patrick, 263

Tremblay, J.C., 43–44

Trois-Rivières Draveurs, 108–14, 262–63

Turner Cup, 11–13, 159–65, *165*, 266

Ubriaco, Gene, 144, 148–49, 155, 157, 158

Vachon, Rogie, 63–64

Van Impe, Ed, 73–74

Veilleux, Steve, 263

visualization techniques, 157–58

Watson, Phil, 73–74, 75

Wickenheiser, Doug, 132, 159

Zubrus, Dainius, 263